6/11

The *Miranda* Ruling

American Psychology-Law Society Series

Books in the Series

Trial Consulting
Amy J. Posey and Lawrence S. Wrightsman

Death by Design
Craig Haney

Psychological Injuries
William J. Koch, Kevin S. Douglas, Tonia L. Nicholls, and Melanie L. O'Neill

Emergency Department Treatment of the Psychiatric Patient
Susan Stefan

The Psychology of the Supreme Court
Lawrence S. Wrightsman

Proving the Unprovable
Christopher Slobogin

Adolescents, Media, and the Law
Roger J.R. Levesque

Oral Arguments Before the Supreme Court
Lawrence S. Wrightsman

God in the Courtroom
Brian H. Bornstein and Monica K. Miller

Expert Testimony on the Psychology of Eyewitness Identification
Edited by Brian L. Cutler

The Psychology of Judicial Decision-Making
Edited by David Klein and Gregory Mitchell

The Miranda Ruling: Its Past, Present, and Future
Lawrence S. Wrightsman and Mary L. Pitman

The *Miranda* Ruling

Its Past, Present, and Future

Lawrence S. Wrightsman and Mary L. Pitman

OXFORD
UNIVERSITY PRESS
2010

OXFORD
UNIVERSITY PRESS

Oxford University Press, Inc., publishes works that further
Oxford University's objective of excellence
in research, scholarship, and education.

Oxford   New York
Auckland   Cape Town   Dar es   Hong Kong   Karachi
Kuala Lumpur   Madrid   Melbourne   Mexico City   Nairobi
New Delhi   Shanghai   Taipei   Toronto

With offices in
Argentina   Austria   Brazil   Chile   Czech Republic   France   Greece
Guatemala   Hungary   Italy   Japan   Poland   Portugal   Singapore
South Korea   Switzerland   Thailand   Turkey   Ukraine   Vietnam

Published by Oxford University Press, Inc.
198 Madison Avenue, New York, New York 10016
www.oup.com

Oxford is a registered trademark of Oxford University Press.

Library of Congress Cataloging-in-Publication Data

Wrightsman, Lawrence S.
The Miranda ruling : its past, present, and future / Lawrence S. Wrightsman and Mary L. Pitma.
p. cm.—(American psychology-law society series)
Includes bibliographical references and index.
ISBN 978-0-19-973090-2   1. Right to counsel—United States. 2. Confession (Law)—United States. 3. Police
questioning—United States. 4. Miranda, Ernesto—Trials, litigation, etc. I. Pitman, Mary L. II. Title.
KF9625.W75 2010
345.73'056—dc22
2010009163

9 8 7 6 5 4 3 2 1

Printed in the United States of America
on acid-free paper

To Saul Kassin, former student, frequent collaborator, and forever a friend.

To Nancy Madeya, whose own accomplishments served as inspiration
                              —kudos!

Series Foreword

This book series is sponsored by the American Psychology-Law Society (APLS). APLS is an interdisciplinary organization devoted to scholarship, practice, and public service in psychology and law. Its goals include advancing the contributions of psychology to the understanding of law and legal institutions through basic and applied research; promoting the education of psychologists in matters of law and the education of legal personnel in matters of psychology; and informing the psychological and legal communities and the general public of current research, educational, and service activities in the field of psychology and law. APLS membership includes psychologists from the academic research and clinical practice communities as well as members of the legal community. Research and practice is represented in both the civil and criminal legal arenas. APLS has chosen Oxford University Press as a strategic partner because of its commitment to scholarship, quality, and the international dissemination of ideas. These strengths will help APLS reach its goal of educating the psychology and legal professions and the general public about important developments in psychology and law. The focus of the book series reflects the diversity of the field of psychology and law, as we continue to publish books on a broad range of topics.

In the latest book in the series, *The Miranda Ruling: Its Past, Present, and Future*, Lawrence S. Wrightsman and Mary L. Pitman focus their attention on one of the most widely known U.S. Supreme Court decisions. In 1966, the Court, in *Miranda v. Arizona*, required police to provide a warning to suspects in custody. Prior to interrogation or questioning, police would now be required to explicitly inform suspects of several rights, including the right to remain silent, that anything they say can be used against them in a court of law, the right to the presence of an attorney, and the right to free counsel if they cannot afford the cost of an attorney. These warnings were viewed as strengthening individuals' constitutional protection against incriminating themselves during police interrogation. This warning is of course familiar to virtually every American, as countless TV shows have shown police dutifully reading these rights to a suspect. Wrightsman and Pitman write about the historical antecedents leading to the decision and critically evaluate the strengths and limitations of the Miranda decision itself. They then assess its impact by analyzing case law and psychological research since Miranda. They find that the majority of cases post-Miranda have served to narrow the Court's original ruling, and challenge the view that many, perhaps most, Americans have that *Miranda* effectively protects the rights of suspects in criminal cases. Indeed, they present compelling evidence that the reality is that this decision has failed to achieve its intended goals. They note that the vast majority of suspects waive their rights, usually with a simple answer of yes when a police officer or detective asks if they understood their rights. Research has shown that many in fact have not fully understood their rights. This is particularly true for vulnerable populations, including juveniles or those with cognitive deficits who may have difficulty understanding warnings that use vocabulary that exceeds their reading level.

Why is ensuring that suspects understand their rights at arrest necessary? A waiver of rights allows an interrogation to continue, and of course, the goal of an interrogation is to produce a confession. While most confessions are valid, there is clear evidence that false confessions also occur. Since these false confessions can lead to erroneous convictions, it is critical that a suspect who waives those rights does so in a knowing, voluntary, and intelligent manner. With this in mind, the authors conclude with policy recommendations for ensuring the protection of rights during police interrogations. This includes restrictions on the use of police deception and lying during the questioning of suspects, videotaping all interrogations, providing attorneys for vulnerable suspects (particularly attorneys who are well versed in the special needs of juveniles, mentally challenged, non-English speaking, and deaf suspects), and allowing experts to testify about the coercive nature of interrogation.

Wrightsman and Pitman provide a compelling case for ensuring that both the courts and researchers continue to focus attention on the issue of arrest rights to ensure that the original goals of the Miranda decision are achieved. Their book will provide both the legal and psychology communities with a cogent analysis of the relevant legal and psychological issues that will inform future law and policy.

Ronald Roesch
Series Editor

Preface

If you asked 100 people at random to give a free association to "Miranda," a few might respond with a girl's or woman's name, but most would make some association with laws or rights. For forty years, "Miranda rights" have not only been a staple of crime programs on television, but they have embedded themselves in American culture. In the words of Richard Leo, "schoolchildren are more likely to recognize the Miranda warnings than the Gettysburg Address" (1996, p. 286). The average American, even the well-educated, highly literate American, assumes that these warnings are here forever. But their existence is less than assured. Had John McCain been elected President in 2008, and assuming that Justice David Souter had still decided to resign at the end of June in 2009, the new member of the Supreme Court could have been the deciding vote in overruling the *Miranda* ruling. As it is, two current justices (Scalia and Thomas) have taken the position that *Miranda* is unconstitutional, and two other justices, Roberts and Alito, are predisposed to restrict, and possibly eliminate, its application.

However, it is not only political conservatives who decry *Miranda*. A number of advocates for defendants' rights have watched as the original goals of the justices who authored the *Miranda* decision have been ignored or emasculated by recent court decisions and police adaptations. Some liberals now advocate the abandonment of Miranda warnings because they do not serve their purpose. Thus, it is time to re-examine what was intended forty years ago, why it has been difficult to achieve, and, most importantly, whether *Miranda* can be resuscitated or whether other procedures need to be implemented to protect suspects' rights against self-incrimination. This book attempts to meet these goals.

Acknowledgments

We are indebted to a number of people who assisted us in the preparation of this book. Professor Ronald Roesch, Senior Editor of the series of books on psychology and the law for Oxford University Press, has been encouraging and enthusiastic about this book's proposal and has provided feedback on the manuscript. As she has in several previous books, Cindy Sexton provided valuable expertise in processing the manuscript; additionally, Charlie Rigdon bailed us out of several computer problems. Professor Saul M. Kassin took the trouble to contact Martin Tankleff to get an answer to a question we posed about that important case. We also want to express further thanks to: Richard Rogers, Professor of Psychology at the University of North Texas, whose extensive investigation of comprehensibility and the many versions of Miranda warnings has allowed us to illustrate the complexity of issues stemming from too many versions and its effect on comprehensibility among the general suspect population and vulnerable suspects, such as juveniles and the mentally retarded and mentally ill. His willingness to provide us with examples of a variety of Miranda versions—to include reading level requirements—played a critical role in our fifth chapter covering comprehensibility of vulnerable suspects. Jill E. Rogstad, Graduate Research Coordinator for Richard Rogers' work with determinants of Miranda warnings and waivers comprehension and reasoning, took on the arduous task of sorting out the extreme versions of Miranda warnings and answering many questions along the way in order to give us just what we needed to make our point clear. She went above and beyond the call of duty. Without her, we could not have gotten the job done. Also, Judge Michael Corriero, retired judge who presided over the

Manhattan Youth Part, a juvenile court within the adult system in New York City and who spent decades working with juveniles, graciously allowed us a telephone interview discussing juveniles and his perception on the cognitive, emotional, and social development of young teens when determining culpability. Judge Corriero is now Executive Director of Big Brothers Big Sisters of New York City. We gained much insight through his book and our phone conversation. We appreciate the University of Kansas School of Law Wheat Library staff for their open door policy. Their U.S. Supreme Court decisions aisle became our home away from home for many months. A hearty thank you is also extended to the Billington Library staff at Johnson County (Kansas) Community College for their generosity of unrestrained research and printing. Their patience and guidance over our fumbling with numerous reels of microfiche made our work a little easier.

Contents

The *Miranda* Ruling

1

The Public Image of *Miranda* and Why It Is Incomplete

> The quality of a nation's civilization can be largely measured by the methods it uses in the enforcement of its criminal law.
> —(Chief Justice Earl Warren, in *Miranda v. Arizona*, 1966, p. 480)

Even casual viewers of television recognize the term "Miranda rights" and the most inveterate watchers of crime shows can readily repeat them: "You have the right to remain silent; anything you say can be held against you; you have the right to an attorney." Citizens *know* that if criminal suspects are not given their "Miranda warnings," any subsequent attempt to prosecute them may be at risk. One law professor even concludes that, "*Miranda v. Arizona* is the Supreme Court's best known criminal justice opinion" (Clymer, 2002, p. 449). In fact, the ingrained nature of these rights was recognized in the year 2000 by then Chief Justice William Rehnquist who, in the case of *Dickerson v. United States*, acknowledged that "*Miranda* has become embedded in routine police practice to the point where the warnings have become a part of our national culture" (2000, p. 2336).

But the public has an incomplete picture of *Miranda*. Most crime shows portray police officers dutifully telling a suspect of his or her rights as the suspect is handcuffed and led away. In most shows there is strong evidence that the suspect is the perpetrator of the crime and that justice is on its way to being fulfilled. On television, the system seems to be working fine. That is, for the television viewer actual perpetrators are being apprehended and still the police are conscientiously informing them of their rights, just as the Supreme Court intended in formulating its *Miranda* decision.

Reality casts a more complicated picture. First, not all suspects are, in fact, guilty and—what is worse—some innocent suspects confess, even when aware of their Miranda rights. Second, police do not always inform suspects of their rights at the time of arrest, and sometimes they do not inform them at all.

The warnings are not always presented in the succinct and understandable way that television portrays them. All in all, what the Court envisioned in its *Miranda* decision is not always accomplished in the real world. The purpose of the Miranda warnings is to prevent suspects from incriminating themselves unless they truly want to. Forty years after the codification of the Miranda rights, we know that 80% of suspects waive their right to silence. Are all of these suspects guilty? No, we know that some are not, although no one can specify what percentage. Those who do waive their rights—whether guilty or innocent—subject themselves to a relentless interrogation, the goal of which is to elicit a confession. But the public rarely witnesses this step in the process.

Has the *Miranda* ruling lost the impact its authors intended? Despite the implicit acceptance by the Court and its leader in the 2000 *Dickerson* decision—a conservative court chaired by a conservative Chief Justice—a number of legal experts who support defendants' rights are concerned that the *Miranda* ruling, decided in 1966, is no longer sufficient to achieve its intended goals. A book published by a distinguished law professor a year after the *Dickerson* decision was titled "*Miranda's* waning protections" (White, 2001b). A recent law review article by one of the most experienced advocates of defendants' rights is titled "Mourning *Miranda*" (Weisselberg, 2008). And, a comprehensive examination by a psychologist/law professor who has observed hundreds of interrogations details how the intent of the law is routinely abrogated by law enforcement officers (Leo, 2008).

Why have Miranda warnings? Here is why: Even suspects of a crime have a right not to be forced to self-incriminate, and in 1966 the majority of justices on the Supreme Court feared that excessive actions by law enforcement officials had caused some suspects who were innocent to confess to a crime and subsequently be convicted. So, we can say that eliminating, or at least reducing, the number of false confessions was a goal of the *Miranda* decision.

What is the truth—does the *Miranda* decision still protect suspects from intrusive interrogation or has it become a toothless tiger? The purpose of this book is to examine the goals of the original decision in the case of *Miranda v. Arizona* and to determine how, in the subsequent half century, the impact of the decision has lessened. The theme of the book is that for a number of reasons, the original intent of the justices in 1966 has not been fulfilled. While some police faithfully subscribe to the intent of the warnings, several obstacles stand in the way of complete implementation. Subsequent chapters will describe each of these obstacles and suggest ways to re-establish the impact of the original ruling.

Disenchantment of *Miranda* by Advocates of Defendants' Rights

Political conservatives and advocates of crime control were quick to criticize the *Miranda* decision. Among them was Paul Cassell, a law professor at the

University of Utah and later a federal district judge. In several articles (Cassell, 1996a, b), he argued that the use of Miranda warnings would seriously diminish the number of criminals who were convicted of crimes, a claim that we will evaluate in a subsequent chapter.

The decision was also criticized because, in the eyes of its critics, it violated basic constitutional principles. Joseph Grano (1993), another law professor, argued that *Miranda* impeded what he saw as the criminal justice system's fundamental goal: the search for truth.

But in the last decade it has been the liberals, the advocates for defendants' rights, who have criticized *Miranda*. Charles D. Weisselberg, a professor of law at the University of California Law School who has studied interrogations for over a decade, has written that, "the Supreme Court has effectively encouraged police practices that have gutted *Miranda's* safeguards, to the extent those safeguards ever truly existed" (2008, p. 1521). Concluding that, "as a protective device, *Miranda* is dead" (2008, p. 1521), Weisselberg's detailed article offers several reasons for this conclusion. These reasons range from faulty assumptions by the justices who wrote the decision to efforts by law enforcement officials to violate the admonitions the justices specified. A recent book by Richard Leo (2008), a psychologist who is a law professor at the University of San Francisco, adds, "Interrogators often minimize, downplay, or de-emphasize the import of the Miranda warnings. The purpose is to trivialize the legal significance of *Miranda*, create the appearance of a nonadversarial relationship, and convey that the interrogator expects the suspect to passively execute the waiver and respond to questioning" (2008, p. 126). The prolific Harvard law professor Alan Dershowitz (2008) even asks in the title of his recent book: *Is There a Right to Remain Silent?* He concludes, based on the decision in a recent Supreme Court case, that the answer is no, if the information gleaned from the accused is not used against the accused in a criminal trial. Finally, Christopher Slobogin, a professor of law at Vanderbilt University who has written extensively on the relationship of psychology to the law, has put it pungently:

> *Miranda v. Arizona* is a hoax . . . Contrary to the predictions of *Miranda's* enemies and the hopes of its proponents; the warnings regime established by that case has had very little impact on the way police conduct interrogations. Confessions continue at virtually their pre-*Miranda* pace. More importantly, *Miranda* has had little effect on police behavior during interrogation. (Slobogin, 2003, p. 309)

Why Advocates of Defendants' Rights have become Disenchanted with *Miranda*

Where did *Miranda* lose its impact? Does the fault lie with the justices who crafted the original opinion in 1966? Or have police systematically tried to bypass the ruling and seen their efforts often given a green light by the courts? Both reasons have merit.

Two Decisions by the Supreme Court Reflecting Current Thinking

It is no secret that certain justices on the Supreme Court would like to do away with Miranda warnings entirely. In a dissent in the *Dickerson* case, Justice Antonin Scalia all but said so, and Justice Clarence Thomas readily joined in his dissent. Justice Scalia called the extension of the defendant's right against self-incrimination from only the courtroom to the station house as, "a doubtful proposition as a matter of both history and precedent" (*Dickerson v. United States*, 2000, p. 2338).

Other justices are willing to circumscribe the application of the warnings. The Court is quite divided on how broadly the rule should be applied, and two of the Court's rather recent decisions reflect the divided nature of the justices regarding the breadth and timing of Miranda warnings. While the facts in the two cases are not in absolute opposition to one another, a majority of the Court decided one case in favor of the police, thus restricting suspects' rights (*Yarborough v. Alvarado*, 2004), while the other curtailed an increasingly frequent police procedure and thus maintained suspects' rights (*Missouri v. Seibert*, 2004). Both were announced in the same month, June 2004.

Yarborough v. Alvarado

The first case involved a 17-year-old named Michael Alvarado, who was involved in an attempt to steal a truck, during which Alvarado's accomplice, Paul Soto, shot and killed the truck's owner. Alvarado helped hide the gun used by Soto. The Los Angeles County detective who was investigating the crime asked Alvarado to come to the sheriff's office for questioning and he obediently appeared, accompanied by his parents (Michael Alvarado lived with his parents and did not have a car). His parents waited in the lobby of the sheriff's department while he was questioned.

The detective took Alvarado to a small room where only two of them were present. After first denying his involvement in the crime, Alvarado slowly began to change his story and eventually confessed to his role in the crime, specifically that he had helped Soto try to steal the truck and to hide the gun after the murder. *He was not read his Miranda rights at any time during the two-hour interrogation.* Twice during this period of questioning the detective asked Alvarado if he needed a break. When they were finished, Alvarado was returned to his parents, who drove him home.

Prior to his trial, Alvarado's attorney tried to have his confession suppressed on *Miranda* grounds, but the judge refused and Alvarado's statements were introduced into evidence at the trial. Both he and Soto were found guilty of first-degree murder and attempted robbery, but Alvarado's charges were later reduced to second-degree murder and attempted robbery because of his role in the criminal acts.

Should Alvarado's conviction be upheld? More specifically, how could his confession be allowed into evidence given that he was not read his Miranda rights? Didn't the original decision say that any self-incriminating statement made by the suspects who had not been given their Miranda warnings would be excluded from evidence? No, the decision was limited to the time while the suspect was "in custody." Upon appeal, Alvarado's claim was initially rejected by the district court; the judge concluded that Alvarado was not in custody and hence the police were not required to Mirandize him while he was questioned. In doing so, the judge relied on a Supreme Court decision made in 1995, in *Thompson v. Keohane*, which required a court to consider the circumstances surrounding the interrogation and then determine whether a reasonable person would have felt at liberty to leave. But, ironically in that decision the Court, by a vote of 7 to 2, ruled that the state (Alaska in that instance) had too casually applied the "in custody" rules and that Carl Thompson was entitled to a new hearing with an independent review by a federal habeas court. The decision in the *Thompson* case was written by Justice Ruth Bader Ginsburg and signed by all the justices except Clarence Thomas and Chief Justice Rehnquist. In his dissent Justice Thomas concluded that the trial judge was in the best position to determine whether, given the specific facts in this situation, a reasonable person would feel free to leave. Thus, iron-ically, the decision that was the basis for the trial judge's ruling *against* Alvarado was in itself a ruling in *favor* of the earlier suspect.

When Alvarado's attorney took the appeal to the next level, the United States Court of Appeals for the Ninth Circuit—the infamous (in the eyes of conservatives) ultra liberal appeals court that includes California and all Western states—reversed the decision, concluding that Alvarado's youth and inexperience should have been taken into account when deciding whether a reasonable person in such a situation would have felt free to leave the interview. The Circuit Court noted that the United States Supreme Court had considered a suspect's juvenile status in other criminal law contexts. For example, in *Haley v. Ohio* (1948), a case prior to the *Miranda* decision, a split court (5 to 4) ruled that the police interrogation violated the Fourteenth Amendment rights of a 15-year-old boy. In that opinion the Court held:

> The age of the petitioner, the hours when he was grilled, the
> duration of his quizzing, the fact that he had no friend to advise
> him, the callous attitude of the police towards his rights combine
> to convince us that this was a confession wrung from a child by
> means which the law should not sanction. (pp. 600–601)

But the interrogation of John Harvey Haley, which occurred in 1948, and that of Michael Alvarado almost 60 years later, were quite different; for example, there were indications that Haley was beaten and kept incommunicado for several days.

After the circuit court reversed Michael Alvarado's conviction, the State of California (in the name of Michael Yarborough, warden of the California prison) appealed the matter to the United States Supreme Court. The high court, by a 5 to 4 vote, reinstated Alvarado's murder conviction, concluding that the presiding trial judge had reached a reasonable conclusion and was not in error. According to the opinion of the Court, Michael Alvarado was not "in custody" and hence issues of youth and inexperience were irrelevant. Justice Anthony Kennedy's majority opinion noted that, "our court has not stated that a suspect's age or experience is relevant to the *Miranda* custody analysis" (2004, p. 2150). (Technically this was true, since the *Haley* decision preceded *Miranda*.) Furthermore, he rejected a suspect's youth as reason for special consideration, writing that,

> The relationship between a suspect's past experience and the likelihood a reasonable person with that experience would feel free to leave often will be speculative. We do not ask police officers to consider these contingent psychological factors when deciding when suspects should be advised of their Miranda rights. (p. 2152)

Such parenthetical statements embedded in Supreme Court decisions (called *dicta*) are often later interpreted by lower courts as precedent. For example, as we will detail later in this book, this is the kind of statement that law-enforcement officials use as justification for their failure to give Miranda warnings in certain situations.

In a dissent in the *Yarborough v. Alvarado* case with which most psychologists would probably agree, Justice Stephen Breyer wrote that the majority opinion defied "ordinary common sense." He asked:

> What reasonable person in the circumstances—brought to the police station by his parents at police request, put in a small interrogation room, questioned for a solid two hours, and confronted with claims that there is strong evidence that he participated in a serious crime—could have thought to himself, "Well, anytime I want to leave I can just get up and walk out?" (*Yarborough v. Alvarado*, 2004, p. 2153)

In the view of Justice Breyer, "Michael Alvarado clearly was 'in custody' when the police questioned him" (p. 2152).

Justice Breyer's dissent was consistent with his questioning during the oral argument, at which he told the Deputy Attorney General of California, "Being a child or an adolescent would make a difference" (*Yarborough v. Alvarado*, transcript of oral argument, p. 5). In fairness, it should be noted that Justice Breyer was arguing against precedent. In 1977, in *Oregon v. Mathiason*, the Supreme Court had ruled, in a *per curiam* decision, that Carl Mathiason's conviction for first degree burglary should be upheld even though he confessed without being given a Miranda warning, because he was not in custody at the time of his confession. [Ordinarily, *per curiam* decisions are brief, with no author indicated, and reflect the summary disposition, reflecting unanimity on the Court. Sometimes, as in the Mathiason case, no oral arguments are held. But in this case, three of the justices—Brennan, Marshall, and Stevens—publicly dissented.]

When Mathiason, a parolee, voluntarily appeared at the police station at the request of a detective, the officer met him in the hallway, shook hands, and took him to an office. He closed the door. Mathiason was told that he was not under arrest. The police officer told him he wanted to talk about a burglary and falsely told him that his fingerprints were found at the crime scene. Mathiason sat quietly for a few minutes and then said that he had stolen the property. This only took about five minutes to transpire. Only then did the detective advise him of his Miranda rights and taped an oral confession. The Supreme Court's decision concluded, "There is no indication that the questioning took place in a context where respondent's freedom to depart was restricted in any way. At the close of the 30 minute interview respondent did in fact leave the police station without hindrance" (p. 496).

Justice Kennedy, in his opinion for the Court in the *Alvarado* case, cites *Mathiason* as a basis for his decision. While some of the facts in Carl Mathiason's and Michael Alvarado's interrogations are the same, some are not—especially the length of the interrogation and the age and experience of the suspect. For some observers, these provide justification for a decision that is different from the one in *Oregon v. Mathiason*.

It is true that the original *Miranda* decision dealt solely with that questioning while the suspect was "in custody." In Chapter 4 we examine the reasons and the ramifications of this decision by the justices, and we go on to trace the meaning of "custody" in the eyes of the courts. But at least for lay people, "custody" is a vague concept. Even Justice Kennedy's majority opinion in the *Alvarado* case acknowledged that, "fair-minded jurists could disagree over whether Alvarado was in custody" (2004, p. 2143). Previous decisions by the Court have used the "reasonable person" standard: does a reasonable person feel at liberty to terminate the interrogation and leave? Always the "fair-minded jurist" himself, Justice Kennedy, in his opinion for the Court, listed facts on either side of the "custody-or-not-custody" question. The following facts, in his view, "weigh against a finding that Alvarado was in custody" (p. 2143):

1. The police did not transport him to the police station or require him to appear at a particular time.
2. They did not threaten him or suggest he would be placed under arrest.
3. His parents remained in the lobby during questioning, suggesting that the interview would be brief.
4. The detective appealed to Alvarado's interest in telling the truth and being helpful to a police officer.
5. As noted earlier, the detective twice asked him if he wanted a break.
6. At the end of the interview he went home.

Other facts, according to Justice Kennedy's opinion, pointed in the opposite direction:

1. Alvarado was interviewed at the police station.
2. He was not told he was free to leave.
3. He was brought to the police station by his legal guardians rather than of his own accord.
4. His parents were rebuffed when they asked to sit in on the interview (*Yarborough v. Alvarado*, 2004).

In his dissent, Justice Breyer gave great weight to several of Justice Kennedy's "facts [that] point in the opposite direction." For example, for Breyer, "the involvement of Alvarado's parents suggests *in*voluntary, not voluntary behavior on Alvarado's part" (p. 2153, italics in original). Even the fact that the detective twice asked Alvarado if he wanted to take a break, in Justice Breyer's view, emphasized "the officer's control over Alvarado's movements [and] makes it *less* likely, not *more* likely, that Alvarado would have thought he was free to leave at will" (p. 2154, italics in original).

Justice Breyer's dissent also recognized Alvarado's youth as a consideration, proposing that at the age of 17, "he was unlikely to have felt free to ignore his parents' request to come to the station" (p. 2154) and that he was "more likely than, say a 35-year-old, to take a police officer's assertion of authority to keep parents outside the room as an assertion of authority to keep their child inside as well" (p. 2154). He argued that the law in general considers a person's youth as a "relevant circumstance" in other situations, for example, in negligence determinations, and he even claimed that the law has developed the concept of "reasonable person" so that courts can "avoid . . . inquiry into subjective states of mind" (p. 2155).

So, in *Yarborough v. Alvarado* we have a decision that weakens the rights of suspects and restricts the breadth of application of the warnings promulgated in *Miranda v. Arizona*. In this decision the three most conservative justices (Rehnquist, Scalia, and Thomas), plus the two justices who were labeled "swing voters" (O'Connor and Kennedy), sided with the state, while each of the four relatively liberal justices (Breyer, Souter, Stevens, and Ginsburg) sided with the defendant.

Missouri v. Seibert

Let us turn to the other decision, also *Miranda*-relevant, made by the Court within days of *Alvarado*: the case of *Missouri v. Seibert* (2004).

Patrice Seibert, of Rolla, Missouri, was considered by the police to be an accomplice in an act of arson of her own trailer home, which caused the death of Donald Rector, age 17. Rector lived with the Seibert family and took care of Seibert's 12-year-old disabled son, Jonathan. The motive for her act of arson seems bizarre. Jonathan, who had cerebral palsy, unexpectedly died in his sleep. Apparently, Seibert feared that she would be charged with neglecting her son—he had bedsores on his body—and she was present when two of her other sons and two of their friends discussed burning the home to conceal the condition of her son's body. Rector was left to die in the fire, so as to avoid the appearance that her son had been left unattended.

Five days later, the police awakened Seibert at 3 a.m. at a hospital where one of her surviving sons was being treated for burns. When the officer was sent to bring Seibert to the police station, the officer's supervisor specifically instructed him not to advise Seibert of her Miranda rights. Upon arrival at police headquarters, Seibert was placed in a small interrogation room, left alone for 15 or 20 minutes, and then questioned. After about 30 or 40 minutes, she acknowledged that the plan was to abandon Rector to die in the fire. Then after a 20 minute coffee and cigarette break, the interrogation continued, now with a tape recorder turned on. As the interrogation was renewed, she was advised of her Miranda rights and signed a waiver form. During this second interrogation she again confessed. The trial judge did not allow the first confession into evidence, but did allow the second.

During the trial the police officer testified that he made a "conscious decision" (p. 2606) to withhold the Miranda warnings before questioning Seibert in hopes of eliciting a confession. He acknowledged that he had been taught this as an interrogation technique and that Seibert's second statement was "largely a repeat of information . . . obtained prior to the warning" (p. 2606). Here is a portion of the interrogation after the break and Seibert's signing of the Miranda waiver:

Officer Hanrahan:	"Now, in discussion you told us . . . that there was an understanding about Donald."
Seibert:	"Yes."
Hanrahan:	"Did that take place earlier that morning?"
Seibert:	"Yes."
Hanrahan:	"And what was the understanding about Donald?"
Seibert:	"If they could get him out of the trailer, to take him out of the trailer."
Hanrahan:	"And if they couldn't?"
Seibert:	"I, I never even thought about it. I just figured they would."
Hanrahan:	"Trice, didn't you tell me he was supposed to die in his sleep?"
Seibert:	"If that would happen, 'cause he was on that new medicine, you know . . . ."
Hanrahan:	"The Prozac? And it makes him sleepy. So he was supposed to die in his sleep?"
Seibert:	"Yes" (*Missouri v. Seibert*, 2004, p. 2606).

After Seibert was convicted and sentenced to life in prison, she appealed her sentence. The Supreme Court of the State of Missouri, by a 4 to 3 vote, ruled that all those statements made by Seibert after her waiver of Miranda rights should also have been excluded from evidence. The Missouri State Supreme Court was quite offended by the police officer's deliberate acts, stating that he had purposefully withheld a Miranda warning and that he had made a conscious decision not to advise Seibert of her rights. They called his action a deliberate "end run" around *Miranda*. Thus the State of Missouri took the appeal to the United States Supreme Court. On June 28, 2004, the last day of the term, the Supreme Court, by a 5 to 4 vote, ruled in Seibert's favor. Justice David Souter, writing for the Court, stated that the facts of the case "by any objective measure reveal police strategy adapted to undermine the Miranda warnings" (2004, p. 2612). It would be natural for a suspect, having confessed once to confess again, Souter reasoned. Furthermore, she "would not have understood that she retained a choice about continuing to talk" (2004, p. 2613).

Justice Souter observed that some police manuals and training programs endorse this question-first or "two-step-tactic" and indeed, Officer Hanrahan admitted that the tactic was advocated not only in his department but also by a national police training organization and by other departments in which he had worked (however, it is *not* endorsed by all police manuals and the one by Inbau and Reid, 1962, to be described in Chapter 7, notes the problems in doing so). Justice Souter wrote: "After all, the reason that question-first is catching on is as obvious as its manifest purpose, which is to get a confession the suspect would not make if he understood his rights at the onset" (pp. 2610–2611).

The *Seibert* decision relied heavily on a case decided prior to *Miranda*, *United States v. Bayer* (1947), which also involved two confessions. In that case, the Supreme Court wrote:

> Of course, after an accused has once let the cat out of the bag by confessing, no matter what the inducement, he is never thereafter free of the psychological and practical disadvantages of having confessed. He can never get the cat back into the bag. The secret is out for good. In such a sense, a later confession always may be looked upon as the fruit of the first. (*Bayer v. United States* 1947, p. 539)

In light of his opinion in the *Alvarado* case, it is worth noting that Justice Kennedy wrote an opinion concurring with the majority opinion written by Justice Souter. In his concurrence Justice Kennedy wrote: "The interrogation technique used in this case is designed to circumvent *Miranda v. Arizona*. . . It undermines the Miranda warning and obscures its meaning" (p. 2614).

While for many, the opinion of the Court in the *Seibert* case seems a sensible one and preserves the original intent of *Miranda*, it was adopted by the narrowest margins: 5 to 4. In contrast, the dissenting opinion (written by Justice O'Connor and joined by Justices Rehnquist, Scalia, and Thomas) carried no weight as legal precedent due to the fact that only four justices signed it, but it is worthy of comment because it gave a different rationale for deciding the case. Justice O'Connor wrote that the intent of the police officer should make no difference "because a suspect could not know what was in the officer's mind" (2004, p. 2618). Rather, the test should be the voluntary nature of the second set of statements; if Seibert gave them voluntarily, they should have been admitted. Justice O'Connor appears to have accepted the claim made by Karen Mitchell, Chief Deputy Attorney General for the State of Missouri, in her oral argument before the Court: "A fully warned and otherwise voluntary statement is not tainted by the existence of a prior unwarned statement even if the officers intentionally initiated questioning without warning" (*Missouri v. Seibert*, oral argument transcript, p. 3). She claimed this for the reason that the officer's intent does not render the unwarned statement actually involuntary.

Under questioning, Mitchell acknowledged a presumption that the *earlier* statement is involuntary. Further questioning—the transcript does not identify the justice but the questioning style is clearly Justice Breyer's—centers on the two-step technique creating a coercive environment in which suspects in effect, "throw up their hands and say it's too late now" (*Missouri v. Seibert*, transcript of oral argument, pp. 11–12). Another justice (probably Justice Stevens) asked Ms. Mitchell: "If your submission is correct, is there any reason why a police department should not adopt a policy that said, 'Never give Miranda warnings until a suspect confesses?'" (pp. 11–12). Later in the oral argument, a justice emphasized the involuntary nature of the second confession; "It seems to me . . . the person would have said, 'What the heck, I've already coughed it up, I may as well do it again'" (pp. 14–15).

Justice O'Connor's emphasis on voluntariness as a sole determination of the admissibility of self-incriminating statements reflects a long standing focus of the courts; Chapter 2 details the emphasis on this factor in decisions by the Supreme Court prior to *Miranda* and, as we will discuss in Chapter 8, recent critics of the *Miranda* decision have once more seen voluntariness as a satisfactory filter for evaluating confessions.

Justice O'Connor's dissent reminds us that, for many people, the voluntary nature of a confession has been, and remains, a salient determinant of the admissibility of that confession. Critics of *Miranda* ask: Why would you need to tell a suspect of his or her rights if the suspect fully intends to confess? Furthermore, judges' and jurors' evaluations of voluntariness extend beyond simply the matter of suspects' confessions. For example, criminal defendants sometimes claim, as a defense, that they were entrapped; that they would not have committed the crime had the police not created an opportunity for them to do it. The case of Keith Jacobson (*Jacobson v. United States*, 1992) is an example. In 1984, Keith Jacobson was a 56-year-old unmarried Nebraska farmer who ordered two magazines through the mail from an adult bookstore; the magazines (titled "Bare Boys I" and "Bare Boys II") contained depictions of nude preteen boys (but the boys were not engaged in sexual activity). At this time, what Jacobson did was not a violation of any state or federal law,

but soon after this, the U.S. Congress passed the Child Protection Act, prohibiting the purchase or possession of child pornography. Over the next two years,
the government, through the use of five fictitious organizations and a bogus
pen pal, aggressively provided a temptation for Jacobson to break the new law
and order child pornography (Edkins & Wrightsman, 2004). After being
sent 9 mailings over a period of 26 months, he finally succumbed, ordering a
pornographic magazine titled "Boys Who Love Boys." He was immediately
arrested.

At his trial Jacobson claimed that he had been induced by the government and that without its instigation, he would not have ordered any child
pornography, thus his claim resembled an involuntary confession, as he
claimed no intent or disposition to commit a crime. However, he was convicted. But he found relief at the Supreme Court level; the majority of the
justices voted to overturn Jacobson's conviction, concluding that it had not
been proven that he possessed the requisite disposition prior to the onslaught
of attempts to get him to misbehave. However, the decision was based on a 5
to 4 vote, and it is instructive to reproduce part of Justice O'Connor's dissent,
as she reflected an assumption that Jacobson was predisposed:

> Keith Jacobson was offered only two opportunities to buy child
> pornography through the mail. Both times, he ordered. Both times,
> he asked for opportunities to buy more. He needed no government
> agent to coax, threaten, or persuade him, no one played on his
> sympathies, friendship, or suggested that his committing the crime
> would further the public good. In fact, no government agent even
> contacted him face to face. The government contends that from the
> enthusiasm with which Mr. Jacobson responded to the chance to
> commit a crime, a reasonable jury could permissibly infer beyond a
> reasonable doubt that he was predisposed to commit the crime.
> I agree . . . Government agents admittedly did not offer Mr. Jacobson
> the opportunity to buy child pornography right away. Instead, they
> first sent questionnaires in order to make sure that he was generally
> interested in the subject matter . . . The Court however, concludes
> that a reasonable jury would not have found Mr. Jacobson to be
> predisposed beyond a reasonable doubt on the basis of his responses
> to the government's catalogs, even though it admits, that, by that
> time, he was predisposed to commit the crime. The government,
> the Court holds, failed to provide evidence that Mr. Jacobson's
> obvious predisposition at the time of the crime "was independent
> and not the product of the attention that the government had
> directed at petitioner." In so holding, I believe the Court fails to
> acknowledge the reasonableness of the jury's inference from the
> evidence, redefines "predisposition," and introduces a new require-
> ment that government sting operations have a reasonable suspicion
> of illegal activity before contacting a suspect . . . There is no dispute
> that the jury in this case was fully and accurately instructed on the

law of entrapment, and nonetheless found Mr. Jacobson guilty. Because I believe there was sufficient evidence to uphold the jury's verdict, I respectfully dissent. (*Jacobson v. United States*, 1992, pp. 554, 555, 556, 561, citations deleted)

We believe that judicial conservatives, in seeing predisposition when in fact the person is pressured to conform, are reflecting the same general assumption that underlies their belief that confessions are voluntary when some pressures exist to confess.

We have portrayed the outcome in the *Seibert* case as one that is supportive of suspects' rights. But we should note that not all observers agree with this conclusion, for several reasons (Moreno, 2005; Thompson, 2006). First, the actual holding in the case is not based on Justice Souter's opinion for the Court but rather on Justice Kennedy's concurrence, since he was the fifth vote and his judgment was on narrower grounds. (In the case of *Marks v. United States*, in 1976, the Court ruled that, "When a fragmented Court decides a case and no single rationale explaining the result enjoys the assent of five justices, the holding of the Court may be viewed as that position taken by those members who concurred in the judgments of the narrowest grounds" [p. 193].) Justice Kennedy's rationale focuses on the *deliberate* nature of the police to circumvent the intent of *Miranda*. He does not rule out all procedures in which police first question without giving the warnings and then question a second time, preceded by the warnings; but only when the "tactic relies on an intentional misrepresentation of the protection that *Miranda* offers and does not serve any legitimate objectives that might otherwise justify its use" (2004, p. 2615). Thus, Justice Kennedy's concurrence does not, like the Souter opinion, rule out other "two-step" procedures by the police. Furthermore, it places the burden on the defendant, who must prove that a police officer acted in bad faith (Moreno, 2005). Law review articles that have evaluated the *Seibert* decision have concluded that intention is difficult to prove—one calls the decision a "terrible idea"—and it does appear that the recent decisions by the lower courts have been more lenient: they have allowed the "two-step" procedure in certain circumstances, and these lower courts have been reluctant to call a "question-first" procedure by the police as an act of "bad faith" or a *deliberate* violation of *Miranda* (Moreno, 2005; Thompson, 2006).

Two conflicting values in our society

Why then did the Supreme Court rule in favor of the suspect in *Seibert* and in support of the police in *Alvarado*? Of course, there are several reasons: The facts and the specific issues differed even though, in a broad sense, both cases dealt with the question of when the Miranda warnings must be administered.

But one reason is that our society has two conflicting values for the goals of the criminal justice system and current members of the Supreme Court disagree about which should predominate. Fifty years ago a law professor,

Herbert Packer (1964, 1968), identified these two goals as *crime control* and *due process*. What is important to those who advocate the crime control model is that law-breakers be apprehended, prosecuted, and convicted. For them, the safety of citizens is paramount, and thus advocates of the crime-control model are willing to cut some slack so that law-enforcement officials can do what they are hired to do. Furthermore, advocates of this model presume that if an individual has been apprehended by the police, he or she likely committed the crime. As Edkins (2007) has observed, it is incorrect to infer that the crime-control model tolerates false convictions. Rather, it supports a thorough crime investigation in order to exclude, as suspects, those who are truly innocent. But it also recognizes that thoroughness may not always be possible, either because of the limited law-enforcement resources or because of laws that limit the investigative actions of the police. But when it comes to a choice, in the eyes of crime-control advocates, it is better to over-convict than to over-acquit. That is, choosing intrusive policing over individual rights is a small price to pay for society's safety.

In contrast, the due-process model places primary value on the protection of innocent persons from the possible abuses of the police and the law-enforcement system generally. Innocence is assumed; the due-process model subscribes to the maxim that "it is better for many guilty persons to go free than for one innocent person to suffer." The due-process model makes a distinction between persons who are factually guilty and those who are legally guilty (Packer, 1964). In each of the above examples, it seems likely that the suspects, Patrice Seibert and Michael Alvarado, were guilty of some crime, of abetting others in a serious criminal act. But given the way they were treated by the legal system, were they the beneficiaries of the due process rights against self-incrimination expressed in the Constitution?

It is because the Constitution provides rights to all individuals, including those suspected of committing a crime, that we have Miranda warnings. Even those persons have a right not to be forced to self-incriminate. In 1966, a majority of the justices feared that excessive actions by law-enforcement officials had caused some suspects who were innocent to confess to a crime and subsequently be convicted. That is why we conclude that the elimination of, or at least the reduction of, the number of false confessions was a goal of the *Miranda* decision.

Not all false confessions are induced by forceful police procedures. Persons admit to crimes they did not commit for a variety of reasons (Gudjonsson, 2003). Why did more than 200 persons falsely confess to the famous Lindbergh baby kidnapping? Among possible motives for false confessions are the desire for notoriety, the unconscious need to expiate guilt, and the inability to distinguish between fantasy and reality (Kassin & Wrightsman, 1985). No innovation will completely eliminate false confessions, but the justices believed, as we do, that if suspects were informed of their rights, some false confessions—these stemming from coercive interrogation techniques—could be prevented.

In the framework of the due-process model, a perfect criminal-justice system would consist of an investigation carried out with the utmost respect for individual rights. It would recognize that at every level human error is a possibility. But a due-process approach does not condone crime, nor does it deny that crime is not a problem in our society. Instead, it recognizes that the system can fail in both its investigations and its trial proceedings, and if there are any qualms about the guilt of the individual, then that person should go free.

Clearly, these two positions are inevitably in conflict with one another. While it is possible that the occasional individual will subscribe to both, ordinarily one position takes precedence over the other. Diverse groups—college students, psychologists, and even Supreme Court justices—show lack of agreement on these issues (Wrightsman, 2001). For example, a number of factor analyses of a 30-item Likert type attitude scale measuring reactions to police tactics, using college students as respondents, revealed two salient factors: one being an endorsement of police activities and the other being a concern for the rights of suspects (Edkins & Wrightsman, 2004). Respondents who agree with the statement "The crime rate is so high that we should give the police the power to catch criminals, whatever it takes" do *not* agree with the statement "If a person was lured by the police into committing a crime, he or she should be found not guilty at trial."

Psychologists and the Two Models

Psychologists, too, are diverse. The Council of Representatives of the American Psychological Association deliberated for two years before adopting a resolution that discouraged its members from employment with organizations in which torture was used against detainees or prisoners. As Kenneth Ring (1971) observed almost 40 years ago, most social psychologists are politically liberal, but not all are. Social scientists who sympathize with the defendant reflect the due-process model; they tend to be skeptical that the defendant truly committed the crime, or that the eyewitness's testimony is truly accurate, or that the confession was truly voluntary. A major concern for politically liberal psychologists is that some defendants will be wrongfully convicted, imprisoned, and even executed (Wrightsman, 2001). Their critics—supporters of the crime-control model—do not share these concerns. Psychologists Michael McCloskey and Howard Egeth (1983) argued that wrongful convictions from mistaken eyewitness testimony reflected only a "small fraction of the 1% of cases in which defendants were convicted at least in part on the basis of eyewitness testimony" (p. 552). Another pair of prominent crime-control oriented psychologists, Vladimir Konecni and Ebbe Ebbesen, approvingly quoted the above and concluded from it "that in the state of California one person is wrongfully convicted approximately every three years because of mistaken eyewitness testimony" (1986, p. 119). (This very low incidence rate is challenged by other experts who study eyewitness accuracy.)

How many errors of omission are we willing to make to avoid making one error of commission? (From the results of the Innocence Project, we know that there have been errors of commission, that innocent persons have been coerced into falsely confessing to a crime [Scheck, Neufeld, & Dwyer, 2001]). Advocates of the due-process model and the crime-control model have different answers to this question. Konecni and Ebbesen (1986) concluded, "One wrongful conviction in three years because of mistaken identification in a state the size of California . . . may be one wrongful conviction too many, but most reasonable people would probably regard it as well within the domain of 'acceptable' risk—acceptable because no workable system of justice is perfect" (1986, p. 119).

Other psychologists would disagree; the magnitude of error, they would say, is much greater. And what is more, for the politically liberal psychologists one wrongful conviction *really is* too many—it is unacceptable. In that regard they seek a standard of perfection in some ways similar to the standard of perfected research consistency sought by their critics. Both seek "zero defects" (Wrightsman, 2001).

An Example of How Two Justices Can Differ

Justices, like all of us, are human beings with differing life experiences and values. These values play a role in their interpretations of the facts of a case and often are reflected in their legal opinions. As one of many possible examples of judicial disagreements, we have chosen a case that dealt with a police interrogation which occurred before the Miranda rules applied, because it not only reflects differing assumptions by two justices, but it reflects the Court's thinking that eventually led to the *Miranda* decision, a topic that is covered in more detail in Chapter 2. The case is *Fikes v. Alabama* in 1957.

A series of rapes of white women occurred in Selma, Alabama, in the late 1940s and early 1950s. All the victims described the assailant as a slender, light-skinned African American. William Earl Fikes, who generally fit the description, was seen prowling through an alley and was taken into custody. He was interrogated off and on over a 10-day period, at which point he confessed. At a trial in 1953 he was convicted and sentenced to die. He appealed his conviction based on a claim that his confession had been coerced and that the interrogation had violated the Due Process Clause of the Fourteenth Amendment, and in December 1956 the Supreme Court held oral arguments on the appeal. Five weeks later the Supreme Court announced its decision— to overturn Fikes' conviction because of the pressures brought upon him to confess, and because of his lack of education, his limited mental ability, and his possible mental illness. The Court's opinion, written by Chief Justice Earl Warren, clearly indicates that Warren believed that all of the circumstances, pooled together, raised reasonable doubt whether Fikes' confession had been voluntary. But the vote was a divided one, 5 to 4—an outcome that presaged the conflicted nature of many future Supreme Court votes on confession cases. Justice John Marshall Harlan II wrote a dissent, questioning whether there had been any violation of Due Process rights. An observer has captured the contrast:

> Taking in the same record and the same facts that the majority of the Court had found shocking, he [Harlan] came to an opposite conclusion. "Concededly, there was not brutality or physical coercion. And psychological coercion is by no means manifest. While the total period of interrogation was substantial, the questioning was intermittent, it never exceeded two or three hours at a time, and all of it took place during normal hours, 'relay-tactics' . . . were not employed . . . I find nothing here . . . which 'shocks the conscience' or does more than offend some fastidious squeamishness or private sentimentalism about committing crime too energetically." (Prettyman, 1961, p. 4)

The Current Composition of the Supreme Court and the Two Models

From their votes on the relevant cases it is clear that the current justices on the Supreme Court are also divided in their allegiance to these two goals of the criminal justice system. In the term beginning in October 2003, the Court dealt with four cases involving Miranda rights, including the *Alvarado* and *Seibert* cases described earlier. In three of these the vote was split 5 to 4, with the four relative liberals always supporting due process and the three conservatives plus Justice O'Connor supporting crime control. In two of the three cases, Justice Kennedy voted with the conservatives—in the *Alvarado* case and the *United States v. Patane* (2004), a case in which the suspect told the police officer not to bother reading him his Miranda rights. In the fourth case, the vote was unanimous. In *Fellers v. United States* (2004), the justices held that the police violated a suspect's Sixth Amendment right to counsel by questioning him at his home but waiting until he was arrested to give him his Miranda warning.

Thus in the three divided vote cases, eight of nine justices were consistent in their adherence to either crime control or due process; only Justice Kennedy was unpredictable. Further support for a divided court is the fact that in two of these cases the Court ruled in favor of the criminal defendant and in two it supported the police procedures.

Since the 2003-2004 term, the Court has generally avoided taking on further *Miranda*-related cases. Only once in the five most recent terms did the Court grant *certiorari* to a case with *Miranda* linkages. In that case, *Wallace v. Kato* (2007), the issue before the Court was the acceptable status of limitations for a suit by a defendant (Andre Wallace) against a police department claiming false arrest. In this case, Wallace had waived his Miranda rights. Of the 69 cases decided during the term that ended in June 2008, none dealt with Miranda rights.

However, in October 2008 the Court granted *certiorari* to a case, *Montejo v. Louisiana*, dealing with a murder suspect, Jesse Montejo, who at first waived his rights to an attorney but changed his mind 5 hours into the interrogation. After a police officer told him that he had "let them down," Montejo revoked his request for counsel and subsequently confessed. In May, 2009 the Supreme Court, by a 5 to 4 vote, upheld Montejo's conviction, ruling that the Louisiana court had acted properly.

Given the diversity—among students, psychologists, and most importantly among Supreme Court justices—a possible explanation for the current state of inconsistency and controversy over the *Miranda* rule is that individuals interpret the law in keeping with their own values. The justices differ as do other groups of people, and so inconsistency is the result.

Overview of the Rest of the Book

The intent of this book, then, is to examine the *Miranda* decision, to identify its antecedents, to explain why the Warren Court decided this case as it did in 1966, to examine whether the expectations of the justices were met, and to trace the modifications made by the Supreme Court in 40 years since the original decision. In doing so, the book examines the current state of interrogations, the reason why the original goals have not been achieved, and some changes in the law that would facilitate achieving these original goals.

The heart of the book presents and evaluates four reasons why the *Miranda* rule does not have the impact that inveterate watchers of television crime dramas believe it does. First, the original decision did not go as far as it might have in specifying protections. Chapter 3 describes the deliberations by the justices in responding to the case of Ernesto Miranda, the various alternatives they considered, and their eventual decision. As Chapter 4 describes, the *Miranda* ruling, despite the criticism elicited in the law-enforcement community, was a compromise. Specifically, it limited the warnings to situations in which a suspect was "in custody," and as we saw in the *Alvarado* case, that restriction permitted the police to question suspects without restriction in a variety of settings.

A second limitation is that many suspects are not able to understand their rights. Incredibly, there are literally hundreds of versions of the Miranda warnings employed in the 17,000 police departments in the United States. Some are only a few sentences in length, while others may encompass 400 words. Some omit one of the warnings. Chapter 5 details the problems in comprehension of the warnings, with emphasis on particular types of suspects at risk, including adolescents, those who have psychological problems, foreign language speakers, and the deaf.

Chapter 6 considers the decisions by the Supreme Court since 1966. As the two cases described earlier in this chapter indicate, the Court has not always moved in the direction of narrowing applications of the Miranda warnings, but that has been the general trend. Major decisions along this path are described. One anomaly in this trend, briefly mentioned at the beginning of this chapter, was the decision in 2000, in *Dickerson v. United States*, in which the Court, led by Chief Justice Rehnquist, upheld *Miranda*. We offer a revisionist view of why this surprising decision was made, and describe cases subsequent to that decision.

Police departments have responded to the requirements of administering a Miranda warning in a variety of ways. As illustrated in the case of *Missouri v. Seibert*, some try to circumvent the original purpose. Chapter 7 analyzes those aspects of training manuals and training programs for police that deal with interrogations. It is not an exaggeration to say that the goal of these—once the police officer is convinced of the suspect's guilt—is to get the suspect to confess. Incidentally, "convinced of the suspect's guilt" poses a problem in and of itself, as our review of the research on the ability to detect deception indicates that police are woefully weak in this regard.

The authors of the original *Miranda* decision were motivated by the belief that America's Constitution provides protection to all citizens against self-incrimination. Can this right be salvaged? The final chapter provides reforms that try to respond to the problems presented in earlier chapters: the elimination of lying and other forms of deception by police, videotaping of interrogations, provision of an attorney for those suspects who are especially vulnerable, and the admissibility of an expert witness to testify about the coercive nature of interrogations. Achievement of such reforms is a challenge, but it reflects the goals of this book.

2

What Led Up to the *Miranda* Decision?

> If the exercise of constitutional rights will thwart the effective-
> ness of a system of law enforcement, then there is something very
> wrong with that system.
> —(*Escobedo v. Illinois*, 1964, p. 484)

Why did the majority of the Supreme Court justices, in 1966, decide that police should be required to inform criminal suspects of their right to remain silent before beginning to question them? To answer this question, two subsidiary matters need to be resolved: What was the nature of police interrogations at that time and what decisions had been made by the Supreme Court prior to *Miranda*?

A Brief Summary of the Long History of Interrogations and Confessions

Hundreds of years ago, physical reactions of the body were used to indicate guilt. The ancient Hindus forced suspects to chew rice and to spit it out on a leaf from a sacred tree; if the rice was dry, the suspect was considered guilty. The Bedouins of Arabia required the licking of an iron; one whose tongue was burned was thought to be lying (Kleinmuntz & Szucko, 1984). Both of these procedures were crude measures of emotion, though not necessarily of lying. And it is worth noting that police—like many of the rest of us—still rely on non-verbal indicators (lack of eye contact, fidgeting, etc.) to assess whether a suspect is trying to deceive.

The police may question a suspect to elicit information about a crime, but their goal is always to extract a confession. Thus, confessions evidence has been a recurring source of controversy in English and American jurisprudence, as the courts have sought a balance between the need to punish perpetrators and the assumption that a suspect is innocent until proven guilty, thus reflecting the conflict between crime control and due process as goals of the legal system. Stephens (1973) articulated a collateral dilemma: Whether our criminal justice system, which assumes the innocence of defendants and requires the government to prove their guilt, is consistent with a practice that permits police to hold a suspect in seclusion and to introduce into evidence statements made under circumstances known only to the accuser and the accused.

According to Wigmore's (1970) historical analysis, the contemporary legal system's use of confessions has evolved through a series of discrete stages, ranging from unqualified admissibility to doubt about their veracity and frequent repudiation. During the 16th and 17th centuries in England, absolutely no restrictions existed about excluding confessions. All admissions of culpability were accepted without qualification. In fact, they were equivalent to a plea of guilt, precluding the need for a formal trial. One statement, in 1607, said it succinctly: "A confession is a conviction" (cited in Wigmore, 1970, p. 293).

Wigmore observed that at least through the middle of the 17th century, the use of physical inducements to confess was the rule, and the evidence so obtained was accepted almost without question. He wrote, "Up to the middle of the 1600s, at least, the use of torture to extract confessions was common, and confessions so obtained were employed evidently without scruple" (1970, p. 294). Franklin (1970) reported that the very first pictures ever drawn of police—found in Twelfth Dynasty Egyptian tombs of about 2000 B.C.—show them administering the third degree to a suspect. In one of the drawings, "a man is being beaten with a stick by one of the policemen, while his legs and arms are being held by three others, a fifth officer looks on supervising the proceedings" (Franklin, 1970, p. 15).

During the period of conquest by the Roman Empire, under Emperor Augustus, soldiers were allowed to apply torture to anyone except citizens of Rome. Jesus Christ received the third-degree treatment; "he was brutally manhandled by those who arrested him, and beaten for not giving the right answers to the high priest" (Franklin, 1970, p. 17).

Deeley (1971) concluded that the Inquisition, instituted by Pope Gregory IX in the 13th century and later led in Spain by the priest Torquemada, was "the forerunner of practices which, are still used in many countries today" (p. 8). Even informants, placed in the suspect's cell by authorities, were used back then. Under the implied blessing of the Roman Catholic Church hierarchy, including Pope Innocent IV, excruciating acts of torture were carried out in search of heretics, primarily Jews. Not only did the methods of physical torture carry forward to the present, but so too do we find vestiges of inquisitors' beliefs in the rightness of their acts—that the ends justify the means.

The Inquisition itself was not abolished until 1809. For more than 600 years its procedures reflected an assumption that threat and psychological coercion could be effective. Eymeric, the Grand Inquisitor of Aragon, laid forth a guide for his brother priests that included five steps; "the threat of torture, taking the victim to the torture chamber, showing him the instruments (the Spaniards called them 'engines'), and explaining in detail how they worked; undressing and preparing the victim, placing him in a machine and tying him down, and finally, the torture itself" (Deeley, 1971, pp. 9–10). At each step, the inquisitor would remind the victim of the folly of remaining silent.

Perhaps surprisingly, given their heinousness, the tactics of inquisitors were closely regulated. Lawyers were required to remain at the side of the heretic, and to note every word he said as he was tortured; they also recorded how long the torture lasted and what specific methods were used. The law was explicit that a man could not be tortured more than once unless new evidence came to light, but torturers could use whatever method they felt suitable to the case—deprivation of sleep, use of the rack, or of what we now know as "water boarding," which caused victims to fear that they would suffocate (Deeley, 1971). When the victim was given a chance to confess, a lawyer would record his willingness or reluctance to talk. As Deeley observed, "in the name of legality, it was possible to carry out the most hideous practices" (1971, p. 12).

In another forerunner of more recent practices, the Holy Office stated that the confessions obtained as a result of such tortures were not valid unless they were later "voluntarily" ratified by the victim. The "two-step" procedure described in the *Seibert* case in Chapter 1 perhaps had its origin in this set of actions—first get a confession, then get the suspect to waive his or her rights so that the confession appears to be sincere.

Joan of Arc, Savonarola, and Galileo were, of course, other famous victims of the Inquisition. Joan was subjected to prolonged and relentless questioning, accompanied by the threat of torture (Franklin, 1970). Savonarola was a priest in Florence who denounced the immoralities of the Papacy. After being tortured in 1498, he agreed to make any confession that his inquisitors sought from him. Galileo was torn between his allegiance to the Church and his observations of the solar system as a scientist. Broken and ill at the age of 70 and having been shown the instruments of torture, he recanted his advocacy of the sun as the center of our solar system.

The Salem witch trials in Massachusetts in 1692 were an American manifestation of the use of torture to generate false confessions. Sleep deprivation, forced exercise such as standing for very long periods, and the insertion of pins into the bodies of the young women, were among the devices used to get them to confess to their possession by Satan. Ann Foster, for example, confessed that the devil appeared to her in the shape of a bird on several occasions (Franklin, 1970).

Shifts in English Jurisprudence

Changes in the reliance on confessions began in England in the 17th century. During the reign of Charles I, from 1625 to 1649, the right against self-incrimination emerged in English common law, "largely in response to repressive measures taken, in the name of law, against some of the king's most persistent critics" (Stephens, 1973, p. 19). Beginning with the period after the Restoration of 1660, there was a slow and gradual amelioration in the procedures used in criminal trials in England. But not until one hundred years later, in 1775, did a judge for the first time place any restrictions on the admissibility of an ordinary confession. And shortly after that, in 1783, the modern view on the admissibility of confessions received what Wigmore (1970) called a "full and clear expression;" that is, the confessions that were obtained through brutality or even through promises or threats were not to be admitted into evidence.

At this point in his historical narrative, Wigmore made a rather astounding statement, given the continuing controversy over admitting coerced confessions at trial: "From this time on (i.e., 1783), the history of the doctrine is merely a matter of the narrowness or broadness of the exclusionary rule" (1970, p. 297). The point is—and Wigmore acknowledged it—that even while the doctrine was espoused that apparently untrustworthy confessions should not be accepted as indications of guilt, in the late 1700s very few confessions were in fact excluded from evidence. The everyday procedures were not consistent with the judicial precedents.

Emerging Distrust of Confessions

In contrast, by the beginning of the 19th century, a time emerged during which the judiciary was generally cynical about all confessions and tended to repudiate them if given the slightest justification. The bases for this distrust of confessions were articulated; they reflected beliefs that the process of procuring proof of an alleged confession through the testimony of a police officer or an informant is of questionable reliability, and thus that it may not really indicate guilt, especially if it has been generated by third-degree tactics or induced by promises of leniency or threats of more extreme punishment. Wigmore (1970) noted that one of the main reasons for distrusting confession evidence arises "when a person is placed in such a situation that an untrue confession of guilt has become the more desirable of two alternatives between which the person was obligated to choose" (p. 344). Historically, many of the false confessions extracted through torture, threats, and promises were probably of this type.

But psychological techniques of interrogation used by modern-day police—accusation, challenges to denials by the suspect, and repetition after repetition of charges—can lead to the same result. Leo (2008) recounts the reaction of one recent suspect, reflecting a choice that a false confession was better than maintaining innocence: "They just keep on and on. Hounding and hounding and hounding. Finally, I just said yes so they'd leave me along . . . I was just tired . . . I thought I was going home. I didn't go home" (Leo, 2008, p. 148). Kassin and Wrightsman (1985) labeled such confessions as coerced-compliant; the suspect confesses even while knowing that he or she is innocent. Coerced-compliant confessions may be given to escape further interrogation, to gain a promised benefit, or to avoid a threatened punishment. Reflecting the temporary nature of compliance to avoid further distress, such confessions are typically withdrawn and hence challenged at pretrial voluntariness hearings.

One significant improvement was permitting the accused to testify, on his or her own behalf, in order to discredit the confession previously given. As Wigmore stated, this development was in response to the unfairness of a system that had virtually told the person, "You cannot be trusted to speak here or elsewhere in your own behalf, but we shall use against you whatever you may have said" (1970, p. 300).

U.S. Supreme Court Decisions in the Late 1800s and Early 1900s

A bright light focused on the suspect's face . . . a rubber hose . . . a hot and crowded cell . . . The threat of further physical force and the promise of deprivation. These and other images—including beatings—contribute to the stereotype of police interrogation. Even the word *interrogation* conjures up unnatural interactions, as Samuel Johnson wrote, "Questioning is not a mode of conversation among gentlemen." The term *interrogation* is still used to describe questioning by police, regardless of whether it is conducted in the police station or in the field, before or after arraignment. The term is preferred over "interviewing" because it reflects a much more active role by the police detective. (Macdonald & Michaud, 1987)

In a thorough review of United States Supreme Court decisions regarding confessions, covering the period from the 1800s to slightly beyond the *Miranda* decision, Otis H. Stephens, Jr. (1973) observed that the initial concern of the Court was toward the "third degree" practices described in the above paragraph. (The origins of the term "third degree" are not clear, but its application to police work apparently originated to indicate a third step in the criminal investigative process, subsequent to arrest and custodial confinement [Franklin, 1970].) What resulted as the most common legal sanction against inappropriate police questioning was to challenge the admissibility of the evidence obtained. But even at that time, the Court had its limits. Three cases in the late 1800s are illustrative. In *Hopt v. Territory of Utah* (1884) the Court presumed that innocent suspects would not ordinarily falsely confess, but if they had been threatened or promised favorable outcomes, the confession could be called into question. But confinement and imprisonment (even in irons) were not, in themselves, grounds to question the authenticity of a confession (*Sparf and Hansen v. United States*, 1895).

The third case, *Bram v. United States* (1897), based on the Fifth Amendment's protection against self-incrimination, barred the introduction into evidence of involuntary confessions produced by interrogations that had threatened the suspect. In their decisions more than 100 years ago, the justices encouraged other safeguards besides the avoidance of threats and physical intimidation; one of these was corroboration. Stephens wrote:

> In addition to its development of safeguards against coerced confessions, the Supreme Court has also endorsed the evidentiary rule requiring corroboration of any extrajudicial confession, admission, or other statement made by the defendant and later introduced as evidence of guilt. Two variations of this rule have emerged: one stressing corroboration of the truth or reliability of the confession; the other requiring independent proof "tending to establish the corpus delicti, that is, the fact that the crime charged has been committed." The second rule is of less protection to the defendant, but the first definition of corroboration is an important safeguard against accepting coerced confessions. (Stephens, 1973, p. 13)

But the requirement of corroboration soon came to be ignored. (Interestingly, its usefulness has been revived by the recent advocate, Richard Leo [2008], in light of the purported inadequacies of the *Miranda* rule. Leo's position is described in Chapter 8). Instead, during the first half of the 1900s, the Court placed its emphasis on the "voluntariness" of a challenged statement, the alleged circumstances of coercion, and the supposed ability of the suspect to withstand pressure from the police. As we will see in the description of decisions by the Court in the 1930s and 1940s, justices differed in their assumptions about human abilities to withstand coercion, even while they were in agreement in their condemnation of *extreme* forms of third-degree methods by the police. Thus, the decision in *Brown v. Mississippi*, decided in 1936, was a landmark case for several reasons.

First, the Court overturned a jury verdict of guilt because the confession was obtained through the use of brutal methods; the decision was written by Chief Justice Charles Evans Hughes and endorsed by every one of the nine justices. Second, the Court's decision asserted that a trial is a mere pretense when the state authorities have contrived a conviction resting solely upon confessions obtained by the use of violence. In the *Brown* case, without the forced confessions of the three defendants, there had been little if any evidence upon which to convict them of murder.

The crime in the *Brown* case occurred in March 1934. A white man, a farmer, was found in his home in Kemper County, Mississippi, brutally murdered. A blood-stained axe and an article of clothing with gray hairs and blood on it were found near the house of one of the three defendants, Henry Shields. All three were African Americans and tenant farmers. A deputy sheriff and a mob of vigilantes took another one of the subsequent defendants, Yank Ellington, to the victim's house and hanged him from the limb of a tree. Taken down, he persisted in disclaiming any part in the murder. He was hanged a second time, and also whipped severely, but did not change his story.

The mob released him, but two days later two sheriff's deputies questioned him and beat him again. Finally, he agreed to sign whatever statement the sheriff chose to dictate. The other two defendants, the above-named Shields and Ed Brown, were put in jail, where they were severely whipped with a leather strap to which metal buckles were attached. Told that this torture would continue until they admitted guilt, they confessed and even altered the details of their confessions to fit the demands of their inquisitors. Their convictions were affirmed twice by the Mississippi Supreme Court (even though on both occasions powerful dissenting opinions were filed). Only after that did the United States Supreme Court overturn the convictions, ruling that those confessions that were generated through the use of brutal and violent inducements could not be admitted into evidence.

The atrocities committed against Ed Brown and the others in the pursuit of a conviction were certainly enough to cause the Supreme Court to outlaw police brutality. But during the 1930s there was also increased pressure by the public to restrain the police. The Wickersham Commission Report, published in 1931, and concurrently, a number of exposes in newspapers and books (Hopkins, 1931) reflected how the third-degree had become a "national scandal" (Leo, 2008). The Wickersham Commission, so named after its chair, former Attorney General George Wickersham, had been appointed in 1929 by President Hoover and was composed of prominent citizens; it published a report in 1931 documenting how the use of beatings of suspects by the police had become widespread.

Although the police generally tried to keep secret their use of physical methods because these violated the norms of acceptable behavior, on occasion accounts would surface, even by police officers themselves. In a book published in 1931, Cornelius Willemse described his approach:

> I opened a drawer of my desk. The prisoner could see blackjacks and lengths of rubber hose. A careful selection, and I drew out a long, black piece of hose, testing it in my hands and then a swish through the air before placing it on top of the desk. A loud moan from the next room, breaking off into sobs. The door opened suddenly. There stood the two detectives, ready for more action. Coats and vests off, shirt-sleeves rolled up, their hair disarranged. "One minute boys. I'll call you when you're needed!" The sound of groans had swelled. As the door closed again there came a stifled shriek. At last I spoke to the prisoner. (1931, pp. 345–346)

The Wickersham Commission made an important contribution by considering that "many things make it clear that a not inconsiderable portion [of suspects who underwent the third degree] are innocent" (1931, p. 161). The Commission's report also alerted the public to the fact that after the police had extracted an involuntary confession from a suspect, they would insert significant and convincing details into the typed statements that the suspect would sign, including a disclaimer that "the statement is made freely and voluntarily and is not made by me as a result of any form of threat or induce-ment" (Hopkins, 1931, p. 283).

In his careful review of the effects of third-degree tactics by the police in the first half of the 20th century, Leo (2008) recognized that it is impossible to pinpoint how many confessions were false; he wrote:

> Though we lack quantitative data on how often police-induced false confessions led to wrongful convictions in the era of the third degree, the qualitative data gives us every reason to believe that it occurred frequently. Not only did American police use the third degree extensively in the early 20th century, but a confession, even then, was also the strongest piece of evidence the prosecution could bring against a criminal defendant at trial. (2008, p. 59)

Inconsistency in the Court's Decisions

As noted, throughout the period of its concern with interrogation procedures, the Supreme Court has demonstrated an inconsistent, shifting policy toward what it considers police behavior that is in conflict with constitutional protec-tions (White, 2001b). Sometimes, it tightened the reins on the police. For example, four years after the *Brown v. Mississippi* decision, in 1940, in *Chambers v. Florida*, the Court extended its prohibition to less violent forms of intimidation, including a prolonged and exhaustive interrogation, frequent threats, and isolation of the suspects from their relatives. (In this case, the suspects had resolutely refused to confess through five days of questioning, only to succumb after an all-night interrogation.)

But until the 1960s, justices who wrote opinions for the Court disagreed about the kind of police pressure that was less drastic than the use of brutality and overt threats. As Stephens noted,

> Intra-Court disagreement has also risen over the point separating legitimate interrogation from unconstitutional coercion. Some justices (frequently a majority) have maintained that this distinc-tion should be made largely on the basis of the individual suspect's supposed ability to withstand the pressure of police questioning. Other members of the Court have insisted on condemning as "inherently coercive" sessions of interrogation that exceed a given number of hours or [prior to *Miranda*] occur in the absence of formal warnings of the right to remain silent and the right to the presence of an attorney. (1973, p. 16)

The inconsistent position of the Court prior to its *Miranda* decision is reflected in its reaction to two cases in 1944; cases that were decided by the Court *only one month apart*. In the first (*Ashcraft v. Tennessee*, 1944), E.E. Ashcraft was suspected of arranging for his wife's murder and was questioned continuously for 36 hours in regard to her death; the detectives came at him in relays, and he was given only 5 minutes respite from questioning during this entire day-and-one-half period. He then, it is claimed, admitted to the murder of his wife, a confession that he recanted at his trial. Justice Hugo Black wrote the opinion for the Court, declaring that the intensity and duration of the interrogation constituted a "situation . . . so inherently coercive that its very existence is irreconcilable with the possession of mental freedom by a lone suspect against whom its full coercive force is brought to bear" (*Ashcraft v. Tennessee*, 1944, p. 154). Five other justices agreed, but not all justices were in agreement with this position. Justice Robert Jackson wrote a minority opinion (endorsed by Justices Felix Frankfurter and Owen Roberts), which reflected the traditional assumption that those suspects who were truly innocent possessed the ability and the will to withstand even this excessive pressure. In his dissent Justice Jackson wrote:

> If the constitutional admissibility of a confession is no longer to be measured by the mental state of the individual confessor but a general doctrine dependent on the clock, it should be capable of statement in definite terms. If 36 hours is more than permissible, what about 24? Or 12? Or six? Or one? All are "inherently coercive." (pp. 161–162)

The forward-looking decision authored by Justice Black did not remain operative; the appeal in *Lyons v. Oklahoma* (1944), decided by the same nine justices just a little more than a month after *Ashcraft*, had a radically different outcome. (Thurgood Marshall, later to become a justice, represented the defendant Lyons.) Justice Jackson was able to persuade a majority of justices, including Chief Justice Stone and Justice Stanley Reed, who wrote the opinion for the Court. The majority upheld the use of continued questioning as long as the individual suspect possessed "mental freedom" at the time of his or her confession. (Lyons and an accomplice were suspected of the murder of a man, a woman, and their 4-year-old son. Lyons was arrested, questioned for two hours, and held incommunicado for 11 days; then he was questioned again for at least eight hours, during which he was physically abused and threatened. He was even shown the "bones" of a murder victim. He then confessed).

Even though the *Lyons* decision was a setback for those concerned with the invidious nature of interrogations, the use of "mental freedom" put an issue on the table. Yes, the two decisions, *Ashcraft* and *Lyons*, so close and yet so disparate, illustrated how much the justices could differ in their assumptions about the capacity of possibly innocent suspects to withstand coercive procedures. But it also opened the door for the justices in the *Miranda* appeal to reconsider the centrality of "mental freedom."

The juxtaposition of the *Ashcraft* decision and the one in the *Lyons* case reflects the dilemma between prohibiting "inherent coerciveness" while not frustrating the police from obtaining credible confessions. Yet, it should be noted that when the Supreme Court, in the 1930s and 1940s, did restrict the admissibility of confessions, the rationale bore little resemblance to the original English common-law rule. As Stephens observed:

> The common-law rule was designed primarily to guard against the introduction of unreliable evidence. It was based on the assumption that a criminal suspect subjected to threats or other forms of intimidation might make a false confession to save himself from further coercion. The common-law rule was thus not aimed at objectionable interrogation practices *per se*, but at the protection of the defendant against an erroneous conviction. The Supreme Court, on the other hand, has been more concerned with the basic fairness of the proceedings against the individual, irrespective of the authenticity of any statement resulting from the interrogation. (1973, p. 17)

As the previous material reflects, the Court has vacillated between dual objectives. For some justices—as we saw reflected in the dissent by Justice O'Connor in Chapter 1—voluntariness remains as the most important, if not the sole, criterion for the admissibility of confession evidence. The major task for legal scholars became to articulate the theoretical rationale for this as a criterion as well as a procedural strategy for its implementation. Why are involuntary confessions excluded? Throughout the various Supreme Court decisions, essentially two reasons were advanced. First is the above-mentioned common-law explanation that involuntary confessions, like testimony given when intoxicated or in response to leading questions, are untrustworthy and unreliable (see Wigmore, 1970: *Stein v. New York*, 1953). Accordingly, the operational test recommended for judges' rulings of admissibility would be whether the inducement had been sufficient to preclude a "free and rational choice" and produce a fair risk of false confession.

The second rationale, first articulated in *Lisenba v. California* (1941), was that "the aim of the requirement of due process is not to exclude presumptively false evidence but to prevent fundamental unfairness in the use of evidence whether true or false" (p. 237). (Ironically, this rationale, expressed by Justice Owen Roberts, came in a majority opinion that ruled against the criminal defendant, who had claimed that brutal tactics had coerced him into confessing. The defendant was charged with murdering his wife and claiming it was an accident in order to cash in on a double-indemnity life insurance policy.) Both scholarly sentiment (McCormick, 1946; Paulsen, 1954) and subsequent case law (e.g., *Rogers v. Richmond*, 1961) have shifted toward this latter emphasis on constitutionally-based procedural fairness, individual rights, and the deterrence of reprehensible police misconduct. As such, although involuntary confessions may be excluded if they are seen as untrustworthy, the criterion is not enough—they also must be excluded if illegally obtained.

Voluntariness is a difficult concept to operationalize because it requires inferences about the suspect's subjective state of mind and embraces the dual concerns of trustworthiness and due process. For example, voluntariness cannot be equated with the probable truth of a confession because the use of this definition could result in the failure to enforce the Due Process Clause of the Fourteenth Amendment (i.e., in instances in which confessions are coerced but subsequently corroborated by additional testimony). In fact, five years before its *Miranda* decision, the Court ruled in *Rogers v. Richmond* that it was a violation of the Fourteenth Amendment for a state court to include the truthfulness of a confession as a component in determining whether it was voluntary (DeClue, 2005). Many courts had adopted a rule-of-thumb approach by which confessions were excluded if induced by a threat or a promise. But this restriction is not comprehensive because it fails to cover other tactics of coercive interrogations that do not involve promises or threats (for example, prolonged detention). Still other courts defined voluntariness as a subjective state of mind and attempted to assess whether the confession was free and rational or the "offspring of a reasoned choice" (*United States v. Mitchell*, 1944). As Justice Frankfurter wrote, "because the concept of voluntariness is one which concerns a mental state, there is the imaginative recreation, largely inferential, of internal, 'psychological' fact" (*Culombe v. Connecticut*, 1961, p. 603).

Graham's (1970) review noted that in the three decades between *Brown v. Mississippi* in 1936 and *Miranda v. Arizona* in 1966, the Supreme Court generated an astounding 36 opinions on the voluntariness of state court confessions, or more than one each year. He concluded, "They covered a wide variety of circumstances, some confessions were upheld and others were thrown out. The result was that state courts could examine the case-by-case authorities of the Supreme Court and could find authority for affirming or rejecting almost any type of confession" (1970, p. 35).

In fact, in 1960, only six years before *Miranda*, the Supreme Court seemed unable to take a firm position that gave direction to the state courts, which had to handle the vast majority of challenges to police interrogations. In *Blackburn v. Alabama* (1960), the Court evaded a precise definition and concluded that a "complex of values underlies the stricture against use by the state of confessions which, by way of convenient shorthand, this court terms involuntary, and the role played by each in any situation varies according to the particular circumstances of the case" (p. 207). The Court reaffirmed this position in a decision the next year, stating that the concept of involuntariness represented a summary expression for all the practices that violated constitutional principles (e.g., the right to a fair trial, the privilege against compulsory self-incrimination) and could be determined only through a comprehensive analysis of the "totality of the relevant circumstances" (*Culombe v. Connecticut*, 1961, p. 606).

The Court indicated that the catalogue of factors that might be relevant to a determination of voluntariness covered a wide range, including characteristics of the accused (e.g., youth, sub-normal intelligence, physical disability, mental illness, intoxication, illiteracy), the conditions of detention (e.g., delayed arraignment, inadequate living facilities, lack of access to a lawyer, friends, or other assistance), and—of course—the manner of interrogation (e.g., lengthy, grueling periods of questioning; the use of relays of questioners; multiple interrogators; physical abuse; deprivation of needs; threats of harm or punishment; and deception). As Justice Frankfurter wrote, "there is no simple litmus paper test" (*Culombe v. Connecticut*, 1961, p. 601). This failure to be explicit led to a disturbing inconsistency in rulings by lower courts. For example, in *Dorsciak v. Gladden* (1967) a confession was excluded because the interrogator told the defendant that the judge "would be easier on him." But in *People v. Hartgraves* (1964) the confession was admitted despite its having followed the interrogator's promise that "it would go easier in court for you if you made a statement."

And while we can decry the lack of a clear rule prior to *Miranda*, we should acknowledge that the laundry list of factors to be considered in judging voluntariness highlighted some aspects that reflect what we consider to be the main problems in implementing *Miranda*, described in subsequent chapters, including the difficulty in comprehension by some suspects and the use of deception by the police.

A hearing to Assess Voluntariness

We have described how voluntariness emerged as a central concept in determining whether a police-generated confession should be admitted into evidence. But how was this to be implemented?

In one of the clarifying decisions made by the Warren Court prior to its *Miranda* decision, *Jackson v. Denno* (1964) made explicit the exclusion of those confessions given against the will of the accused. In fact, in this case the Court held that criminal defendants have a due-process right that entitles them to a pretrial hearing; its purpose is to determine whether any confessions they have made to officials were voluntarily given and were not the outcome of physical or psychological coercion, which the United States Constitution forbids. Only *if* the fact finder—almost always a judge, although it could be a jury different from the trial jury—at this coercion hearing determines that a confession was in fact voluntary, may it be introduced as evidence at the trial. (Prior to this time, in many states the jury would decide the voluntariness of a confession and hence whether it could be used in deciding guilt or innocence.)

Requiring a judge or some other fact-finding body to screen confessions is a sensible idea, as well as a life-saving one for some defendants. But the rule did not completely resolve the problem. Left unclear in the *Jackson v. Denno* decision was what should be the standard of proof by which the fact finder judged voluntariness. This question reflected the fact that states had differed in their threshold for admitting confessions into evidence. Some states had adopted a stringent criterion that voluntariness must be proved *beyond a reasonable doubt*. In contrast, other states had set the bar lower, specifying proof of voluntariness by a mere *preponderance of the evidence*. The Supreme Court felt it necessary to resolve this discrepancy, but it did not do so until 1972, when conservative appointees had replaced several justices of the Supreme Court. In *Lego v. Twomey* (1972), it ruled that only a preponderance of the evidence in the direction of voluntariness was necessary to admit a confession into evidence.

Because the *Lego v. Twomey* decision set in place the lowered standard for admitting confessions into evidence—and it is still the law of the land—we think it is worthwhile to describe the facts of Lego's crime and subsequent interrogation. The following description is taken from the Supreme Court opinion. Note that the fact finder is presented with conflicting testimony from the defendant and the police regarding what occurred during the interrogation. This is typical, and that is one reason why the decision in this case was so important.

> Petitioner Lego was convicted of armed robbery in 1961 after a jury trial in Superior Court, Cook County, Illinois. The court sentenced him to prison for 25 to 50 years. The evidence introduced against Lego at trial included a confession he had made to police after arrest and while in custody at the station house. Prior to trial, Lego sought to have the confession suppressed. He did not deny making it but did challenge that he had done so voluntarily. The trial judge conducted a hearing, out of the presence of the jury, at which Lego testified that police had beaten him about the head and neck with a gun butt. His explanation of this treatment was that the local police chief, a neighbor and former classmate of the robbery victim, had sought revenge upon him. Lego introduced into evidence a photograph that had been taken of him at the county jail on the day after his arrest. This photograph showed that petitioner's face had been swollen and had traces of blood on it. Lego admitted that his face had been scratched in a scuffle with the robbery victim but maintained that the encounter did not explain the condition shown in the photograph. The police chief and four officers also testified. They denied either beating or threatening the petitioner and disclaimed knowledge that any other officer had done so. The trial judge resolved this credibility problem in favor of the police and ruled the confession admissible. At the trial, Lego testified in his own behalf. Although he did not dispute the truth of the confession directly, he did tell his version of the events that had transpired at the police station. The trial judge instructed the jury as to the prosecution's burden of proving guilt. He did not instruct that the jury was required to find the confession voluntary before it could be used in judging guilt or innocence. On direct appeal the Illinois Supreme Court affirmed the conviction. (*Lego v. Twomey*, 1972, pp. 480–481)

Thus each side's statement is self-serving and this becomes a "who-do-you-believe" case. Justice Byron White was chosen to write the majority opinion in the *Lego v. Twomey* case. He wrote:

> While our decision (in *Jackson v. Denno*) made plain that only voluntary confessions may be admitted at the trial of guilt or innocence, we did not then announce, or even suggest, that the fact-finder at the coercion hearing need judge voluntariness with reference to an especially severe standard of proof. (p. 478)

This decision was clearly a blow for defendants, who would have preferred a more rigorous threshold to be required before such potentially damaging testimony would be introduced to the jurors. (The *Lego* decision did permit any state to develop a more stringent standard if it so desired.)

In *Lego v. Twomey*, the Supreme Court reasoned that the sole aim of the previous *Jackson v. Denno* decision was to exclude evidence that was illegally obtained and hence violated the individual's right to due process, not because of the possible untruthfulness of a coerced confession. In fact, it assumed that jurors can be trusted to use potentially inaccurate confessions cautiously. Specifically, in *Lego v. Twomey*, the Court justified the latter position by saying: "Our decision was not based in the slightest on the fear that juries might misjudge the accuracy of confessions and arrive at erroneous determinations of guilt or innocence . . . Nothing in *Jackson* questioned the province or capacity of juries to assess the truthfulness of confessions" (1972, p. 485).

Do Jurors Really Discount a Possibly Coerced Confession?

Guided by a faith in jurors' capacities, the Supreme Court justified a lower threshold by which the fact finder may admit a confession whose voluntariness is in some question. Thus the Court assumed that jurors would be able to disregard testimony if they questioned the motivations behind it. Is that assumption by the Supreme Court well founded?

This is a problem in attribution, a topic that has been central to the interests of social psychologists for a number of years. Jurors are, after all, confronted with a behavior (a confession) whose cause is unclear (is it sincere and self-initiated or is it an example of the coerced-compliant type?). If a defendant confesses while under severe threat during an interrogation, that confession may be viewed either as a reflection of the defendant's true guilt or a means of avoiding the negative consequences of silence. Ideally, jurors employing what a leading attribution theorist (Kelley, 1971) has called the *discounting principle* would have more doubts about the truth and reliability of this kind of elicited confession than they would about one made in the absence of threat as a plausible cause; that is, they would "discount" or give less weight to the confession—perhaps they would even disregard it—because it was generated by the threat of force.

But discounting does not always occur. A number of social-psychological studies have reported that when making attributions about the causes of another's behavior, most people do not give sufficient importance to the situation as a determinant; instead, they accept the behavior at face value (Jones & Nisbett, 1972). That would mean that in the present situation they would conclude: "He confessed, so he must be guilty." A series of experiments by Jones and Harris (1967) had participants read an essay or hear a speech presumably written by another student. These speeches and essays reflected certain attitudes. In one study, participants read an essay in which the communicator either supported or criticized the Castro regime in Cuba. Some respondents were told that the communicator had freely chosen to advocate this position; others were told that the communicator had been assigned to endorse this unpopular decision by a political science instructor. But even when the participants thought the communicator had no choice but to write the essay, their impressions about the communicator's true beliefs were still markedly influenced by the particular position he had espoused. *It seems that what you say is more influential than why you say it.*

The parallels between this research procedure and the coerced confession are striking. In both, observers (research participants or jurors) are faced with a verbal behavior, which they may attribute either to the actor's true attitude or to the pressures emanating from the situation. Yet, although the Supreme Court assumed that jurors would reject the involuntary confessions as not to be trusted and thus not allow it to guide their decisions, the program of research by Jones and Harris suggests that jurors might not totally reject the confessions when considering the actor's true guilt.

The Cases that Led Up to *Miranda*

In the 1960s, the Supreme Court moved toward establishing more objective criteria for the admissibility of confession evidence. Up to that point, the refusal of the police to permit the accused to consult with an attorney was regarded as part of the "totality of relevant circumstances" for judging voluntariness. Then, in one of the first of the radical shifts, the Court ruled in 1964 in *Massiah v. United States* that if the accused had been indicted, all incriminating statements elicited by government agents in the absence of counsel were inadmissible. (Winston Massiah was an alleged drug dealer who had been released on bail and had hired a lawyer; he was tricked by an informant to make self-incriminating statements about the crime.) In this decision, the Supreme Court ruled that government actions had breached the Sixth Amendment's provisions that "in all criminal prosecutions, the accused shall enjoy the right to have the assistance of counsel in his defense." As Graham has observed, "This ruling was a narrow one in that the situation was unlikely to recur. But the holding established the precedent that fully voluntary admissions can be ruled out for the failure of the police to respect a suspect's right of counsel prior to trial" (1970, pp. 163–164).

The decision in *Massiah* followed directly from the Court's decision in *Gideon v. Wainwright* the year before. Clarence Gideon had been tried for breaking and entering a pool hall in Panama City, Florida, and stealing some money from the cigarette machine and jukebox. He had been convicted and was serving a five-year term in a Florida prison in 1963 when the Supreme Court ruled on his appeal. It was not his first offense; Gideon had served time on four previous occasions, mostly for burglary. A candid assessment must label him a small-town thief who lived on the edges of society.

At his trial, Gideon had asked the judge to appoint an attorney to defend him because he had no money to pay one. The judge, in accordance with the laws in Florida, had refused. Free attorneys were provided only if there were special circumstances in the case—if, for instance, the offense was a very serious one or if the defendant's mental abilities were limited. So Gideon had lacked the benefit of a lawyer's assistance during his trial. He lost, as we have seen, and eventually—from his prison cell—he filed a pauper's appeal to the United States Supreme Court. His contention, laboriously printed in pencil, was that the United States Constitution guaranteed the right of every defendant in a criminal trial to have the services of a lawyer. Gideon's efforts were a long shot, the vast majority of appeals every term are pauper's appeals (almost all from prisoners) and the Supreme Court agrees to consider less than 1% of them. But Gideon's appeal was one of the very few that the Court chose to review.

When Gideon's case was argued before the Supreme Court in January, 1963, he was represented by Abe Fortas, a prominent Washington attorney who later was named a Supreme Court justice himself. Fortas argued that it was impossible for a person to have a fair trial unless he or she was represented by a lawyer. He also observed that the "special circumstances" rule was very hard to apply fairly. Twenty-two state attorneys general wrote friend-of-the-court appeals to support Fortas' argument. Among these were Thomas Eagleton and Walter F. Mondale, who were the attorneys general of Missouri and Minnesota at the time.

The attorney representing the State of Florida at Gideon's oral argument, Bruce Jacob, had an uphill battle. Chief Justice Warren, who, when a prosecutor in California had provided a lawyer for every defendant, asked: "Mr. Jacob, I suppose that of those 5,200 prisoners now in your jails who were not represented by counsel, that a vast majority of them are not only poor but are illiterate. Would that be a fair observation?" Jacob replied: "My observation is that—in all honesty, my observation is that there are some [Warren interjected: "Some?"] but I have no idea how many" (Irons & Guitton, 1993, p. 191).

Clarence Gideon did not have to wait long for a decision. On March 18, 1963, the Supreme Court announced its ruling, and on the main issue it was unanimous: Gideon had the right to be represented by an attorney, even if he could not afford one. Justice Hugo Black's opinion stated: "That the government hires lawyers to prosecute and defendants who have the money hire lawyers to defend are the strongest indications of the widespread belief that lawyers in criminal cases are necessities, not luxuries" (*Gideon v. Wainwright*, 1963, p. 344).

Nearly two years after he was sentenced, Clarence Gideon was given a new trial, and with the help of a free, court-appointed attorney, he was found not guilty. Gideon lived the rest of his life (he was 51 at the time of the crime) almost free of legal tangles; his only subsequent difficulty came two years after he was freed when he pleaded guilty to a vagrancy charge in Kentucky. He died in 1972.

The *Gideon* and *Massiah* decisions set something major in motion. On virtually an annual basis over the next few years, the Warren Court chose to expand the rights of suspects. The next petitioner to become a test case was Danny Escobedo, a 22-year-old Mexican-American laborer living in Chicago, who was accused of murdering his sister's husband. A few hours after the killing, he was arrested without a warrant and interrogated. While being questioned by the police, he asked repeatedly to see his lawyer but was refused. In actuality, his lawyer was trying to contact him during the interrogation that lasted almost 20 hours, but the police ignored his requests.

Escobedo was tricked into admitting his guilt, or at least he so claimed, during this long period of questioning, and his confession was used against him at his trial. The jury found Escobedo guilty; he was sentenced to a prison term of 20 years to life.

Were his rights violated when the police denied his request for a lawyer who could have advised him during the interrogation? The Supreme Court, in June 1964, said yes: because the police did not warn Escobedo of his right to remain silent as guaranteed under the Fifth Amendment and denied him the aid of a lawyer in violation of the Sixth Amendment, statements of his that the police elicited during the questioning should not have been introduced into the evidence against him at his trial. Accordingly, now in the absence of a confession that was admissible in court, Escobedo's conviction was overturned and he was released because the prosecutors concluded that they did not have a strong case against him without the confession.

In the *Escobedo* decision, the Supreme Court broadened the application of the Fifth and Sixth Amendments, thus giving suspects greater legal protections at earlier stages in a criminal investigation. In contrast to the *Gideon* ruling, however, this further extension of rights was by no means unanimous; the *Escobedo* majority was by the narrowest of margins, 5 to 4. In writing the majority decision, Justice Arthur Goldberg declared that once suspects became the focus of investigation, they were entitled to legal assistance; otherwise the trial would be nothing more than an appeal from the suspect's interrogation. Justice Goldberg was not convinced that broadening the right to counsel would discourage confessions and hamstring the enforcement of the law; as the quotation from the decision at the heading of this chapter reflects, his focus reflected a belief that it is wrong for our legal system to obstruct the exercise of constitutional rights.

Danny Escobedo's life did not proceed swimmingly from that point on, even though he was set free (Formanek, 1985). He later claimed that he was constantly harassed by the Chicago police. He was arrested 16 more times, but most of the charges eventually were dropped. Then he was convicted of conspiracy to sell amphetamines and spent five years in prison. And two days before Christmas in 1983, he was charged with taking indecent liberties with a 13-year-old child while he lived with her and her mother; he was convicted and sentenced to 12 years in prison. Two years later, in 1985, having been freed on bond while appealing his indecent liberties conviction, he was charged with two counts of attempted murder during a shooting in a Southside Chicago tavern. He was arrested in 2001 in Mexico, for violation of federal probation; at that time he was approximately 65 years old.

These decisions culminated in the *Miranda v. Arizona* decision in 1966. But that decision, like the one in *Escobedo*, reflected a divided Supreme Court, and so Chapter 3 describes the crime, the appeal, and the decision in detail.

3

The Decision in *Miranda v. Arizona*

The person in custody must, prior to interrogation, be clearly informed that he has the right to remain silent, and that anything he says will be used against him in court; he must be clearly informed that he has the right to consult with a lawyer and to have a lawyer with him during interrogation, and that, if he is indigent, a lawyer will be appointed to represent him.
—(*Miranda v. Arizona*, 1966, p. 437)

Social psychologists operate from a fundamental principle, first espoused by one of their field's founders, Kurt Lewin, "Behavior is a function of the person and the situation." In this chapter the "behavior" we consider is the Supreme Court's decision to grant suspects the right to be warned of their rights to silence and to an attorney; specifically, it is the behavior of a majority of the justices who signed on to the opinion for the Court, prepared by Chief Justice Earl Warren. So when social psychologists say that a behavior comes from both the situation and the person, they are implying that a given action requires environmental conditions that permit the action to occur as well as internal qualities of the person, in order for the action to take place. In 1966 there was ample evidence that police in many jurisdictions continued to resort to physical brutality to elicit confessions (*Miranda v. Arizona*, 1966, p. 446); furthermore, many police departments had switched to a psychologically-oriented interrogation that still was coercive. The *Miranda* decision (on pp. 448–456) described the tactics advocated by the various police training manuals available at that time (we will describe these and their more recent counterparts in Chapter 7). But even if a certain situation exists, there is no guarantee that the actors (in this instance, the Court's justices) will behave in a certain way. Humans are a variable group. Some will have qualities that direct them to take action given a certain situation and others will not. We have already seen in Chapter 2 that in many situations the judgment whether or not a confession was voluntary is in the eye of the beholder, and potential actors who differ in their support of due process and crime control will differ in their response to a given situation.

In actuality, the bare minimum—only 5 out of 9 justices—voted in favor of adopting what we now call the Miranda rights. If President Eisenhower had not appointed Earl Warren to the Supreme Court to repay a campaign debt—but had appointed a more traditional conservative instead—the appeal by Ernesto Miranda would have been decided in the opposite way.

When the justices hold their conference on a particular case, a few days after its oral arguments, they take a preliminary vote. The closeness of the vote has an influence on just how the eventual decision is worded. The author of an opinion for which the tentative vote was unanimous has a lot of freedom to write an expansive, unconditional opinion. Even if one or two justices object and threaten to change sides if the draft is not revised, the opinion drafter can ignore their objections (and even their support) and still retain the majority necessary to make his or her draft the opinion for the Court. But when the tentative vote is 5 to 4, the opinion drafter must be careful to craft an opinion that does not cause defections. William Brennan, who was on the Court from 1956 to 1990, was able to write drafts and revisions that accommodated the concerns of those whose initial vote sided with him; sometimes he had to write 10 to 15 drafts, but he was so successful that he earned the reputation of being an effective conciliatory force on the Court. In the matter of *Miranda*, Earl Warren had to take into account the lack of unanimity among his colleagues.

Thus the *Miranda* decision, despite the criticism it instantly received from those who favored the crime-control model, was a compromise. The Court could have adopted more stringent measures that would have severely inhibited interrogations. The purpose of this chapter is to describe the process through which the decision was developed, including the differing viewpoints of the various justices. But first we begin with the facts of the case that led to the decision.

The Crimes of Ernesto Miranda

The "*Miranda* case" stemmed from what has become, in the United States, an all too typical occurrence with an all too disturbing outcome. Late on a Saturday night, March 2, 1963, an 18-year-old woman finished her job at the refreshment stand at the Paramount Theater in downtown Phoenix, Arizona. After taking a bus to near her home, she started walking the remaining distance. By then it was just past midnight; a man grabbed her, placed something sharp against her neck, dragged her to a parked car, tied her hands behind her, laid her down on the back seat, and tied her ankles together. He told her to lie still. He drove the car out into the desert, where he unbound her and raped her. Then, as he waited for her to get dressed, he demanded whatever money she had. She gave him the four $1 bills from her purse.

The young woman was one of 152 rape victims in Phoenix in 1963. There had been only 123 the previous year and even fewer, 109, in 1958. By 1970 there were more than 300 a year. These figures are a microcosm of those, countrywide, that eventually contributed to reversing the trend set forth by the Warren Court decisions and re-establishing crime control as the dominant value in the Court's decisions for the next 40 years.

But national implications of a court decision were far from the minds of the Phoenix police when they had the victim look at a lineup on Sunday morning. She had described her attacker as a Hispanic-American male, 27 or 28, 5'11", and weighing 175 pounds. He was of slender build, she said, medium complexion, with black, short hair. She further described him as wearing Levis, a white T-shirt, and dark-rimmed glasses. The police composed a lineup of likely-looking choices, but the victim failed to identify anyone. She was very shy; apparently of limited intelligence, she had dropped out of school after failing for several years.

But the victim's brother-in-law, a week after the rape, spotted a car like the one the victim had described (a 1953 Packard). He pointed it out to her and she said yes, it did look like it. As the car sped away, they were able to reconstruct enough of the license plate for the police to trace it. The car was registered to a young woman who had a friend named Ernesto Miranda. He fit the description; he was a Hispanic-American in his early twenties.

When the police located the car, they saw a rope strung along the back of the front seat, just as the young woman had described it. Police records also generated the information that Miranda had several previous criminal convictions, including one for assault with the intent to commit rape. A person with a long history of criminal activity, back to age 14, he had been charged with attempted rape at the age of 15.

So the police put together a new lineup. They took three Hispanic Americans, all about the same height and build, to stand with Miranda. But he was the only one wearing a short-sleeved T-shirt; he was the only one with eyeglasses; and he was the only tattooed man in the lineup. Still, the young woman could not identify her assailant, although she felt that Number 1, Ernesto Miranda, had a similar build and features. Nor could another victim, a woman involved in a similar crime three weeks earlier, who viewed the same lineup.

Frustrated, the police then took Miranda to an interrogation room. "How did I do?" Miranda asked. "Not good Ernie," a police officer replied. "They identified me, then" Miranda asked. "Yes Ernie, they did," replied the detective. "Well," said Miranda when faced with the false information, "I guess I better tell you about it then" (Stuart, 2004, p. 6). No attorneys were present, no witnesses, no tape recorders. The police later reported that Miranda voluntarily confessed, that he "admitted not only 'that he was the person who raped this girl' but that he had attempted to rape another woman and to rob still another" (Baker, 1983, p. 13).

At that point the police officer, Carroll Cooley, began to question Miranda. He handed him a standard form, after having already filled in the top four lines: SUBJECT: Rape DR 63-8380, STATEMENT OF: Ernest Arthur Miranda;

TAKEN BY: C. Cooley, #413-W. Young #182; DATE: 3-13-63; TIME: 1:30 p.m.; PLACE TAKEN: Interr. Room #2. At the top of the standard form was a paragraph that read:

> I,_____, do hereby swear that I made this statement voluntarily and of my own free will, with no threats, coercion, or promises of immunity, and with full knowledge of my legal rights, understanding any statement can be used against me.
> I, _____, am_____ years of age and have completed _____grade in school.

Miranda wrote his name, recorded his age as 23, and the grade completed as eighth.

Then, in the space below, he wrote:

> Seen a girl walking up street stopped a little ahead of her got out of car walked towards her grabbed her by the arm and asked to get in car. Got in car without force tied hands and ankles. Drove away for a few miles. Stopped asked to take her clothes off. Did not, asked me to take her back home. I started to take clothes off her without any force and with cooperation. Asked her to lay down and she did. Could not get penis into vagina got about 2; (half) inch in. Told her to get clothes back on. Drove her home. I couldn't say I was sorry for what I had done but asked her to pray for me.

When he had finished, Miranda signed a form again at the bottom, beneath the comment: "I have read and understand the foregoing statement and hereby swear to its truthfulness." Detectives Cooley and Young signed the document as witnesses (Stuart, 2004, pp. 6–7).

But Miranda described the interrogation quite differently:

> Once they get you in a little room and they start badgering you one way or the other, 'You better tell us . . . or we're going to throw the book at you'. . . that is what was told to me. They would throw the book at me. They would try to give me all the time they could. They thought there was even a possibility that there was something wrong with me. They would try to help me, get me medical care if I needed it . . . And I haven't had any sleep since the day before. I'm tired. I just got off my work, and they have me and they are interrogating me. They mention first one crime, then another one, they are certain I am the person . . . Knowing what a penitentiary is like, a person has to be frightened, scared. And not knowing if he'll be able to get back up and go home. (Baker, 1983, p. 13)

Whichever story one believes, Ernesto Miranda emerged from the questioning a confessed rapist. Since the young woman had actually been unsure of identifying Miranda, the police summoned her to the interrogation room to hear Miranda's voice. As she entered, one of the police officers asked

Miranda, "Is that the girl?" "That's the girl," he replied, believing that she had already identified him in the lineup.

The Trial for Robbery

Miranda was first brought to trial in June of 1963. This was not for the charge of raping the movie theater attendant but instead for the charge of robbery of another young woman five months before. (When the woman seemed to be successfully resisting his assault, he took the money in her purse—$8—and left.) Not being able to afford a lawyer (and being a beneficiary of the recent *Gideon* decision of a year before), Miranda was assigned a 73-year-old lawyer, a sole practitioner, who readily took the assignment of representing indigent criminal defendants even though most of his experience was in civil court. He was paid a total of $50 to represent Miranda; trials such as this one, which included confessions by the defendants, usually lasted only one day. But prior to the trial, Miranda's attorney filed a solitary motion, that Miranda would plead the insanity defense. This caused the defendant to be evaluated by two prominent Phoenix psychiatrists. Contrary to the defense attorney's hope, they both concluded that Miranda was not insane, that according to the report of one of them, "he was aware of the nature and quality of his acts and he was aware that what he did was wrong" (Stuart, 2004, p. 9). However, each did not give him a full bill of mental health, concluding that he had "an emotional illness and that his judgment and reasoning were impaired" (Stuart, 2004, p. 9).

At this first trial, during cross-examination the officer who had been in charge acknowledged that he had not told Miranda about his rights to an attorney. Although at this trial Miranda was not charged with rape, his attorney ineptly asked the police officer if his conversation with Miranda concerned rape. This permitted the prosecution to bring out that Miranda had admitted to the police that raping the woman was his original intention, but she had "kind of talked him out of it . . . and he had changed his mind and he said he decided just to take her money" (Stuart, 2004, p. 12). This gaffe also meant that when the robbery victim subsequently testified, she could describe Miranda's efforts to rape her.

In this first trial, for robbery, Miranda took the stand in his defense and acknowledged that on the day of the crime he had interacted with the victim, that he had helped her get her car started, and that she had asked him if he wanted to go home with her, but when they arrived there and he put his hand on her thigh, she bit him on the cheek. At this point, he claimed, he "got disgusted, got out of her car, and went around to the back of the car and asked her if she had any money. She grabbed her purse . . . took the money out and give [sic] it to me" (Stuart, 2004, p. 13).

The jury at the robbery trial deliberated only briefly before reaching a unanimous verdict of guilt. Since Miranda was to be tried for rape of the theater attendant the next day in the same courtroom with the same lawyers and judge, sentencing was deferred. (A different jury decided Miranda's fate in the rape trial.)

The Trial for Rape

In a highly unusual maneuver, the prosecution in Miranda's rape trial waived its opening statement, and the defense did too, so the jurors only gradually learned of the facts of this case. Immediately placing the victim on the stand, the prosecutor used a series of questions to piece together a narrative of what happened to the young woman as she walked home from her movie-theater job. After describing the act of penetration, she then identified Miranda.

Upon cross-examination, Miranda's court appointed attorney continued his inept behavior from the first trial; he asked the victim, "You are a very young girl, do you know the difference between rape and seduction?" "Yes," the victim answered. "If you know the difference, did the defendant rape you or did he seduce you?" "He raped me," the victim answered immediately and authoritatively (Stuart, 2004, p. 18). Once again the police detective testified, and Miranda's confession was admitted into evidence.

Miranda's attorney, in his closing argument, reflected the all-too-frequent strategies of placing the burden of proof on the victim and attempting to denigrate her reputation. He told the jury:

> I could be wrong and that is either this young lady—and she is a nice-looking young lady—but she is human like you and I—and that is whether or not she resisted until she could resist no longer. That is the meat of the coconut, and I want to say this to you. You men don't know too much about that because you are not nervous and you don't thread needles, but a nervous person can't thread a needle if the needle is moving. Thank you. (Stuart, 2004, p. 21)

The jury in Miranda's rape trial, like the first jury, only deliberated briefly, and in less than an hour returned a unanimous guilty verdict. On June 20, 1963, Miranda was sentenced to 20 to 30 years for kidnapping and rape; he was also sentenced for a slightly shorter time for the $8 robbery charge, but this sentence was to run concurrently with the others.

The First Level of Appeals

Despite his faults as a trial strategist, Miranda's defense attorney should be commended for his willingness to pursue an appeal in what seemingly was a cut and dried case. In August 1963, two months after the trials, he appealed Miranda's convictions to the Arizona Supreme Court. But in a 21-page opinion, the court rejected all of the claims of error. Specifically, the court discarded the claim that the confession should not have been admitted into evidence, stating that the police "had informed him of his legal rights and that any statements he made might be used against him" (Stuart, 2004, p. 41).

In examining the constitutional issues related to Miranda's appeal, the Arizona Supreme Court had to consider the United State Supreme Court's decision in *Escobedo v. Illinois* which had just been announced, but found it inapplicable because, in contrast to Danny Escobedo, Ernesto Miranda had been advised of his rights. "He had not requested counsel and had not been denied assistance of counsel. We further call attention to the fact that . . . the defendant Miranda had a record, which indicated he was not without courtroom experience" (Stuart, 2004, p. 42). In summary, this court was explicit: "We hold that a confession may be admissible when made without an attorney if it is voluntary and does not violate the constitutional rights of the defendant" (Stuart, 2004, p. 42).

The Appeal to the United States Supreme Court

The decision by the Arizona Supreme Court in April of 1965 could have terminated what has become "the Miranda story." Most of the losing parties in appeals at that level do not pursue their appeals further (and among those that do, few receive satisfaction). According to the detailed history of the *Miranda* case by Gary Stuart (2004), the one person responsible for keeping the *Miranda* case alive was Robert Corcoran, counsel to the Arizona branch of the American Civil Liberties Union (and later a justice on the Arizona Supreme Court). He became interested in the case in the summer of 1965, only a few months after the announcement by the Arizona Supreme Court of its decision. Stuart described his motivation:

> Corcoran, like many others, viewed *Escobedo* as another incremental change, consistent with past standards, and so he became hopeful that *Miranda* might be the next step in the effort to further expand the *Escobedo* doctrine to include cases wherein the suspect had *not* asked for a lawyer. (2004, p. 43, italics in original)

Beyond the Warren Court's clear involvement in the rights of those individuals suspected of crimes, Corcoran had another reason why he thought the Supreme Court would consider an appeal by Miranda: the California courts (in *California v. Dorado*, 1965) had just extended *Escobedo* to cases in which the defendant had not asked for a lawyer, concluding that "the defendant must be advised that he does have the right to counsel and that anything he does say may be used against him" (1965, p. 952). The United States Supreme Court, in choosing which of the many appeals it will decide, looks with favor on those that reflect inconsistent rulings between two lower courts.

Corcoran then enlisted the energies of two prominent Phoenix attorneys: John P. Frank, a noted constitutional scholar who had clerked for Justice Hugo Black and had taught at Yale Law School; and John Flynn, a very effective litigator. He also wrote to Ernesto Miranda, urging him to retain the law firm where these two attorneys worked, and Miranda enthusiastically agreed. John P. Flynn thus became responsible for preparing the brief to the Supreme Court;

such briefs, called petitioner's briefs, are limited to 50 pages, and there is an art to writing an effective one.

Frank had to decide the basis on which to frame the appeal; he saw the matter as a constitutional issue, but which amendment best applied? The Fifth Amendment guarantees the privilege against self-incrimination; several recent cases favoring defendants were based on the Due Process Clause of the Fourteenth Amendment. But he chose to place his foundation on the Sixth Amendment, which dealt with the rights to trial. He framed the central question of his brief as follows: "Whether the confession of the poorly educated, mentally abnormal, indigent defendant, not told of his right to counsel, which was not requested, can be admitted into evidence over specific objection based on the absence of counsel?" (Stuart, 2004, p. 47).

When a petitioner's brief is submitted to the Supreme Court, the other party—in this case, the State of Arizona—is given opportunity to respond with a brief of the same length, the purpose of which is to argue that the Supreme Court should not take the case. In response to the *Miranda* appeal, Arizona Assistant Attorney General Gary Nelson agreed that only the Sixth Amendment applied, but he questioned the accuracy of the descriptive phrases "poorly educated" and "mentally abnormal."

In retrospect, it seems inevitable that the Court would grant *certiorari* to a case like Miranda's, given its decision in the *Escobedo* case two years before, as that case raised many uncertainties about the validity of confessions and the procedures used by police in confronting suspects. Shortly after that decision, the Clerk of the Supreme Court had been marking certain appeals "E.C." for "Escobedo cases." By late November 1965, approximately 140 such cases had accumulated (Graham, 1970). On November 22, 1965, the Supreme Court granted *certiorari* to the *Miranda* appeal and four other similar cases.

It is true that the *Escobedo* opinion did not give clear guidance to the police. Law professor and confessions expert Yale Kamisar described it as "accordion-like," writing that,

> At some places the opinion seemed to say that a person's right to
> counsel is triggered once he or she becomes the "prime suspect" or
> once the investigation shifts from the "investigatory" to the "accusa-
> tory" stage and begins to "focus" on the suspect. At other places,
> however, the opinion seems to limit the case's holding to the specific
> facts preceding Escobedo's confession. (Kamisar, 1992, p. 260)

The Oral Arguments

The oral arguments for *Miranda* and its similar cases began on Monday, February 28, 1966. Because there were five cases, each with two opposing lawyers, the oral arguments were spread over three days, and generated a 280-page transcript. (Forty years ago, the Court permitted each side up to an hour and a half, as opposed to the 30-minute limit in effect today.)

Although John Frank, the legal scholar, had prepared the petitioner's brief, he believed that the oral argument for Miranda should be delivered by someone with superior oratorical skills, his partner John J. Flynn. When Flynn approached the podium at 10 a.m. that Monday, he faced nine justices, four of them appointed by Republican presidents (Chief Justice Earl Warren, Associate Justices William Brennan, John Marshall Harlan, II, and Potter Stewart, all appointed by President Eisenhower) and five appointed by Democratic presidents (William O. Douglas and Hugo Black, appointed by Franklin Roosevelt; Tom Clark, by Truman, Byron White, by Kennedy; and Abe Fortas, by Johnson). Common wisdom and empirical evidence (Rowland & Carp, 1996; Wrightsman, 2006) says that judges appointed by Democratic presidents support defendant's rights while judges appointed by Republican presidents protect the police. But among these nine men there were several anomalies; two of the Republican-generated appointees eventually supported Miranda and two of the Democratic appointees supported Arizona.

In recent years the style of the justices at oral arguments has been to interrupt the advocates fairly quickly into their presentations. For example, in Chief Justice Rehnquist's last two terms, the average number of words uttered by petitioners' advocates before they were interrupted by one of the justices was 111 words—actually, given how attorneys speak, only about three sentences (Wrightsman, 2008). But John Flynn found to his delight that he was able to complete his opening phase without a single interruption; he covered the facts of the case and asserted that the issue was not whether to warn but when to warn. He summarized by telling the justices, "I believe the record indicates that at no time during the interrogation and prior to the confession—his oral confession—was he advised of his right to remain silent, of his right to counsel, or of his right to consult with counsel" (Stuart, 2004, p. 55).

Then, as John Frank recalled many years later, "Flynn paused briefly at this point to examine the faces of the justices, perhaps expecting a question, perhaps even inviting one. None was offered, however, and so he resumed, now with the intention of distinguishing *Miranda* from *Escobedo*" (Stuart, 2004, p. 55). Again, no justice interrupted, so he continued for a few more minutes, until a first question came from Justice Potter Stewart, who asked, in effect, at what point does a suspect have a right to a lawyer. Flynn used the opportunity to emphasize the disparity in suspects; he replied:

> I think that the man at that time has the right to exercise, if he
> knows, and under the present state of the law in Arizona, if he's rich
> enough, and if he's educated enough, to assert his Fifth Amendment
> right, and if he recognized that he has a Fifth Amendment right, to
> request counsel. But I simply say that at that stage of the proceed-
> ing, under the facts and circumstances in *Miranda* of a man of
> limited education, of a man who certainly is mentally abnormal,
> who is certainly an indigent, that when that adversary process came
> into being that the police, at the very least, had an obligation to

extend to this man not only his clear Fifth Amendment right, but to afford to him the right to counsel. (Irons & Guitton, 1993, p. 216)

So once again the dilemma was raised; the petitioner's brief spoke of Sixth Amendment rights, but here Flynn was insisting that it was the "Fifth Amendment, not the Sixth, that made *Miranda* different from its predecessors [including] *Gideon and Escobedo*" (Stuart, 2004, pp. 55–56). While Justice Stewart attempted another question, Flynn persisted:

Under the facts and circumstances in *Miranda*—of a man of limited education, of a man who certainly is mentally abnormal, who is certainly an indigent—that when the advocacy process comes into being that the police, at the very least, had an obligation to extend to this man . . . his clear Fifth Amendment right, to afford to him his right of counsel. (Stuart, 2004, p. 56)

When Justice Stewart finally got another question in, it initiated a response that later was transformed by the Court opinion into the warnings now well known by most American citizens. Justice Stewart: "And what would the lawyer advise him that his rights then were?" Mr. Flynn:

The right not to incriminate himself, and the right not to make any statement at all. Furthermore, the right to be free from questioning by the police department, that he had the right to ask, at an ultimate time, to be represented adequately by counsel in court, and that if he were indigent, too poor to employ counsel, that the state would furnish him counsel. (Stuart, 2004, pp. 56–57)

While Miranda's attorney had a highly successful oral argument, his adversary, Gary Nelson, representing the State of Arizona, did not fare so well. First, he had barely begun his presentation when he was interrupted. And the question, by Justice Fortas, was of the "Are you still beating your wife?" type: "Let us assume that he was advised of these rights. In your opinion does it make any difference when he was advised?" (Stuart, 2004, p. 59). Nelson's answer, reflecting the totality of circumstances, was unsatisfactory to Justice Fortas, who seemed to have his mind made up—well he might, having argued Clarence Gideon's case before he was appointed to the Court.

Duane Nedrud, another attorney representing the respondents, had an equally difficult time. He asked the Court not to "encourage" defendants to consult lawyers before talking to the police, because any defense lawyer "is going to prevent a confession from being obtained." Chief Justice Warren pounced on that, "Are lawyers a menace?" Nedrud was unable to answer directly, instead responding, "Mr. Chief Justice, a lawyer must, in our system of justice, *must* attempt to free the defendant. This is his job" (Irons & Guitton, 1993, p. 221, italics in original).

Interestingly enough, one of the ten attorneys who participated in these oral arguments was Thurgood Marshall. Given his support of the rights of the underprivileged and minorities, as exemplified by his role in the NAACP's protest of racial segregation in the public schools and his advocacy for African-American parents in *Brown v. Board of Education* 12 years before, one might assume that he represented one of Miranda's fellow criminal defendants. But at that time he was Solicitor General of the United States (having been appointed by President Johnson) and he was representing the FBI in the case of *Westover v. United States*. This case dealt with the length of time Carl Westover had been detained by the FBI and the lack of counsel during a protracted interrogation. Marshall told the justices that the suspect had been fully informed of his rights. Justice White asked: "Suppose . . . the person being interrogated is given such a warning and says, 'I want a lawyer'?" Stuart described the exchange as follows:

> To this Marshall responded with the standard, FBI-policy answer: "This statement says that if he wants to see an attorney he can do it before he talks."
> "If he says, 'I don't know anyone, I don't know a lawyer, I can't afford one but I still want to talk to one,' what happens then?" Justice White asked.
> To which Marshall answered: "If he says he still wants to talk to one it would be my position the agent has to say, 'We do not have a lawyer and we have no means of furnishing a lawyer.'"
> "Will the agent then go on and interrogate him?"
> "The agent would then say, 'In view of the fact that we can't give you a lawyer and we can't pay for a lawyer for you do you still want to talk?' He then is in a position I think to say, 'If I don't get a lawyer I don't talk,' and that is the end of it."
> "What if he says, 'No, I don't want to talk.' Is the interrogation over?"
> "Yes, Your Honor, I think so," Marshall responded.
> This was an admission that would not likely have come from any of the other government lawyers in the case, but it is entirely consistent with Marshall's view of individual rights. (2004, p. 71)

Marshall was appointed to the Supreme Court the next year, in 1967.

The Struggle within the Court to Adopt *Miranda*

Chief Justice Earl Warren announced the *Miranda* decision in the Supreme Court courtroom on Monday, June 13, 1966. Typically, the justice who authored the opinion for the Court gives only a brief overview of the decision. But Warren read the entire 60-page opinion—it took nearly an hour—and in a voice laden with emotion, he announced at the onset, "If a person in custody is to be subjected to interrogation, he must first be informed in clear and unequivocal terms that he has the right to remain silent" (Stuart, 2004, p. 81). Doubtless his emotion reflected the struggle within the Court to achieve an outcome that Warren sought.

The decision was endorsed by only the bare minimum—five justices—needed to make it the law of the land. Liva Baker's (1983) extended treatment of the *Miranda* case describes these five as "the justices born to families in humble circumstances looking at the interrogation room through the eyes of the defendant" and says "the Court had divided along class lines" (p. 166). To call the families of all five of the majority justices as from "humbler circumstances" may be a stretch—William Brennan's father was a labor organizer and very influential in New Jersey political affairs—but it is true that their backgrounds did not reflect the wealth of, for example, Justice John Marshall Harlan, II, whose grandfather had also been a Supreme Court Justice. We grant Baker's main point that justices differ in the perspective they take. In fact, those justices who, in her words, viewed the issues in *Miranda* "through the eyes of the policeman" (p. 166)—specifically Harlan, Byron White, Tom Clark, and Potter Stewart—subscribed to the crime control model described in Chapter 1, while the five justices in the majority reflected a concern with due process.

Proposed Sources of the Ideological Split within the Court

Let us examine more thoroughly whether the split in *Miranda* votes truly reflects a socio-economic-class split in the backgrounds of the justices. In an earlier book, one of us (Wrightsman, 2006) concluded that only four of the justices chosen in the last half of the twentieth century were members of families with working-class backgrounds. Of these, only one, Earl Warren, was on the Court in 1966. Warren's father worked on the railroad; the family had little money. Earl Warren's father once told him, "My boy, when you were born I was too poor to give you a middle name" (Schwartz, 1995, p. 436). While Justice Brennan's father stoked a coal-fired furnace in a New Jersey brewery, "the home in which Brennan grew up was not the typical working class environment" (Wermeil, 1995, p. 446) because his father worked in the local union and was elected four times to the governing body of the City of Newark. Both Brennan's parents were avid readers, including the classics. Abe Fortas's father was a cabinet-maker who operated his own shop. William O. Douglas was the son of a successful Presbyterian minister, but his father died when Douglas was 6 years old and his family was left with few financial resources, though we question if this would characterize him as being from the working class. While Hugo Black grew up in rural Alabama, his father's ancestors were merchants and his mother came from a landholding family.

We do not disagree with a characterization of each of these justices having a deep-set ideology favoring defendants' rights, but we note that their origins differed. Brennan's father doubtless instilled in him a sensitivity to the rights of common laborers and the underprivileged. Fortas doubtless experienced being a victim of discrimination because he was Jewish. Douglas had to overcome physical disabilities in order to succeed, and Black, while an attorney in Birmingham, oriented his practice toward working people and labor unions (Black, 1995). Earl Warren's support of defendant's rights is the most surprising because for many years as a district attorney in Alameda County, California, and as Attorney General of California, he vigorously prosecuted criminals and was known as a crusader against vice and violent crime (Schwartz, 1995).

But despite Warren's long experience as a prosecutor (or perhaps *because* of that experience), he distrusted the police. The opinion spends several pages detailing how police training manuals designed interrogations to elicit confessions. The opinion even described the use of trickery, noting how police are instructed to use fictitious witnesses who view a lineup and then identify the suspect. It also explains how the police manuals advised police when a suspect refuses to discuss the matter or asks for an attorney.

So how do the backgrounds of those five compare with those of the four in the minority on *Miranda*? Potter Stewart came from a prosperous and well-established Cincinnati family; his father was a prominent trial attorney and Republican politician (Kujovich, 1995). Byron White's father managed the local outlet of a lumber supply company in Wellington, Colorado. Shortly after he was appointed to the Supreme Court he recalled that, "by the normal standards of today we were all quite poor, although we didn't necessarily feel poor because everyone was more or less the same. Everybody worked for a living. Everybody. Everybody" (Hutchinson, 1995, p. 461). White did manual labor in the beet fields of Colorado during the summers while in high school. Tom C. Clark grew up in Dallas, Texas; both his parents came from distinguished Southern families and his father, a well-respected lawyer, was President of the Texas Bar Association. Like Stewart and Clark, John Marshall Harlan's father was an attorney (he was also a Chicago alderman and once was the Republican candidate for mayor of Chicago). Harlan spent his childhood in residential private schools (Lewin, 1995).

So Baker's distinction is generally supported by an analysis of family lineages, although we would suggest that it is not just one's socio-economic class, but one's idiosyncratic experiences as a child that directs one into certain ideological viewpoints.

Between the Oral Arguments and the Decision's Announcement

Given the split in votes, it is entirely likely that much discussion took place between the time of the initial vote, probably on March 4 (the Friday after the oral arguments), and the announcement three and a half months later. But Baker noted that, "Remarkably, for an opinion that had such a high potential for public controversy, it had changed very little from the first draft circulated a month before" (1983, p. 167). How did the decision get put together? Interestingly, Chief Justice Warren, in his autobiography (1977), devoted only one paragraph to this case. Baker stated that "Warren put the document together himself, his memory refreshed by the oral argument tapes. The rewriting of an early ambiguous reference to a lawyer's presence in the interrogation room, the toning down of a derogatory comment on police practices, and some minor editing put the first draft into its final form" (p. 167).

If, indeed, the first draft had been circulated only a month before its announcement, that means that in the earlier two and a half months there must have been extensive discussion of the nature of the opinion, its breadth, and its basis. It is true that the four dissenters generated three dissenting opinions, one of five pages by Justice Clark, one of 22 pages by Justice Harlan (joined by Justices White and Stewart), and one of 20 pages by Justice White (joined by Justices Harlan and Stewart). These dissents will be described subsequently, but first it is important to summarize the 62-page opinion of the Court.

The Essence of the Decision

In choosing a constitutional basis for the adoption of the Miranda warnings, Chief Justice Warren applied the Fifth Amendment to the Constitution, not the Sixth Amendment. The Fifth Amendment concerns the privilege against self-incrimination—"no person should be compelled in any criminal case to be a witness against himself." Warren applied this provision to the pretrial interrogation, reasoning that, "the atmosphere and environment of incommunicado interrogation, as it exists today, is inherently intimidating and works to undermine the privilege against self-incrimination" (*Miranda v. Arizona*, 1966, p. 436). This privilege, said the decision, guarantees the individual the "right to remain silent unless he chooses to speak in the unfettered exercise of his own free will" (p. 436). Thus, promised the Court, the following should occur:

> The person in custody must, prior to interrogation, be clearly
> informed that he has the right to remain silent, and that everything
> he says will be held against him in court; he must be clearly
> informed that he has the right to consult with a lawyer and to have
> a lawyer with him during interrogation; and that, if he is indigent,
> a lawyer will be appointed to represent him . . . If the individual
> indicates, prior to the questioning, that he wishes to remain silent,
> the interrogator must cease; if he states that he wants an attorney, the
> questioning must cease until an attorney is present . . . Where the
> individual answers some questions during in-custody interrogation
> he has not waived his privilege and may invoke his right to counsel
> thereafter. (p. 437)

The Court went on to say that if an interrogation is done without the presence of an attorney and if the suspect does confess, the burden—in the words of the opinion, a "heavy burden"—rests on the government "to demonstrate that the defendant knowingly and intelligently waived his right to counsel" (p. 437).

Thus to summarize, the Court specified the following rights, which we have numbered because subsequent chapters describe how particular police departments have worded them (or, in the case of #5, ignored them):

1. You have the right to remain silent.
2. Anything you say can and will be held against you in a court of law.
3. You have the right to an attorney.
4. If you cannot afford an attorney, one will be appointed to you free of charge.
5. If at any point you wish to terminate the questioning, you may do so.

The Court required police interrogators to follow these and then to ask the suspect two questions: Do you understand these rights? Having these rights in mind, do you wish to speak to me? Only if the suspect had waived his or her rights might an interrogation proceed.

Especially given the problems to be described in Chapters 4 and 6, it is essential to mention that the Court limited these requirements to the treatment of those suspects who were in police custody. Chapter 1, in describing the case of *Yarborough v. Alvarado*, demonstrated that custody is an elusive concept. In *Miranda* the Court stated: "By custodial interrogation, we mean questioning initiated by law enforcement officers after a person has been taken into custody or otherwise deprived of his freedom of action in any significant way" (p. 444).

So far, so good. But the opinion went on to say, "Unless adequate protective devices are employed to dispel the compulsion inherent in custodial surroundings, no statement obtained from the defendant can truly be the product of free choice" (p. 457). Thus, in order to dispel the compulsion, safeguards must be provided. This seemed to blur—even obliterate—the importance of the distinction between voluntary and involuntary admissions, and one of the dissenters jumped on it (see Justice White's dissent described subsequently in this chapter).

Was Michael Alvarado "taken into custody"? One might argue that, given that the police had asked him to come in for questioning, he had not been "taken" into custody. Was he "deprived of his freedom of action?" The answer to this question is even stickier; we do not know of the physical layout of the room in which Alvarado was questioned, but most police departments place suspects in a chair in a distant corner of the interrogation room and "surround" the suspect with police, thus discouraging the suspect who wishes to leave.

The Dissents in the *Miranda* Decision

As noted, there were four justices who refused to support Warren's draft of the opinion, and three of these wrote dissenting opinions. The Court strives for uniformity, and if not that, for consensus. For example, in the *Brown v. Board of Education* decision, Chief Justice Warren felt that it was essential that the decision be unanimous, and he finally was able to persuade the laggards through Herculean efforts. But unanimity is achieved in only 30% to 40% of decisions. Both concurring opinions and dissenting opinions may weaken the impact of the Court's opinion; concurrences in effect say the majority decision is correct but for the wrong reasons. (There were no concurring opinions in the *Miranda* case.) Dissents, of course, reject the perspective of the majority. They do not carry the weight of law, though they can have the effect of rallying those troops who lost the battle but still aspire to win the war on a later day. Chief Justice Warren was particularly disturbed that Justice Clark chose to write a dissent, because until the last minute, Clark appeared to have sided with the majority.

Justice Clark's dissent

Justice Tom Clark had long been a supporter of the law-enforcement community, and his brief, five-page dissent reflected his view that the opinion of the Court unjustifiably maligned police officers and hampered their efforts to apprehend criminals; thus his dissent exemplifies the position of crime control as a value. Typical of some advocates of the crime-control orientation, he downplayed the impact of police training methods and was critical of the majority opinion's citation of them as indicators of the systematic use of custodial interrogation to obtain confessions. Justice Clark wrote:

> The materials it [the majority opinion] refers to as "police manuals"
> are, as I read them, merely writings in this field by professors and
> some police officers. Not one is shown by the record here to be the
> official manual of any police department, much less in universal use
> in crime detection. (1966, p. 499)

In actuality, manuals had been in existence since 1940 and to imply their primary authors were "professors" and hence academic rather than practical belied their impact. Training manuals and the Reid School (which developed the most influential manual, by Inbau and Reid, first published in 1962) have systematized police interrogations into a high art, such that they have significantly contributed to the diminished effectiveness of the *Miranda* ruling. Chapter 7 describes their procedures in detail. Justice Clark's dissent also downplayed the incidence of illegal procedures by the police; "the examples of police brutality mentioned by the Court are rare exceptions to the thousands of cases that appear every year in the law reports" (1966, pp. 499–500). Again, to diminish the incidence of errors is a staple of the crime-control model and is reminiscent of the statements in Chapter 1 that only a very few false convictions occur (and that these are the price we pay for an efficient law-enforcement system).

Justice Clark was so offended with the majority opinion that he even decided to reply in print, beyond the dissent, and so edited his dissent before it appeared in the official publication, *United States Reports*, saying:

> The police agencies—all the way from municipal and state forces to
> the federal bureaus—are responsible for law enforcement and

public safety in this country. I am proud of their efforts, which in my view are not fairly characterized by the Court's opinion. (Graham, 1970, p. 191)

Justice Harlan's dissent

In his 22-page, eloquently-written dissent, Justice Harlan took more of an intellectual stance than did Justice Clark (and re-affirmed his reputation, among friends and foes alike, that he was "a judge's judge"). He questioned the extension of the Fifth Amendment rights to the pretrial phase, and also felt that the decision was impulsive and premature, given that new rules and "long-range and lasting reforms" in criminal procedure were at that time being considered by the American Bar Association, the American Law Institute, and the President's Commission on Law Enforcement and Administration of Justice.

But like Justice Clark, he also warned that the decision would inhibit effective crime investigation, he wrote:

> What the Court largely ignores is that its rules impair, if they will not eventually serve wholly to frustrate, an instrument of law enforcement that has long and quite reasonably been thought worth the price paid for it. There can be little doubt that the Court's new code would markedly decrease the number of confessions . . . How much harm this decision will inflict on law enforcement cannot fairly be predicted with accuracy . . . We do know that some crimes cannot be solved without confessions . . . and that the Court is taking a real risk with society's welfare in imposing its new regime on the country. The social costs of crime are too great to call the new rules anything but a hazardous experimentation. (1966, pp. 516–517)

Justice White's dissent

Justice White had been in the minority in the *Escobedo* case, having criticized the Court for barring admissions from suspects, whether they had been voluntary or not. He picked up on this theme in his *Miranda* dissent, posing the hypothetical situation in which a police officer asked a suspect who had just been taken into custody whether he had anything to say. His dissent was predictable from the content of his questions during the oral argument, in which his inquiry about whether Miranda was "compelled" to give the statement he did lead Flynn to respond, "Not by gunpoint . . . . He was called upon to surrender a right that he didn't fully realize that he had" (Irons & Guitton, 1993, p. 217).

Justice White's concern was the effect of the ruling on the expression of a confession that was truly voluntary; he wrote:

> Although in the Court's view in-custody interrogation is inherently coercive, the Court says that the spontaneous product of the

coercion of arrest and detention is still deemed to be voluntary. An accused, arrested on probable cause, may blurt out a confession which will be admissible despite the fact that he is alone and in custody, without any showing that he had any notion of his right to remain silent or of the consequences of his admission. Yet, under the Court's rule, if the police ask him a single question such as "Do you have anything to say?" or "Did you kill your wife?" his response, if there is one, has somehow been compelled, even if the accused has been clearly warned of his right to remain silent. Common sense informs us to the contrary. While one may say that the response was "involuntary" in the sense the question provoked or was the occasion for the response and thus the defendant was induced to speak out when he might have remained silent if not arrested and not questioned, it is patently unsound to say the response is compelled. (1966, pp. 533–534)

Like Justices Clark and Harlan, Justice White felt that the *Miranda* decision would further weaken the capacity of law enforcement to apprehend and convict criminals. He wrote that the majority opinion "will return a killer, a rapist, or other criminal to the streets" (1966, p. 542) to commit more crimes and he pointedly made clear in his dissent that he had "no desire whatsoever to share the responsibility for such an impact on the criminal process" (1966, p. 542).

It is clear from reading these excerpts that the dissenters felt strongly that *Miranda* was a mistake. Chief Justice Warren, ever the in-touch leader, was aware of their position and thus wrote an opinion that was moderate in its requirements, albeit occasionally extreme in its prose. Chapter 4 describes the implications of the wording of the decision.

Was *Miranda* to be Retroactive?

So, Ernesto Miranda was to get a new trial. But was the requirement to warn suspects of their rights retroactive? How many persons in prison, having been convicted on the basis of a confession, could claim that they had not been informed of their rights? The Court had mixed feelings about retroactivity, depending on "the exigencies of the situation" (Baker, 1983, p. 174). It did not make its ruling in *Mapp v. Ohio* (on the exclusionary rule) retroactive but it did in *Gideon v. Wainwright*. A week after its decision in *Miranda* (in which it had left open whether the decision was retroactive), the Court settled the matter; in *Johnson v. New Jersey* (1966), another confessions case, it ruled that neither *Escobedo* nor *Miranda* would be applied retroactively. The Court announced that the *Escobedo* decision affected only those defendants for whom the trial began after June 22, 1964, the date of that decision, and *Miranda* applied only to defendants for whom the trial began after the date of the *Miranda* decision.

Out of luck were the 144 criminal defendants whose "*Escobedo* cases" had been held over by the Clerk of the Supreme Court. The only beneficiaries of the *Miranda* decision were Ernesto Miranda himself plus the defendants in the other cases argued at the same time as Miranda's: Michael Vignera, Carl Calvin Westover, and Roy Allen Stewart. (Each of these three were either convicted on re-trial, even without a confession, or pled guilty to a lesser charge.)

Whatever Happened to Ernesto Miranda?

Because of the Supreme Court's decision in his appeal, Ernesto Miranda was given a new trial in 1967. But even though his confession was not permitted to be part of the evidence in this new trial, he was once again convicted; one reason being that the prosecution had uncovered new evidence against him.

Between 1967 and 1976 Miranda served some prison time, was released, and continued to have run-ins with the law. At the age of 34 he was an ex-con, an appliance-store delivery man, and probably a drug dealer. On the night of January 31, 1976, he was playing poker in a flophouse section of Phoenix. A drunken fight broke out involving two illegal Mexican immigrants. As he tried to take a knife away from one of them, Miranda was stabbed in the stomach and again in the chest. He was dead on arrival at the hospital.

Miranda's killer fled, but his accomplice was caught. Before taking him to police headquarters, two Phoenix police officers read to him—one in English, one in Spanish—from a card. They conscientiously read him his Miranda rights and then asked him, "Do you understand these rights? Will you voluntarily answer my questions?"

Thus, ironically ended the life, but not the legacy, of Ernesto Miranda.

4

Limitations of the Original Opinion

Question: "Should suspects have a right to have a lawyer present before being questioned by the police?"

Answer: "Suspects who are innocent of a crime should. But the thing is you don't have any suspects who are innocent of a crime. That's contradictory. If a person is innocent of a crime, then he is not a suspect."—Edwin Meese, then Attorney General of the United States in 1985.

—(Stuart, 2004, p. 100)

Reactions to the Announcement of the *Miranda* Decision

When the *Miranda* opinion was announced in June 1966, the reaction was immediate and frequently described as calamitous. Advocates of crime control prophesied an abrupt change in conviction rates. Some law-enforcement officials vehemently decried the decision, claiming it would hamper the police and the arrest of lawbreakers (Donohue, 1998). Baker described some of the reactions:

In Boston, the police commissioner, Edmund L. McNamara, mourned that "criminal trials no longer will be a search for truth, but a search for technical error." In Philadelphia, Police Commissioner Edward J. Bell declared that, "the present rules and interpretations, whether or not intended, in fact protect the guilty. I do not believe the Constitution was designed as a shield for criminals." In Cleveland, Ohio, Chief of Police Richard Wagner, alluding with some skepticism to the provision in *Miranda* that spontaneous statements and confessions were by no means barred, rumbled that, "there is no such thing as a voluntary statement. While the Supreme Court justices say it is, they have made it impossible to obtain one." An unidentified patrolman in Wisconsin suggested the justices thought innocent persons were being unduly harassed, forgetting the general public has the right to protest if they felt they were being harassed. Also they are protecting the criminal's rights. "There is nothing in the rule about the rights of the innocent public." And William H. Parker, Los Angeles police chief, predicted *Miranda* would effectively end the use of confessions in convicting criminals. (Baker, 1983, p. 176)

These comments by individual law-enforcement officials were supported by more extensive polling; Cassell summarized the results of some of the early surveys:

> Cyril Robinson conducted a nationwide survey in 1966 of police and prosecutors of the effects of *Escobedo* and *Miranda*. Most police and prosecutors who responded thought that the percentage of suspects who refused to make a statement had increased and that the percentage of suspects confessing had decreased after police were required by *Escobedo* to warn suspects of their rights. In New Haven, the Yale students interviewed the detectives involved in most of the interrogations they observed during the summer of 1966 and an additional twenty-five detectives six months later. The students reported that the detectives unanimously believed that *Miranda* will unjustifiably help the suspect. They also reported that the detectives "continually told us that the decision would hurt their clearance rate and they would therefore look inefficient." Otis Stephens and his colleagues surveyed law-enforcement officials in Knoxville, Tennessee, and Macon, Georgia, in 1969 and 1970. Virtually all of the officers surveyed believed that Supreme Court decisions had adversely affected their work and most attributed this negative influence first and foremost to *Miranda*. Law student Gary L. Wolfstone sent letters in 1970 to police chiefs and prosecutors in each state and the District of Columbia. Most agreed that *Miranda* raised obstacles to law enforcement. In "Seaside City", James Witt interviewed 43 police detectives sometime before 1973. Witt reported that the detectives "were in almost complete agreement over the effect that the Miranda warnings were having on the outputs of formal interrogation. Most believed that they were getting many fewer confessions, admissions, and statements." (Cassell, 1996a, pp. 1089–1090)

But it should be noted that each of these surveys were conducted within 5 or 6 years of the *Miranda* decision (Schulhofer, 1996b). Still at that time, their seemingly unanimous sentiment did not escape the attention of politicians. Richard Nixon, preparing for his campaign for the presidency in 1968, castigated the Court for its position that was "soft on crime," claiming that *Miranda* and other Warren Court decisions "had the effect of seriously hampering the police in our country" (Donohue, 1998, p. 1150).

Not to be lost in the criticisms of the decision by conservatives was the fact that the burden of proof was now on the government to prove that a defendant had waived his or her rights. The opinion made this clear:

> Since the State is responsible for establishing the isolated circumstances under which the interrogation takes place and has the only

means of making available uncorroborated evidence of warnings given during incommunicado interrogation, the burden is rightly on its shoulders. (*Miranda v. Arizona*, 1966, p. 425)

Recall that in the *Jackson v. Denno* decision two years before (described in Chapter 2), the Court had ruled that defendants who had recanted their confessions had a right to a pretrial hearing to assess the voluntariness of their confessions. But that decision left open who had the burden of proof; the judge was to objectively weigh the evidence from each side. Now police felt they were more on the defensive, even if the decision had proclaimed that "our opinion is not intended to hamper the traditional function of police officers in investigating crime" (1966, p. 477) and "Our decision in no way creates a constitutional straightjacket which will handicap sound efforts at reform" (*Miranda v. Arizona*, 1966, p. 467).

Three Stages

The above reactions by police, prosecutors, and even a soon-to-be elected President were forty years ago. Since then, reactions have changed. In fact, three stages can be identified: first, the initial negative reaction described above; second, a debate whether *Miranda* really changed police practices and the frequency of confessions; and third, a realization on the part of due-process advocates—who had initially welcomed the decision—that the decision was of little impact.

Why this remarkable reversal in attitudes occurred demands explanation, but it will take us four chapters to thoroughly resolve it, as we will describe several reasons why—in the eyes of advocates, if not the public—the *Miranda* decision has become a "paper tiger." This chapter will offer support for the first explanation that despite its endorsement from due-process supporters and the dire predictions of law-enforcement officials, the original decision was a compromise, that it had built-in limitations which restricted its application. We devote a separate chapter to the problems of suspects understanding their Miranda rights. In Chapter 6 we review Supreme Court decisions on the Miranda warnings since 1966, the conclusion being that their general thrust has been to erode the application of the warnings. And in a fourth chapter dealing with the restrictions on achieving the goals of *Miranda*, we examine the tactics used by the police during interrogations and how they have sought to circumvent the original goals of *Miranda*. But first we return to the initial reactions.

The Dissents by the Justices

The dissents to the decision, described in Chapter 3, offered two main criticisms: that police are doing not just a necessary job in questioning suspects but that they are doing it in a legally-acceptable way (Justice Clark), and that the decision would frustrate the police efforts and decrease the number of confessions (Justices Harlan and White). In contrast, the justices who endorsed the Miranda warnings were primarily concerned with the abundance of false confessions that resulted from police coercion. One wonders if, in their private conferences, they speculated about what percentage of suspects would waive their rights to remain silent or have a lawyer present. They probably would have been surprised to learn that about four out of every five still waived such rights, even when given their Miranda warnings (Leo, 1996b; Schulhofer, 1999). They doubtless assumed that some decrease in the number of confessions would occur, but they probably considered that a salutary outcome, because the Miranda warning would be a safeguard against false self-incrimination.

Empirical Findings

Has the availability of Miranda warnings thwarted the police and reduced the conviction rate? We have described how the police originally expected so, but several viewpoints exist (Thomas, 1998).

For example, it has been argued that police have learned how to accommodate to the warning; some ways they do so will be described in Chapter 7. Specifically, it has been observed that police become adept at introducing the warning so casually that suspects waive their rights without full knowledge; other police find ways to continue questioning suspects even when they refuse to answer. Observers of interrogations have concluded that one of the goals of many of them is to prevent the suspect from invoking his or her right to an attorney (Simon, 1991).

But two other positions have generated a long-running and acrimonious dispute. These positions have used empirical data to substantiate their claims, but the data and findings cited by the two sides conflict with each other. The debate has been fought on several grounds; for example, how often do false confessions occur despite the suspect being given a Miranda warning? For example Richard Leo and Richard Ofshe (1998) described 60 examples of what they saw as false confessions between 1973 and 1996, all of which occurred after the installation of Miranda waivers. Leo (2001a) considered these to be only the tip of the iceberg. Confessions occur in an estimated 45% to 55% of all criminal cases (Thomas, 1996). As DeClue (2005) has observed, no one knows what percentage of interrogations generate false confessions, but the empirical data suggest it is sizeable. Bedau and Radelet analyzed 350 cases of wrongful convictions (40% led to a sentence of death) and concluded that 49 or 14% involved false confessions. More recently, as part of the Innocence Project, researchers found that of the first 62 persons exonerated on the basis of DNA evidence, 15 or 24% had falsely confessed (Sheck, Neufeld, & Dwyer, 2001). But other scholars and researchers have questioned whether the classification of cases by Bedau and Radelet really reflect wrongful convictions or the cases described by Leo and Ofshe reflect *false* confessions (Cassell, 1999a).

The 60 cases identified by Leo and Ofshe share one characteristic: the individual was arrested primarily because the police obtained an incriminating statement from the individual "that later turned out to be a proven, or highly likely false confession" (Leo & Ofshe, 1998, p. 436). For each of these cases, no compelling evidence corroborated the defendant's admission of guilt. In some of these cases the suspect confessed to a crime that, it was later found, had not even happened. In Austin, Texas, in 1990, Billy Gene Davis twice failed a polygraph test and then confessed that he had killed his girlfriend, who later turned up alive in Tucson, Arizona. In others, police extracted a confession from individuals who could not have committed the crime. For example, Leo and Ofshe describe three cases in which flawed interrogations generated confessions from men who, it was later revealed, were in jail or in prison at the time of the crime.

Sometimes the interrogation is so intense that the innocent suspect comes to internalize that the events occurred just as the police describe them. The case of Peter Reilly is an example (Barthel, 1976; Connery, 1977). Reilly was 18 years old when he returned home one night in 1973 to find that his mother had been brutally murdered and sexually mutilated. He called the police, who questioned him and administered a polygraph test. They interrogated him over a 25-hour period; he was questioned without legal counsel. Transcripts reveal a fascinating transition in Reilly's responses—from denial through confession and self-doubt to a statement that "it really looks like I did it." Two years later, after Peter Reilly had been sentenced to as many as 16 years in prison, it was revealed through independent evidence that Reilly could not have committed the murder. Twenty years later Connecticut police continued to insist that Reilly brutally killed his mother; they refused to make public their files on the case.

Others of the 60 cases reviewed by Leo and Ofshe are classified as false confessions because the true perpetrator was later identified. After 21 hours of interrogation produced a confession, Paul Reggetz spent 11 months of incarceration before one of his neighbors confessed to killing Reggetz's wife and children. In 1990, a mentally retarded teenager, Donald Shoup, was interrogated and confessed to murder and robbery, but while he was awaiting trial, the true killer confessed.

Leo and Ofshe use a category of innocent confessions for which the public has become familiar: convicted defendants who were exonerated on the basis of scientific evidence. They describe five examples among numerous ones uncovered by the Innocence Project. They carefully note that for some of their 60 cases, the falsity of confession is "highly probable, but not certain", in most of their cases the defendant's narrative of the "facts" after his or her admission showed discrepancies with the actual facts (the cases of Bradley Page, Tom Sawyer, Martin Tankleff, and five others).

But the classification of these 60 cases as "false" confessions that led to "wrongful" convictions was disputed by Paul Cassell (1999a). Narrowing the focus to 29 of these cases and choosing nine for detailed consideration, Cassell concluded "that each of the nine persons were, in all likelihood, entirely guilty of the crimes charged against them" (1999a, p. 525). We have chosen one of these for analysis here: the case of Martin Tankleff, because it received a great deal of publicity in 1988, when the crime occurred, and again in 2007 and 2008 when an appellate court reversed his conviction and the prosecutor dropped all charges against him. (Tankleff had been in prison for 19 years when this happened.) The interrogation in this case was, in our opinion, one of the most egregious uses of lying and manipulation by the police, a matter that will be described in detail in Chapter 7.

Leo and Ofshe describe the interrogation of Martin Tankleff as follows:

> After 5 hours and 30 minutes of accusatory interrogation in 1988, Suffolk County, New York police obtained a confession from Martin Tankleff, then 17 years old, to brutally stabbing and murdering his parents. No evidence linked Tankleff to the crime, and his post-admission narrative did not match the facts of the case. Instead, Tankleff's narrative matched (indeed it was) the flawed theory of the crime that police detectives held at the time of Tankleff's interrogation. Tankleff confessed to killing his parents with a dumbbell and a watermelon knife, yet both items tested negative for blood traces, hair, and fibers. Medical testimony established that the head injuries to Martin's father were caused by a hammer. Tankleff confessed to beating his mother with a dumbbell and then fighting with her, which would have been consistent with the defensive wounds on her arms, but Tankleff's body was unscratched and the absence of any bruises suggested that he had not been in a life-or-death struggle with anyone. Tankleff confessed that he took a shower to wash away the substantial bloodstains the killings would have left on the perpetrator, but no blood residue or hairs from his parents were found in the shower. Tankleff had one bloodstain on his shoulder that could have been acquired when he discovered the bodies, but would have been washed away if he had showered to remove the substantial bloodstain that likely marked the killer. Tankleff confessed to assaulting his parents between 5:35 a.m. and 6:10 a.m., but his mother's time of death was established to be much earlier. Tankleff confessed to killing his mother and then walking through the house before attacking his father, but none of his mother's blood was found along this pathway. The killer used gloves, but Tankleff's confession made no reference to gloves. Tankleff confessed that after showering he removed his father from the chair and did not shower again, yet, Tankleff's clothes were not bloodstained. His confession was not corroborated by the physical evidence that should have linked him to the crime (if, in fact, he were guilty) and was merely a regurgitation of the factually errone-ous theory the detectives admitted they had initially held. Nevertheless, a jury convicted Tankleff of two counts of second-degree murder. Tankleff's judge sentenced him to prison for 50 years to life. (Leo & Ofshe, 1998, pp. 458–459)

Cassell, in describing this case, emphasizes a different set of facts. He first describes events prior to the crime, including "an ugly public argument with his [Tankleff's] father" (1999a, p. 573) a few days before. He notes that later in the same day that Tankleff confessed, "a detective overheard Tankleff acknowledge to his sister that he committed the crime" (p. 574).

Leo and Ofshe would call this admission, if it existed, and the actual confession, as products of a kind of brain-washing by the police. At his trial, Tankleff disputed his confession and continued to insist on his innocence, even as he was convicted and imprisoned. In December 2007, his conviction was vacated by the Appellate Division of the New York state courts, and in July 2008 a judge signed off on a motion by the New York State Attorney General to dismiss all charges against him.

Another matter which led to an extensive dispute was the effect of the *Miranda* ruling on convictions. Paul Cassell, while a law professor at the University of Utah, accumulated extensive data which he interpreted as reflecting a reduced clearance rate after the institution of the Miranda warnings, meaning that a greater percentage of suspects were not convicted and remained out on the streets. In one of his articles (Cassell, 1996b), a graph of arrest rates for violent and property crimes, drawn from several jurisdictions, showed a sharp reduction in the proportion of violent crime cases that were reported to have been cleared by the police ("cleared" refers to a case in which an arrest has been made or the crime has been solved). The rates from 1950 to the mid-1960s hover close to 65%, with an occasional dip to 60%. But from 1965 to 1970 they precipitously drop to close to 45%, and remain between 45% and 50% through the 1980s and early 1990s. This evidence, as well as other types reported in his various articles, led Cassell to conclude that implementation of Miranda warnings had seriously undermined the ability of police to fight crime. He wrote that "one out of every four violent crimes that was 'cleared' before *Miranda* was not cleared after" (1996a, p. 1090) and went on to say, "over the long haul, law enforcement never recovered from the blow inflicted by *Miranda*" (1996a, p. 1091). He concluded that 28,000 arrests for violent crimes and 79,000 arrests for property crimes were lost as a result of the Miranda warnings.

A regression analysis done by Cassell and Fowles (1998) concluded that the clearance rate for violent crimes began to fall sharply beginning in mid-1966, just after the *Miranda* decision had been announced.

Cassell, who later became a federal judge, maintained on the television program *Sixty Minutes* that *Miranda* was the most harmful decision to law enforcement in the last 50 years (White, 2001b). He also claimed that the incidence of *false* confessions is largely limited to those suspects who are mentally retarded or disturbed (Cassell, 1999a).

Others have disagreed, arguing that Cassell's conclusions are based on selective cases and that the actual declines in clearance rates are not so large (Schulhofer, 1996a; White, 2001b). Schulhofer (1996a) conceded that, "something important happened to law enforcement in the 1960s" (1996a, p. 280) but that "we cannot seize upon *Miranda* as the presumptive cause of the changes, as if there were no other important development during the period" (1996a, p. 280). He noted that other factors could have contributed to, or even primarily caused, the changes in the clearance rates from the 1960s to the 1990s. He wrote:

> Because the clearance rate is defined as the percentage of all reported crimes that police solve, increases in the amount of reported crime tend to drive down the clearance rate, even if police remain highly effective and solve as many cases as they did prior years. (1996a, pp. 280–281)

For example, crime rates grew steadily in the late 1950s and began to soar in the mid-1960s—apparently due at least partly to an increase in the number of young males—and police resources couldn't keep up. Schulhofer reported, for instance, that in 1955 there were 121 police officers for every 100 reported violent offenses, but only 45 in 1970 and just 28 in 1996 (Schulhofer, 1996a, p. 288). "There was less time available to investigate each case, and more crime reports had to be left unattended, simply because of lack of resources" (1996a, p. 281).

Schulhofer thus concludes that what Cassell attributed to *Miranda* is better explained as the interaction between increased crime rates and lessened availability of police. He bolstered this claim by producing data that the *number* of crimes (as contrasted with the clearance *rate*) that were cleared increased steadily from 1950 to 1974. Likewise, the data on crimes cleared per dollars of law-enforcement expenditure showed no dip as a result of the *Miranda* decision, "not even a temporary pause in the rate of increase" (p. 286). Schulhofer concluded by saying "after thirty years of experience with Miranda rules and intensive efforts of critics to muster arguments against them, the burden that *Miranda* supposedly imposed on law enforcement once again proves undetectable in the relevant empirical evidence" (1996a, p. 287).

Did *Miranda* decrease the number of confessions or not? Another point of view, posited by Thomas (1996, 1998), is a "steady-state" theory, that "*Miranda* persuades some suspects to make voluntary statements that sometimes turn out to be incriminating, at the same time that it permits roughly the same number of suspects to resist the inherent compulsion of police interrogation" (1998, p. 323).

As Kassin (1997) and Thomas (1998) have observed, differences in the data samples used and in the ideological viewpoints of the advocates have driven the extensive exchange in the literature about just how much *Miranda* has affected confession rates and conviction rates (Cassell, 1998, 1999b; Cassell & Hayman, 1996; Leo & Ofshe, 1998; Ofshe & Leo, 1997). Therefore, conclusions based on empirical findings are not enough; many of the instigators of empirical studies do so with a partisan background. Can an objective assessment of the diverging empirical claims be found?

John J. Donohue, III, a law professor at Stanford and an expert on analyzing the effects of legal interventions, was asked by the editors of the *Stanford Law*

Review to examine the regression analysis done by Cassell and Fowles (1998) that had concluded that the *Miranda* decision had dramatically reduced clearance rates. Donohue entered the fray which, as he wrote, had generated a "lively, contentious, and voluminous literature" (1998, p. 1148) as a disinterested observer, but his experience in such evaluations caused him to begin with an assumption that,

> In general, it is hard to find *any* direct effect of a legal intervention and when impacts are found they tend to be rather small. The complex forces that shape major social phenomena do not tend to shift dramatically or quickly in response to a legal intervention. (p. 1149, italics in original)

After examining the data and controlling for possible other factors, Donohue wrote,

> Based on my review of all the statistical evidence, I would venture that there is some evidence that the *measured* violent crime clearance rate is 10-12% lower in the post-mid-1966 period than would have been expected based on various time-series regression models. (1998, p. 1170)

But the decrease in clearance rate for most of the specific types of crimes is not statistically significant; he noted that for seven of the nine crime categories the falling clearance rates are fully explained by "higher crime, relatively fewer public resources, and a long-term downward trend that started in 1950" (p. 1170).

Of special interest is one type of crime—the most serious type, murder. Cassell and Fowles had conceded that on the basis of their regression findings, *Miranda* did not reduce clearance rates for murders as it did for other types of cases. It seems plausible that given the increase in sheer amount of crime in that time period and the diminishing police resources, as Schulhofer noted, police would expend a greater percentage of their resources on the most serious of crimes.

While Donohue accepts some drops in clearance rates for some types of crimes over this time period, he is less able to attribute the cause to the *Miranda* decision. He returns to his disclaimer presented early in his article—that there are many methodological problems, confounds with other explanatory variables, and questionable crime data, such that "one is left with an unbridgeable uncertainty about how much confidence to repose in any of the statistical results" (Donohue, 1998, p. 1172).

The Realization of *Miranda's* Ineffectiveness

Despite the controversy over the statistical data that carried over into the late 1990s, many of the original critics of the *Miranda* decision began changing their positions. Some did so because their fears were not warranted. As of

1988, less than 1% of criminal cases had been dismissed because of confessions generated without receipt of Miranda warnings (Stuart, 2004). Even more importantly, most suspects were waiving their rights. As noted earlier, an estimated 80% of suspects agreed to talk to the police detectives without restrictions. The shift in acceptance became so prevalent that Gary Stuart, in his book on the *Miranda* case, wrote that, "Today [in 2004] *Miranda* appears to have more proponents than detractors" (p. 103). And of recent years, the detractors are those who, 40 years ago, would have endorsed the decision. Why has this shift in opinion occurred? One reason traces back to the original decision, and its limitations.

Limitations in the Original Decision

Despite the protests of the crime-control advocates, Justice Fortas, a supporter of *Miranda*, characterized it as a "conservative decision" (Graham, 1970, p. 182). In the words of Stephen Schulhofer, *Miranda* "was a compromise. It was carefully structured to preserve police interrogation as an investigative tool and preserve the shrouds of secrecy that protect the practice from the prying eyes of judges and the public" (2006, p. 179). It is a useful exercise to consider just what the options of the Court were in 1966. At one extreme, the justices could have prohibited interrogations completely. But they considered that to be too extreme; United States citizens value due process but they also view a role for the police to investigate crimes fully. It is true that, as Baker has observed, the Court "took the unprecedented step of imposing stringent rules on law enforcement officers" (1983, p. 167). But the Court could have adopted more radical requirements; for example, it could have required an attorney to be present at every interrogation. Certainly it had set such an innovation in motion with its *Gideon* decision that provided indigent defendants an attorney at trial. The financial costs would have been huge but the requirement would curtail the excesses of police. The amicus brief from the American Civil Liberties Union had urged the Court about the absolute necessity for a lawyer to be present at all stages of investigation and prosecution. Interestingly, Chief Justice Warren relied upon the ACLU brief in developing the basis for his opinion; the language in that part of his opinion was even identical to that in the ACLU's amicus brief (Baker, 1983). But Warren balked at endorsing the ACLU's efforts to require an attorney's presence. Suspects would be offered an attorney but they didn't have to accept the offer.

If the requirement of a lawyer's presence was too extreme, the Court could have insisted that the police tape record every minute of every interrogation (in 1966 it would have to have been audiotape). As Schulhofer has observed:

> Nothing in *Miranda* prevents a state from requiring its police to
> videotape their interrogations whenever possible. Indeed no
> conceivable law-enforcement interest—at least no *legitimate*

law-enforcement interest—stands in the way of such a requirement. Yet to this day only a handful of jurisdictions require videotaping, and only a handful of police departments preserve videotapes showing anything more than the end result—the confession itself, but not the dynamic that produced it. (2006, p. 179, italics in original)

Why did the Court not adopt such requirements? Perhaps the justices felt that the establishment of the warnings would be sufficient to protect suspects from coercion. Graham (1970) suggested that the justices thought that, "in-custody interrogation was being virtually eliminated" (1970, p. 183). He further concluded:

The Supreme Court had deliberately given the impression that it had dealt police interrogation a grievous blow, when the justices had to know that it had really only dealt a tap on the wrist. The motive for this can only be assumed. The justices may have felt that constitutional rights are always watered down in practice, and that the only proper course for the Court is to insist on the ideal and hope for the best. They may have thought that by attacking all police interrogation, they might at least eliminate some of its worst abuses. They might have planned to eliminate interrogation by degrees, tightening the loopholes in future decisions until no suspect could be questioned outside the presence of his lawyer. (Graham, 1970, pp. 183–184)

Specific Limitations

Beyond considering alternatives, this chapter suggests that several limitations existed in the decision.

No requirement that Miranda rights be given immediately

The *Miranda* decision was explicit that no interrogation could occur until suspects had been advised of their rights. But it was not specific that the warnings should be given promptly upon arrest or the invocation of custody. Suspects may be kept waiting for long periods, thus increasing their willingness to waive their rights. For example, in a later case, *Rhode Island v. Ellis* (1980), the Court ruled that police officers who had discussed the suspect's case with each other on the way to the police station, while in the suspect's presence, were not "interrogating" the suspect.

No retroactive application

The *Gideon* decision had been announced in March 1963, providing all future indigent defendants with a defense attorney paid for by the state. What about all those indigent defendants in prison in March 1963 who had been denied legal assistance when they were tried and convicted? Should they be covered retroactively and thus get new trials? The Court ruled yes, and more than 1,000 convicts in Florida alone were freed (Graham, 1970). (In other states the retroactivity of this decision was not an issue because at the time of *Gideon* many states already had provided for indigent defendants to receive trial assistance; the importance of the *Gideon* decision was that this became mandatory in *all* states.) What about retroactivity for suspects not given any Miranda warnings?

As mentioned in Chapter 3, a week after *Miranda* the Court ruled in *Johnson v. New Jersey* that neither *Escobedo v. Illinois* nor *Miranda v. Arizona* would be applied retroactively. There was some discussion by the justices as to just when the cutoff points should be; eventually, for *Escobedo* claims, they ruled that the *Escobedo* decision affected only those cases in which their trials had begun after June 22, 1964, the date of that decision. For *Miranda*, only those eligible were defendants whose trials began after the date of the *Miranda* decision. Since that had been only one week earlier, very few defendants other than Ernesto Miranda and those in the other cases argued at that time benefitted. As Justices Black and Douglas put it in their dissent in a similar case, "The Court's opinion cuts off many defendants who are now in jail from any hope of relief from unconstitutional convictions" (*Linkletter v. Walker*, 1965, p. 652). Chief Justice Warren also wrote the opinion for the Court in *Johnson v. New Jersey*, but he backtracked from the *Miranda* decision of a week before: "Retroactive application of *Escobedo* and *Miranda* would seriously disrupt the administration of our criminal laws. It would require the retrial or release of numerous prisoners found guilty by trustworthy evidence in conformity with previously announced constitutional standards" (*Johnson v. New Jersey*, 1966, p. 721). No one would question a conclusion that making *Miranda* retroactive would create a hornet's nest of claims of convicts that "I would have never confessed if I had known my right to remain silent," but for Warren to describe previous convictions as based on "trustworthy evidence" seemed quite inconsistent with *Miranda's* description of the shabby tactics of police who were unfettered by any requirement to inform suspects that they could, in fact, remain silent.

Limited to "in-custody" interrogations

The *Miranda* decision was explicit that the warnings had to be given after "a person has been taken into custody or otherwise deprived of his freedom of action in any significant way" (1966, p. 436). Why this limitation? Did the justices not envision that police could question suspects at the crime scene or on the way to the station house (or did those qualify as "in custody")? Did they envision the subjective nature of a deprivation of freedom of action as illustrated in the *Yarborough v. Alvarez* case described in Chapter 1?

Some confessions are spontaneous; the offender may appear at the police station and state that he or she wants to confess to a crime. An example is

Bernhard Goetz, the so-called "subway vigilante" who shot and injured four young men who, in his opinion, were going to rob and maim him. Goetz voluntarily appeared at a Concord, New Hampshire police station several days after the Manhattan shooting to turn himself in. The Court did not want to inhibit such spontaneous actions (although it could be argued that even these individuals deserve to be Mirandized, and, in fact, Goetz was read his rights at the Concord police station).

Other offenders may confess in response to the first approach by a police officer who is only seeking information about the crime. The key concern for the Warren Court was whether the individual was compelled to incriminate himself or herself, and the justices evidently felt that such a possibility significantly increased while the suspect was in custody. (They also apparently assumed that no questioning would occur until the suspect was at the police station or otherwise confined.)

But limiting the rights to "in-custody" interrogations has opened a Pandora's box of problems, and it has permitted the more recent Court—not as concerned with due process as the Warren Court—to broaden the admissibility of "unMirandized" confessions. The decision in the 1991 *Arizona v. Fulminante* case is an example. It dealt with a confession given to an informant while the criminal was in prison for another charge. The defendant, Oreste Fulminante, was suspected of the murder of his 11-year-old stepdaughter. On September 14, 1982, Fulminante called the Mesa, Arizona, Police Department to report his stepdaughter, Jeneane Hunt, missing. Jeneane's mother was in the hospital and during this time Fulminante was caring for the child. Two days later the girl's body was found in the desert east of Mesa. She had been shot with a large weapon twice in the head at close range. Officials could not determine whether or not she had been sexually assaulted because her body was severely decomposed.

Fulminante told the police a number of inconsistent stories about his stepdaughter's disappearance and his relationship with her; at times he blamed the child for problems in the family's relationship. He became a suspect in the killing, but charges were not filed against him, so he left for New Jersey. But while there, he was charged with possession of a firearm by a felon, was convicted, and sent to a federal prison in New York. In prison, he met Anthony Sarivola, a former police officer and a fellow inmate who was also a paid informant for the Federal Bureau of Investigation. Fulminante did not know that the Arizona authorities were pursuing him, and that Sarivola had agreed to play a game of deception in order to elicit a confession from Fulminante.

Sarivola masqueraded as an organized crime figure; he and Fulminante became friends. Sarivola heard that Fulminante was suspected of murdering a child and brought up the topic a number of times. Each time Fulminante denied any involvement in his stepdaughter's death. He on one occasion told Sarivola that bikers who were looking for drugs killed her, and another time he offered that he did not know what happened. Sarivola told Fulminante that he knew that the other inmates were giving him a hard time because they had heard that he was a child molester and murderer, and so he offered to protect

Fulminante if Fulminante told him the truth about the murder. Sarivola later testified that Fulminante told him that he had driven his stepdaughter to the desert on his motorcycle, where he choked her, sexually assaulted her, and made her beg for her life, before he shot her twice in the head.

Here was a confession that had been given outside of police jurisdiction, although it was elicited by questioning instigated by police suspicion of the respondent's guilt. Obviously, Fulminante was not given any type of "Miranda warnings."

At his trial back in Arizona, Fulminante's confession was ruled voluntary and therefore admitted into evidence. Fulminante was found guilty and sentenced to death. His appeal to the Arizona Supreme Court led that body to reverse his conviction on the grounds that his jailhouse confession had been made under the pressure of a plausible threat of violence.

When Arizona brought an appeal to the United States Supreme Court, the justices agreed with the Arizona Supreme Court that Fulminante's confession was made as a result of a threat, but the Court also made a ruling that extended beyond Fulminante's situation, it ruled that coerced or involuntary confessions fell under the "harmless error" rule. That is, generally, if someone is convicted and the court or police have committed an error, the error is not enough to cause the appellate court to overturn the conviction *if there is other evidence that would have led to a conviction anyway*. In the past the Court had taken the position that a coerced confession is fundamentally different from other types of erroneously admitted evidence to which the harmless error rule had been applied; that is, in the past the Court had ruled that admitting a coerced confession is never "*harmless.*" But in the *Fulminante* decision, for the first time, the Court ruled that coerced confessions fell under the "harmless error" rule (White, 1992). Justice White, one of the dissenters in *Miranda*, wrote a strong dissent to the *Fulminante* decision, stating that "the majority of the Court, without any justification, overrules this vast body of precedent without a word and in so doing dislodges one of the fundamental tenets of our criminal justice system" (*Arizona v. Fulminante*, 1991, p. 1254).

A loss of morale and a sense of confusion in the police

An initial casualty of *Miranda* was a loss of morale in the police. As Baker observed:

> *Miranda* was another sign of the fundamental distrust undeserved
> by men whose work demanded a high degree of physical stamina,
> courage, alertness, common sense, intelligence, and good judgment
> and in return exacted a high emotional toll, men who every day
> stood between society and the criminal, putting their lives on
> the line. As one observer put it, police looked at *Miranda* and felt
> a "slap at policeman everywhere . . . a personal rebuke". (1983,
> p. 177)

Police had a great deal of mistrust of the Supreme Court anyway, contrasting the justices' lives in an "ivory tower" (or "marble palace," as the Supreme Court building is often referred to) with the police officer's life on the mean streets.

But another reaction by the police was confusion. Just what could they do—and not do—under *Miranda*? Thus began the use of wallet-sized cards by police—now familiar to viewers of television crime shows—which the officer retrieved and read to the suspect. The wording of these was not uniform from one jurisdiction to another, as Chapter 5 demonstrates, and the Supreme Court gave no guidance as to exactly what to say.

The justices apparently listened to the concerns reflected in this chapter. But instead of clarifying, they essentially did nothing. Over the next few years, they accepted very few cases that dealt with police interrogations. Meanwhile, the composition of the Court began to shift. Although William Brennan remained on the Court until 1990, the other justices who had contributed to the *Miranda* majority were soon gone—Earl Warren and Abe Fortas in 1969, Hugo Black in 1971, and William O. Douglas in 1975. The Republican domination of the White House from 1968 to 1980 permitted the appointment of justices who were assumed to be less sympathetic to defendant's rights, and especially beginning in the 1980s the Court welcomed petitions dealing with Miranda rights so that it could begin to restrict their application.

5

Problems with the Comprehension of *Miranda* Rights Among Vulnerable Suspects

> As we have seen, some types of individuals—the mentally handicapped, the mentally ill, and juveniles in particular—are especially vulnerable to the pressures of accusatorial interrogation. They tend to be more easily led into giving involuntary or unreliable statements and are thus disproportionately represented in the documented false confessions cases.
> —Leo, 2008, p. 312

The majority opinion in the *Miranda* case specifically focused on protecting suspects taken into custody from noxious interrogation practices by police that compel inculpatory statements or confessions. In order to accomplish this, the Supreme Court authorized "procedural safeguards" that would serve to reinforce suspects' Fifth Amendment right against self-incrimination and right to counsel. The opinion illustrated at great length the malignant nature of interrogation procedures and indicated that this very nature played an "essential" role in the majority's decision (*Miranda v. Arizona*, 1966, p. 445). Recognizing that an overwhelming, oppressive atmosphere of domination by the police could render individuals psychologically, emotionally, and judgmentally incapacitated, the Supreme Court strictly required that those suspects taken into custody be "adequately and effectively apprised of their rights" (1966, p. 450). This apprising must also be "in clear and unequivocal terms" (1966, pp. 467–468). The Court believed that through the components of the Miranda warnings, suspects would become informed of their rights and the consequences of waiving those rights. Whatever the individual's background, such awareness would assure a "real understanding and intelligent exercise of the privilege," thus enabling suspects to thwart intimidation by the police and to avoid compelled incriminating statements (1966, pp. 468–469).

But does being made "aware" truly produce the level of understanding anticipated by the Court? Do the warnings, as given, permit suspects "whatever their background" to know what exercising their rights to silence or to counsel implies, or to resist domineering interrogation tactics, or to "voluntarily, knowingly, and intelligently" waive their rights? This chapter reviews extensive research that leads us to conclude the answers to the above questions are a resounding no. Not all suspects possess the capabilities that would assure a rational and intelligent exercise of waiving their rights. Vulnerable groups, such as juveniles, the mentally retarded and mentally ill, deaf, and non-English-speaking suspects, struggle with comprehending the very warnings that were constructed to protect them.

Not only do these vulnerable groups have some inherent limitations in their ability to comprehend written and oral material, but police jurisdictions have compounded the problem of comprehension by developing numerous, often wordy, versions of the warnings. The United States has literally thousands of versions of the warnings among its various police jurisdictions. Many of these are far more verbose and far less comprehensible than those well known by watchers of television crime programs. Before describing this problem in detail, we provide some background on the way that the court system has treated juveniles, since they comprise the category that is numerically most vulnerable to problems in understanding their rights.

The Comprehension of Miranda Warnings by Juveniles

> Annually, more than 1.5 million juvenile offenders are arrested and routinely Mirandized with little consideration regarding the comprehensibility of these warnings.
> –Rogers, Hazelwood, Sewell, Shuman, & Blackwood, 2008, p. 63

Awareness that adolescents have special problems in comprehension can be traced back to the founding of the juvenile courts under the Juvenile Court Act of 1889. Research by developmental psychologists of that period permitted society to understand the specifics of children's shortcomings in logic and reasoning. The establishment of juvenile courts meant that children were no longer tried and, if found guilty, possibly sentenced to death as were adults (Snyder & Sickmund, 2006). Children actually became children in the eyes of justice—for the most part. Many juvenile-court judges assumed the role of *parens patriae* (the state acting as parent), ready and willing to help errant children find their way into society as productive members. In most states, children (defined as under age 18) were seen as "essentially good" but lacking moral and cognitive maturity. These courts recognized that children fell far short of adults in their understanding of legal procedures. While this recognition provided positive change, an underlying negative side existed.

Juvenile-court judges often had complete autonomy over procedures and outcome of cases, deciding what "treatment" would "benefit" each child. Children were denied due process protections, such as the requirement of an indictment by a grand jury, the provision of bail, the privilege against self incrimination, the right to confront accusers, and a speedy and public trial. In many jurisdictions children had no right to counsel (*Kent v. United States*, 1966). Needless to say, they had no constitutional rights; whether they understood their legal situation was not considered to be relevant. Children were questioned without a parent or attorney present. Many children—confused and challenged in deciphering reality from police characterizations—readily confessed whether they were guilty or not.

Critics gradually began to sense dangers within a system that disregarded the protections of due process and ignored the usual courtroom procedures. Menacing interrogation practices plus denial of due process led the Supreme Court, in the mid-1900s, to grant *certiorari* to several appeals claiming that children had not been adequately protected.

Cases Leading to the Clarification of Juvenile Rights

One focus of the Court, even prior to *Miranda*, was the capacity of children to tolerate interrogations. In *Haley v. Ohio*, decided in 1948, 15-year-old John Harvey Haley confessed to his role in a murder after police beat him and unrelentingly questioned him for 5 hours. It took 3 days after he confessed for an attorney to get permission by police to counsel him, and 5 days before his mother laid eyes on her son. Justice William O. Douglas, in the *Haley* opinion, stressed "That which would leave a man cold and unimpressed can overawe and overwhelm a lad in his early teens" (1948, p. 600), making him no match for police tactics. Justice Douglas, emphasizing Haley's youth, questioned his ability to fully appreciate any advice given him by the police without guidance from an attorney. The Court overturned his conviction, finding that police had violated his Fourteenth Amendment protection by coercing a confession from him.

By the 1960s, a shift toward juvenile rights went into full swing. Fourteen years after delivering the opinion on *Haley v. Ohio*, Justice Douglas expressed similar sentiments in the case of *Gallegos v. Colorado* (1962). This case involved a child of 14, originally charged with "assault to injure" an elderly man but later charged with murder after the victim died from sustained injuries (1962, p. 49). Gallegos signed a formal statement of confession "before his victim died, before being brought before a judge, and after he had been held for five days without seeing a lawyer, parent, or other friendly adult" (1962, p. 49). Again, Justice Douglas reiterated concerns relating to the petitioner's age and his ability to adequately "know, let alone, assert" his constitutional rights (1962, p. 55). Justice Douglas explicitly defined critical deficiencies in capabilities with this young defendant:

> He cannot be compared with an adult in full possession of his senses and knowledgeable of the consequences of his admissions. He would have no way of knowing what the consequences of his confession were without advice as to his rights – from someone concerned with securing him those rights – and without the aid of more mature judgment as to the steps he should take in the predicament in which he found himself. (*Gallegos v. Colorado*, 1962, p. 54)

Justice Douglas acknowledged that the Supreme Court justices had nothing to guide them in their decisions of such cases other than the totality of the circumstances—age, education, background, circumstances while under police custody, and mental health. A few years later in 1966 and 1967, the Supreme Court ruled on two more juvenile cases dealing with due process rights, with *Miranda v. Arizona's* decision sandwiched between them. In both cases the Supreme Court questioned the legitimacy of police and judicial procedures used to commit each juvenile defendant and reviewed the Due Process Clause of the Fourteenth Amendment in relation to juvenile rights.

In the first of these, *Kent v. United States* (1966), Morris A. Kent, Jr., a 16-year-old "victim of severe psychopathology" (1966, p. 545), charged with housebreaking, robbery, and rape, faced adversaries on both ends of the system—police procedures and judicial negligence. Police first fingerprinted and then subjected this highly troubled teenager to 7 hours of interrogation before notifying his parents or the juvenile court. Without probable cause, Kent then spent a week in a detention home for children before arraignment. The travesty of this case centered on Judge Orman W. Ketchum's philosophical abandonment of *parens patriae* and his determination to waive a child with "rapid deterioration of personality structure and possible mental illness" over to the U.S. District Court for trial. Judge Ketchum held no hearing, gave no reason for waiving, and most astoundingly, never conferred with Kent, his parents, or his attorney. Kent's counsel filed for a motion to reverse and retain his client under juvenile court jurisdiction in order to obtain psychiatric treatment. He also motioned for access to Kent's Social Services files that he had previously been denied. Judge Ketchum never ruled on either motion. No hearing, no inquiry by the judge with Kent or his attorney, and no motion ruling, yet Judge Ketchum claimed he made a "full investigation" prior to waiver. Justice Fortas, in his decision for the Supreme Court, noted serious inadequacies within some juvenile courts, specifically in relation to compliance with the Juvenile Court Act. He asserted:

> There is evidence, in fact, that there may be grounds for concern
> that the child receives the worst of both worlds: that he gets neither
> the protection accorded to adults nor the solicitous care and
> regenerative treatment postulated for children. (*Kent v. United
> States*, 1966, p. 556)

The majority's opinion held that to consider the validity of waiver that could differentiate between 5 years in confinement and a possible death sentence, young Kent was entitled to a hearing with counsel present, counsel's right to access records or statements considered by the court, and a statement from the judge explaining reasons for the juvenile court's decision to waive. Based on constitutional principles, the Supreme Court found that none of these conditions were met. Within a few months of the *Kent* decision the Supreme Court ruled on *Miranda v. Arizona*. Decisions from *Miranda* and questions raised in *Kent* played well into the ruling of *In re Gault*, (1967) therein completing the shift from safeguards afforded juveniles under juvenile court jurisdiction to safeguards afforded juveniles under constitutional due process.

Similar to Morris Kent, Gerald Gault found himself sucked under a wave of judicial arbitrariness that plagued the juvenile courts. A 15-year-old, Gault made the poor decision to pass the time of day by making prank phone calls to a neighbor woman. The woman reacted by calling the police and accusing Gault of making indecent remarks. Police apprehended Gault, questioned him, and then placed him in a detention home while never notifying his parents. An initial informal hearing for Gault took place in the juvenile judge's chambers with his mother and probation officer attending. The hearing lacked formality in every aspect imaginable, with no transcripts or recording made of statements by Gerald Gault, the judge, mother, or probation officer, no memorandum of the substance of the proceedings prepared, and no complainant present. Gault was then sent back to the detention home and released 4 days later. No record existed as to why he was detained or why he was released. At his second hearing, the judge formally charged Gault with making "lewd phone calls" and sentenced him to the State Industrial School for 6 years (until he reached his 21st birthday).

Gault's alleged confession of making lewd remarks put him away for 6 years. There was no other evidence to convict him—the complainant never attended either hearing or talked directly with the judge. Had he been 18 years old, he would have paid $5 to $50 in fines or faced imprisonment for no more than 2 months. With Gault's confession playing the sole role in his fate, the Supreme Court chose in 1967 to review the procedure. In its *In re Gault* (1967) decision the Court concluded that:

> The constitutional privilege against self-incrimination is applicable in the case of juveniles as it is with adults . . . the greatest care must be taken to assure that the admission was voluntary, in the sense, not only that it was not coerced or suggested, but also that it was not the product of ignorance of rights or of adolescent fantasy, fright, or despair. (1967, p. 56)

With its declaration that constitutional privileges are applicable to juveniles, Justice Fortas discussed the possibility of "special problems" (1967. p. 56) surfacing with regard to children waiving their rights. From *Gault* onward, children were no longer exempt from safeguards under *Miranda*. Children received entitlement to "being made aware" of rights to silence, counsel, and waiving those rights just like adults. As predicted by Justice Fortas, problems did surface, especially among police.

Police Irritation and Transformation of *Miranda*

Shortly after the announcement of the *Gault* decision, the National Council of Juvenile Court Judges conducted a four-week "summer college" held at the

University of Colorado to help judges and jurists "adjust" to the Supreme Court's decision of *In re Gault*. Denver Judge Ted Rubin, attending the event, cautioned that the change from *Gault* "will cost money and irritate police as well as judges" (Time Magazine, 1967, p. 68). Police irritation with the *Gault* decision, however, could simply have been run-off from the initial irritation with *Miranda*, described in Chapter 7. The requirement to be advised of rights served to intentionally balance the level of fairness between suspects and interrogators. For police, however, this requirement obviously sabotaged the overall structure of interrogation techniques. Informing suspects of their rights to silence and counsel conflicted with the very essence of interrogation—unadulterated psychological "manipulation, deception, and fraud" (Leo, 2008, p. 120). Police had to find a way to work with *Miranda* but maintain power over suspects.

Along with Judge Rubin's caution came recognition of necessary change— predicting that in the long run benefits would outweigh the costs. Rubin conceded to the fact that "flexible and informal deliberations deny consistent legal protection to the child" (Time Magazine, 1967, p. 68). This inconsistency resulted in confusion, leaving children unable to understand their situation or the system (p. 68). Police did not then and still today do not hold similar sentiments. The court system changed but police techniques have remained immutable. Police interrogators are psychologically conditioned to keep their guard up in order to maintain full control over the interrogation environment and quench any resistance by suspects. It did not take long for them to figure a way to transform *Miranda* into just another interrogation "tool" to work for instead of against them (Leo, p. 281). As discussed in Chapter 7, police eventually devised "multiple strategies to avoid, circumvent, nullify, or simply violate *Miranda* and its invocation rules" (Leo, p. 281).

Youthfulness, the Leading Cause of Juveniles' Inability to Comprehend their Miranda Rights

Richard Leo (2008) has succinctly stated the problem:

> Youth (especially young children) also lack the cognitive capacity and judgment to fully understand the nature or gravity of an interrogation or the long-term consequences of their responses to police questions. Juveniles also have limited language skills, memory, attention span, and information-processing abilities compared to adults. (p. 233)

When speaking about judging juvenile offenders, former New York Judge of Manhattan's Youth Part, Michael Corriero, begins with the question, "how many of you have ever been fourteen?" (Corriero, 2006, p 20). Could any adult, reaching back in memory to age 14, be able to affirm that he or she would have had the ability to invoke or waive rights to silence and counsel "knowingly, intelligently, and voluntarily" while being subjected to police tactics described so far in this chapter? Many adults would most likely answer no. Corriero notes I Corinthians 13.11: "When I was a child, I spoke as a child, I understood as a child, I thought as a child . . ." as he argues his position for judging children as children opposed to judging them as adults. When determining criminal culpability of juveniles, Judge Corrierio urges us to keep in mind that, "the cognitive, emotional and social development of adolescents is incomplete and that . . . boys well into their teens have difficulty curbing their impulses, thinking through long-term consequences and . . . resisting the influence of others" (2006, pp. 42–43). When investigating comprehensibility of Miranda warnings by juveniles, we must recognize that development plays the same role here as it does with criminal culpability and competence to stand trial.

Evidence about limited capacities of comprehension among juveniles

How many times do parents ask their teenager, "what were you thinking?" after some ill-fated incident? In most cases, this is not as much a question as it is a statement. While parents may be dumbfounded over their child's actions, it can be safe to assume that most parents intuitively know the difference between their own logic and that of their young offspring. As we have previously illustrated through several Supreme Court decisions, the justices recognized cognitive, developmental, and comprehension deficiencies among children and adolescents. Research reveals a wide range of disparities between juvenile and adult comprehension when given the option to waive or invoke rights. Grisso (2003, p. 156) found that over 90% of juvenile suspects waive their rights compared to 58% of adults. Rogers, Hazelwood, Sewell, Shuman, and Blackwood (2008) concluded, "Typical juvenile Miranda warnings are far beyond the abilities of the more than 115,000 preteen offenders charged annually with criminal offenses" (2008, p. 75). Rogers et al. also addressed the "clinical realities" (p. 79) of cognitive abilities and mental disorders on Miranda comprehension with juveniles. Approximately 70% of youths within the juvenile justice system qualify for mental disorder diagnosis (2008, p. 79). In summary, Rogers and his colleagues stated:

> The synergistic effects of poor reading comprehension, low intelligence, and comorbid mental disorders are likely to have catastrophic effects on Miranda comprehension and subsequent reasoning. Reading comprehension alone may render most Miranda warnings ineffective for the majority of juvenile offenders. (2008, p. 80)

Leo (2008) identified developmental traits of young children characteristically similar to those who are mentally retarded. Both groups are highly compliant, generally naïve, and easily misled to comply. They are usually unable to tolerate high levels of interpersonal stress, easily confused, and predisposed to submission toward adults (2008, pp. 233–234).

What behavioral scientists have recognized for decades, the Supreme Court made concessions to in its decision in *Roper v. Simmons* (2005). Quoting *Eddings v. Oklahoma* (1982), the Roper Court agreed that, "Youth is more than a chronological fact. It is a time and condition of life when a person may be most susceptible to influence and to psychological damage" (1982, p. 115), reminding us that minors lack the "experience, perspective, and judgment" that adults have (1982, p. 116). In support of respondent Christopher Simmons, sentenced to death row for a murder committed at age 17, testimony submitted to the Supreme Court by the scientific community as *amici curiae* (friends of the court) presented more tangible evidence of concrete differences between adolescent and adult mental processes that are anatomically based. According to the Brief of the American Medical Association et al. as *Amici Curiae* in support of Simmons, (2005), "Adolescents' behavioral immaturity mirrors the anatomical immaturity of their brains . . . that adolescents are immature not only to the observer's naked eye, but in the very fibers of their brains" (2005, p. 10).

Magnetic resonance imaging (MRI) studies of the brain's structure reveal that particular regions of the brain mature in various stages throughout childhood, into late adolescence, and early adulthood, (2005, p.16). Children predominantly utilize the amygdala, a part of the limbic system referred to as "the emotional center of the brain," responsible for "primitive emotional impulses of aggression, anger and fear." The amygdala works as our security system. When detecting danger it arouses our instincts to either fight or flee "without conscious participation." Adults, on the other hand, use what scientists describe as the "executive functioning" portion of the brain that is not fully developed until early adulthood. The frontal lobe regulates behavior and impulses, assesses risks, and processes moral reasoning. It helps us "mediate more complex information-processing functions such as perception, thinking, and reasoning" (2005, pp. 11–13). With this area underdeveloped in children, "perspective and temperance" are also underdeveloped until late adolescence (2005, p. 7). Thus, primitive emotions rule the child who functions more on impulse rather than on the basis of higher-level cognitive processes. During a *Frontline* interview by the Public Broadcasting System (2002), neuroscientist Jay Giedd, Chief of the Unit on Brain Imaging in the Child Psychiatry Branch at the National Institute of Mental Health, conveyed:

> Right around the time of puberty and on into the adult years is a
> particularly critical time for the brain sculpting to take place . . .
> I think that [in teen years] part of the brain that is helping organiza-
> tion, planning and strategizing is not done being built yet . . . It's
> sort of unfair to expect [adolescents] to have adult levels of organi-
> zational skills or decision-making before their brains are finished
> being built. (p. 2)

Giedd emphasized children should not be viewed as "stupid or incapable of things." Adults have the ability to regulate thinking with logic and reasoning generated from a brain fully matured. Adults also have an advantage with more years of life's experiences. Children, with less experience in life, process events with a brain that reacts on fight or flight impulses, especially when under duress. This deficiency in maturity and life's experience allows interrogators to easily trick juveniles into believing that waiving rights will make their situation tolerable or even bring circumstances to an end. During a phone interview one of the present authors had with Judge Michael Corriero, when asked about the capabilities of street-wise juveniles with high rates of recidivism, Judge Corriero stressed that street-smart juveniles are just as easily tricked by police interrogators as those who have little or no history with authorities.

The vulnerability of adolescents under stress

Research indicates that cognitive deficiencies are more salient when experiencing stress (Brief as *Amici Curiae* in support of Simmons, 2005, p. 8). Interaction between situational stressors and elevated emotions create havoc within the minds of juvenile suspects when under the influence of police interrogators who push for suspects to waive their rights. Cognition is affected in turn, thus diminishing already underdeveloped logic and critical thinking processes. For *Miranda* to serve as a safeguard against the unrelenting grip of interrogators, juvenile suspects must have more than a "factual understanding of the word" (Feld, 2006, p. 43). To have an ability to make the rational decisions required to invoke or relinquish rights, suspects—juveniles and adults alike—need the brainpower to appreciate the consequences that would follow their decision. Feld indicates that, "juveniles often fail to appreciate the significance and function of rights." Adolescents appear to have difficulty handling even the "basic concept of a 'right' as an absolute entitlement that can be exercised without adverse consequences." Some juveniles interpret their "rights" as something given to them by interrogators who can also take those rights away (Feld, 2006, p. 43). Confusion with *Miranda* reigns over juveniles and permeates throughout the legal and judicial system. A strong indicator of this confusion is the remarkably high numbers of different versions of Miranda warnings.

Too many Versions of Miranda Warnings

When custodial interrogation is imminent and it's time to give the suspect a Miranda warning, what exactly do you have to say? The answer is, nothing exactly. –Rutledge, 2006, p. 1

Jurisdictions have created numerous versions of Miranda warnings—some have separate versions for juveniles; others do not. The lower courts and U. S. Supreme Court have ruled inconsistently with regard to valid waiver of rights of juveniles. Thus the most vulnerable of suspects are at a great disadvantage when confronted with the task of making very serious choices. To the devoted Lenny Briscoe fan ("Law & Order" character portrayed by the late Jerry Orbach), this may come as a bit of a surprise. Most avid crime-show viewers could most likely recite the standard phrases "you have the right to remain silent . . ." as heard on TV, with just as much ease as it takes to recite a favorite nursery rhyme. In reality, however, there is nothing standard about Miranda warnings.

The Written Warning

Extensive research by Richard Rogers and his colleagues (Rogers, Harrison, Shuman, Sewell, & Hazelwood, 2007; Rogers, Hazelwood, Sewell, Harrison, & Shuman, 2008) on the comprehensibility of Miranda warnings has found that numerous variations of written warnings exist throughout the 50 states—too numerous to obtain a full count. For the general suspect population, Rogers et al. found 886 different written Miranda warnings among 945 federal, state, and county jurisdictions (2008, pp. 125–126). There are also inter-jurisdictional variations. In the city of Pittsburgh, Pennsylvania, which is the county seat of Allegheny County, suspects taken into police custody would receive one set of warnings; if taken into custody with the sheriff's department, suspects would be read a different set of warnings. For suspects taken into custody at the university or railroad, two more versions would be issued. All four departments are located on the same street within walking distance from each other. It appears that differences between these four warnings consist of word length and complexity. Two versions have right to waive components and two do not: The following examples represent the two different versions of Miranda warnings with waiver components:

Warning 1:

> You have the right to remain silent. Anything you say can and will be used against you in a court of law. You have the right to speak to an attorney and have him present before and during questioning. If you cannot afford an attorney, one will be appointed free of charge before or during any questioning, if you so desire. Do you understand each of these rights I have explained to you, yes or no? Having these rights in mind do you wish to speak to me now, yes or no?

This warning set contains 92 words and appears simple in complexity. The next warning set contains 172 words with terminology more abstruse compared to the first.

Warning 2:

> Under the law, you cannot be compelled to answer, and you have the right to refuse to answer any questions asked of you while you are in custody. If you do answer any such questions, the answers given by you will be used against you in a trial in a court of law at some later date. You are also entitled to talk to a lawyer and to have

him/her present before you decide whether or not to answer questions and while you are answering questions. If you do not have the money to hire a lawyer, you are entitled to have a lawyer appointed without cost to consult with you and to have him/her present before you decide whether or not you will answer questions and while you are answering questions. You can decide at any time, before or during the questioning, to exercise these rights by not answering any further questions or making further statements. Knowing these rights, are you willing to answer questions without the presence of a lawyer?

According to the findings by Rogers and his colleagues, Miranda warnings in differing jurisdictions stretch from 49 to 547 words; they differ in reading grade level from elementary school to post-college, depending on the composition of each individual Miranda component (2008, p. 125). The waiver component of one's rights to remain silent and to an attorney can contribute considerably to the complexity and word length of warnings. Riverside, California's waiver component "Do you wish to talk to (me) (us) now?" consists of nine words requiring reading competency at the third- grade level. In contrast, Grayson, Texas, includes a waiver component that contains 65 words requiring a suspect to have reading competency at the post-college level:

> Prior to and during the making of any statement, you have and do hereby knowingly, intelligently, and voluntarily waive the above explained rights and do make the following voluntary statement to the law enforcement officer named on this document of your own free will and without any promises or offers of leniency or favors, and without compulsion or persuasion by any person or persons whomsoever.

WRITTEN JUVENILE MIRANDA VERSIONS: Richard Rogers and his colleagues (Rogers, Hazelwood, Sewell, Shuman, & Blackwood, 2008) also examined the content of Miranda warnings for juveniles from 109 counties in 29 states. Word length ranged from 52 to 526 (64 to 1020 with a right to waive component included) and a reading grade-level requirement from elementary school to post-college, again, depending on the composition of each individual Miranda component (2008, p. 63). Illustrated by the following examples, we find significant contrasts between jurisdictions—specifically with waiver of rights components. The Marshalltown, Iowa, Police Department's juvenile version of the Miranda waiver component alone consists of 14 words requiring a sixth-grade reading competency: "Do you understand each of these rights? Do you wish to talk with me?" At the other end of the spectrum, we have Sheridan County, Montana's, juvenile waiver component containing 99 words and requiring post-college reading competency:

> If you are 16 years of age or older, you can waive these rights without talking to your parent (or guardian) or an attorney. If you are not

yet 16 years old, and you and your parent (or guardian) do agree
that you should answer our questions before talking to a lawyer, you
and your parent or guardian must sign a waiver. If you are not yet
16 years old and you and your parent (or guardian) do not agree
that you should answer our questions before talking to a lawyer, you
can waive your rights only if you and your attorney sign this waiver.

Not only is the above waiver component lengthy, it rambles—an adult
could get lost in its clutter. A child might tune-out after the second sentence
if not at the first mention of the word "waive."

Comprehending Miranda warnings requires more than recognition of
words. Rogers and his colleagues noted that in order to gain a genuine understanding of warnings, juveniles "must be able to integrate the whole message
and apply its meaning to their own case" (2008, p. 78). This could be difficult
because most teenage offenders never make it through high school, they read
at an average fifth or sixth-grade level, and have low IQ scores (2008, p. 79).
In jurisdictions that do not have juvenile versions and only offer more complex components, as the Grayson, Texas, waiver component mentioned earlier, we doubt that juvenile suspects could adequately comprehend legalese
content that many adults may find indecipherable.

The oral warnings

A survey was conducted by the office of the Los Angeles County
Superintendent of Schools involving 863 youngsters between the
ages of 14 and 17. One interesting result was that 75.2% of the
people in the survey said they did not understand the rights as read
to them by policemen. –Briere, 1978, p. 242

Verbal Miranda warnings are often no easier comprehended than written
ones and can possibly be more problematic. Juvenile mental processing capabilities do not get any sharper with oral warnings. Also, police may deliberately manipulate verbal warnings to confuse suspects. In the case of *Fare v.
Michael C.* (1979), it is apparent that in spite of prior history, 16-year-old
respondent Michael C. appeared confused as to his right to see his probation
officer in lieu of counsel. Furthermore, the police interrogator tried to extract
a confession out of Michael C. by promising to answer his question only after
the respondent waived his rights.

Q. Okay, do you wish to give up your right to remain silent and
   talk to us about this murder?
A. What murder? I don't know about no murder.
Q. I'll explain to you which one it is if you want to talk to us about
   it . . .
Q. Do you want to give up your right to have an attorney present
   here while we talk about it?
A. Can I have my probation officer here?

Q. Well I can't get a hold of your probation officer right now. You have the right to an attorney.

A. How I know you guys won't pull no police officer in and tell me he's an attorney.

Q. Huh?

Q. Well, I'm not going to call Mr. Christianson tonight. There's a good chance we can talk to him later . . . If you want to talk to us without an attorney present, you can. If you don't want to, you don't have to. But if you want to say something, you can, and if you don't want to say something you don't have to. That's your right. You understand that right? (*Fare v. Michael C.*, 1979, pp. 710–711)

Michael C. eventually talked. In the 5 to 4 decision, in favor of Fare, the majority opinion could not find any indication that Michael C. "was of insufficient intelligence to understand the rights he was waiving" and that his request to talk to his probation officer was not a *per se* invocation of his right to an attorney (1979, p. 727). In dissent, Justice Lewis Powell reminded the majority of *In re Gault* charging that "care must be taken" when judging juvenile waivers. In Justice Powell's opinion, Michael C. "demonstrated that he was immature, emotional, and uneducated and . . . likely to be vulnerable to skillful, two-on-one, repetitive interrogation" (1979, p. 733). We concur with this opinion.

A case from the Supreme Court of the State of Delaware, *Smith v. Delaware* (2006), illustrates how Family Courts can play an adversarial role against juveniles' best interest. Fourteen-year-old James Smith was charged and found delinquent on two counts of second degree rape and one count of second-degree unlawful sexual contact with a 3-year-old little girl by Family Court. James had trouble reading, had a full scale IQ of 67, indicating mild mental retardation, and "word recognition and arithmetic skills equivalent to second grade," demonstrating significant cognitive deficits (2006, pp. 4–5). During 45 minutes of questioning without his parents or counsel present, the police detective chose to read James his rights because he had difficulties with reading. Miranda warnings read to James by the detective stated:

Okay, number one you have the right to remain silent. And what that means is you can be quiet if you want to. You don't have to answer anything if you don't want to. Anything you say can and will be used against you in a court of law. It just means whatever we're talking about today you know is legal, you know whether it happens from here on out whatever we talk about you know is pertinent to what's going to happen okay. You have the right to talk to a lawyer and have him present with you while you're being questioned. If you can't afford to hire a lawyer one will be appointed to represent you. If you wish one we've already talked to your mom about that and that's fine. At any time during this interview if you wish to discontinue your statement you have the right to do so. All that means is at any time we're talking if you want to talk to me or you don't. You understand these things I explained to you? (2006, p. 3)

James answered the detective with "uh huh." The detective deciphered this response as a waiver and had James print his name on the form—he could not sign in cursive. Getting no confession out of James, the detective gave him the ultimatum, "The only way we're walking out of here is if you're straight up and honest with me and we deal with this and then I can help you" (2006, p. 4). James confessed.

The Delaware Supreme Court remanded the case back to the Family Court and ruled that James did not understand his rights and should have a new trial. This case illustrates how easy it is for interrogators to take full advantage of vulnerable juveniles. James obviously had mental deficiencies; the detective knew of these deficiencies but continued to do what he had been trained and conditioned to do—to get the confession any way he could.

Police Attitudes

Investigation into police practices and perceptions of juvenile suggestibility by Meyer and Reppucci (2007) documents police attitudes toward the comprehension levels of juveniles during interrogation. Meyer and Reppucci surveyed 332 law enforcement officers. Officers were surveyed on interrogation and developmental knowledge. Approximately 41% of those participating had bachelor degrees and close to 61% had a child or children. We focus on the Developmental Knowledge Survey from this research, specifically police perception in the areas of comprehension and suggestibility and psychosocial immaturity. Results indicate some contradictions in perception among police officers. When considering comprehensibility outside interrogation, police agreed that children lack understanding with words commonly used by adults. In contrast, when asked about comprehensibility within interrogation, officers indicated that, "all ages understand their rights and intent of interrogations" (2007, p. 774). Police recognized developmental differences but seem to prefer to disregard that knowledge inside the interrogation room. As to suggestibility and psychosocial immaturity, police acknowledged diminished developmental capacities and diminished psychosocial maturity, but this knowledge also remained outside the interrogation context (2007, p. 775).

Police attitudes determine the nature and direction of any interrogation. In many cases this unrestrained power produces dangerous side effects for vulnerable children until someone, usually an attorney, intervenes against such flagrant abuse. When dealing with juveniles, Walker, Brooks, and Wrightsman (1999) caution, "the court must attempt to balance the privilege of preventing self-incrimination with the reality of the child's developmental status and the rehabilitation goals of the juvenile justice system" (1999, p. 203). Suggesting the *per se* approach over the "totality of the circumstances," Walker et al.

emphasizes the need for a "skilled lawyer," one well versed in juvenile law, to be present before and during questioning (1999, pp. 104–105). We highly agree.

How has the System Fared Since *In Re Gault* over 40 Years Ago?

Not well. Why? By taking into consideration cases already discussed thus far to include the Marty Tankleff case introduced in Chapter 4 and expanded on in Chapter 7, by dissecting two more recent high profile juvenile cases with police interrogation tactics remaining unfettered, and prosecutors attempting to try children as adults at the tender age of eight, we suspect a shift may be reverting back to 18th and 19th Century mentality prior to the juvenile reform stance of the Progressive era.

> The current practice of incommunicado interrogation is at odds with one of our Nation's most cherished principles—that the individual may not be compelled to incriminate himself. Unless adequate protective devices are employed to dispel the compulsion inherent in custodial surroundings, no statement obtained from the defendant can truly be the product of his free choice. (*Miranda v. Arizona*, 1966, pp. 457–458)

The Warren Court constructed *Miranda's* safeguards to serve as a precautionary threshold separating suspects from immediate interrogation. They recognized then that those targeted by police for questioning did not have a fighting chance unless "protective devices" existed to keep these people outside of interrogation doors until they had full understanding of their rights. Once inside and without the knowledge of rights to silence and an attorney, suspects became subjected to high levels of coercion and intimidation resulting in confessions or inculpatory statements. Under *Gault*, children were finally granted these same safeguards. Along with this grant came admonishment from the Supreme Court that great care must be taken to ensure that confessions or statements made by children do not result from coercion. Today, are these safeguards extended to juveniles fully respected and enforced by police and the courts? From our investigation, no. We will discuss two high-profile cases that represent many previous and existing cases of police violating *Miranda's* safeguards. When police fraudulently shove juveniles around the protective threshold, into interrogation rooms, slamming and locking the doors behind them, children suffer tremendous damage before attorneys are called in to intercede on behalf of their young clients.

First, we look at a case involving three teenage boys, Michael Crowe, Joshua Treadway, and Aaron Houser, all arrested for their involvement in the 1998 murder of Michael's sister Stephanie. By converging on the scathing nature of police interrogation tactics used on these children, we demonstrate the pernicious effects suffered by each child.

Interrogation is a high stakes game, too much pressure and an innocent person might confess to a crime they didn't commit. (Tanner, 2008, March 10)

INTERROGATION OF MICHAEL CROWE   The world watched in disbelief as 14-year-old Michael Crowe falsely confessed to murdering his 12-year-old sister Stephanie. In fact, this case turned into a made-for-cable drama in 2002—*The Interrogation of Michael Crowe*, produced by Hearst Entertainment. Those viewing police interrogation videos witnessed young Michael struggle to understand what was happening to him, why police were telling him that they had proof that he indeed killed his sister with a knife, even though he had no memory of killing her. After following this case throughout its various stages and authoring a six-part series for the *San Diego Union-Tribune*, staff writers Sauer and Wilkens (1999) reflect:

> The nightmare began for the Crowe family . . . when Stephanie was found stabbed to death on her bedroom floor. It grew exponentially in the days to follow when her brother, Michael, then 14, and two of his friends, Joshua Treadway and Aaron Houser, were charged with conspiring to kill her. . . . It is a tale of tragedy and loss, of mindsets shattered and decisions made in the quest for justice and their consequences. (1999, May 11, p. A-1)

The entire ordeal became overwhelming for the Crowe family. Given no time to adequately digest the death of Stephanie and probably everyone still in shock, all members of the Crowe family were taken to police headquarters, then required to strip down and be photographed by police. Adding to existing trauma, police separated Michael and his surviving sister Shannon from their parents by placing them in a local children's center. As both children cried out from fear and confusion while forcefully taken away, Cheryl Crowe, their mother, asked them to be "strong" and to "trust" police—they only wanted to "help" (p. A-1).

During two days of separation and unbeknownst to his parents, police questioned Michael twice for long periods of time. Detectives already had their minds set that Michael and his friends Joshua Treadway and Aaron Houser participated in the murder. Detectives became suspicious with what they considered Michael's "unaffected" demeanor over his sister's stabbing. He also told police that he had gotten up during the night to take Tylenol for a headache but did not see his sister on the floor by the open door to her bedroom. Detectives found this tough to believe. Michael's first "interview," just one day after Stephanie's death, lasted three and a half hours. The wearing down process began with this first round of questioning.

Police interrogated Michael without advising him of his Miranda rights and without the presence of an attorney. At one point Michael was asked to take a "truth-verification exam." Police were referring to a Computer Voice Stress Analyzer (CVSA) that detects tremors within the voice, supposedly identifying "stressed or deceitful" responses. Early on in the questioning Michael began showing signs of uneasiness. When probed by police Michael responded:

> I've spent all day away from my family. I couldn't see them. I feel like I'm being treated like I killed my sister, but I didn't. I feel horrible. I'm being blamed for it. Everything I own is gone. (Sauer & Wilkens, 1999, May 12, p. A-1)

After CVSA testing, the detective administering the exam lied to Michael, informing him that there appeared to be indicators of deception with his answers. Upset with this news, Michael insisted that he had been truthful with all answers. The more Michael denied his involvement the more police accused him. Police began feeding lies to Michael about blood being found in his room telling him that "science is in our favor . . . Technology is on our side" (p. A-1). Sobbing, Michael continued to maintain his innocence. After hours of unrelenting accusations, however, Michael became unsure of reality. As he began to buckle from persistent pressure he wailed,

> Why are you doing this to me? I didn't do this to her. I couldn't. God. Why? I can't believe myself anymore. I don't know if I did it or not. I didn't, though. . . . I don't think—if I did this, I don't remember it. I don't remember a thing. . . . What's going to happen to me now? Even though I don't even know that I did it. What's going to happen? (p. A1)

Three and a half hours passed before police returned Michael Crowe to the children's center. According to a social worker, she recalled that "Michael was emotionally drained, so tired he could barely walk" (p. A-1). Police, apparently not happy without a confession, decided to interrogate this very broken child again the next day. This time questioning lasted six hours.

The National Geographic Channel produced a documentary titled, *Science of Interrogation* (Tanner, 2008, March 10). Excerpts from police interrogating Michael Crowe served to exemplify how conditions created by police set the stage for the young suspect to falsely confess. Watching Michael squirm in his chair with no advocate to act on his behalf, hands cloaked around his face as he sobs, and wrenched in agony from the psychological beating police forced him to endure, could make the most callous tear-up if not scream in outrage. Those interviewed by National Geographic were Stan B. Walters and Richard Leo. Walters indicated that "under the right conditions people will make false confessions" (2008, March 10). Using insidious tactics throughout the entire 10 hours or so of interrogation, the very police who Michael's mother instructed him to "trust," created the perfect conditions for his false confession.

> What do you want me to do? I haven't lied to you. . . . I don't remember what I did . . . I tried to tell you. . . . You keep asking me

questions I can't answer. . . . I can't remember what I did . . . you
keep saying I did it . . . I can't remember. (2008, March 10)

With Michael's state of mind extremely distraught, coercion finally took
its toll. Police attacked Michael's lack of memory calling it "selective" and that
he could not remember because there were "two parts" to Michael: a good
and a bad. The good Michael did not remember what the bad Michael did.
This suggestion threw Michael into an emotional and psychological tailspin.
By the time police offered him the choice of "two paths;" one of punishment
in prison and the other of leniency and help, Michael informed detectives
that "I have this overwhelming feeling I killed her . . . I don't know why I feel
that way," wherein the detective responded calmly, "let me hear about it"
(2008, March 10). Motionless, with his head and shoulders slumped forward,
Michael then confessed that, "I got a knife went into her room and I stabbed
her" (2008, March 10).

Watching as police interrogated Michael, Richard Leo stated the
following:

> They have beaten him down. . . . This is nothing short of child
> abuse. . . . He is crying he is having a breakdown. . . . This is
> psychological torture . . . This is a painful scene to watch, it's an
> egregious interrogation an absolutely awful interrogation. (2008,
> March 10)

While the interrogation of Michael Crowe entails much more than what
we have presented, our purpose in discussing this case focuses on deliberate
disregard for Michael's constitutional rights by police. Sitting in front of
two police detectives, isolated from parents, with no chance of obtaining an
attorney, being relentlessly attacked with an accusation after every claim of
innocence, and forced to write an apology letter to his sister Stephanie,
constitutes nothing short of psychological rape. Michael had no place to
run, his parents had no clue as to his situation—they were given no opportunity to rescue their son from individuals they believed would keep their
children safe.

The other two suspects, Joshua Treadway and Aaron Houser, both
15-year-olds at the time of the murder, underwent similar interrogation.

INTERROGATION OF JOSHUA TREADWAY   Joshua Treadway spent close to 20 hours
with interrogators. After detectives finished with him, Treadway also falsely
confessed, implicating both Crowe and Houser. Police administered the
CVSA test with Treadway, just as they did Michael Crowe, and lied about
results as well. Deception permeated throughout this interrogation. When
Joshua, crying and scared, asked to see his mother, police threatened him with
dire consequences if questioning ceased:

> If you want to conclude this conversation, we can do that OK?
> But now you're no longer faced with the opportunity of getting the

truth out. Cause what's gonna happen is once I leave here, the only possible conclusion is that you have a knife that was used to kill a 12-year-old girl and it was in your bedroom, OK? (Sauer & Wilkens, 1999, May 13, p. A-1)

In Joshua's case, police also duped his father into encouraging his son to cooperate fully with detectives. Michael Treadway believed that without Joshua's cooperation his son was going straight to prison. Today, Michael Treadway wrestles with never insisting on his son's invocation of his rights. He tells Sauer and Wilkens,

> We had no experience with this. You watch "60 Minutes," or "20/20" on TV and these kids spend one night in juvenile hall and they are gang-raped or commit suicide in their cells. And so my goal was: Keep him out of Juvenile Hall. So you cooperate. (p. A-1)

Joshua did just what his father asked of him—he cooperated anyway that he could in order to get out from under the threat of prison. In fact, when tested with the CVSA around 4:00 a.m., Joshua diligently tried to "work with the instrument" (p. A-1). If the truth indicated a lie, Treadway told a lie to indicate a truth. Young Joshua Treadway became trapped in a moral dilemma; tell the truth and go to jail, tell a lie, implicate his friends, and maybe go home. When he denied involvement police would push, suggesting their own fabrications of how he was involved, such as being a "lookout." At one instance, after not hearing what they wanted, an interrogator demanded: ". . . Josh, you've got to stop. You've got to stop denying. Look at me, OK? . . . You're thinking too much. You're not listening to me . . . Let's talk about the lookout thing" (p. A-1). The interrogation process took on an evolutionary nature from that point; as detectives made suggestions, Josh followed along with whatever he believed they wanted to hear. Through police prompting, Joshua eventually found himself presenting a step-by-step account of his involvement and the roles Michael Crowe and Aaron Houser played as well. It all turned out to be false in the end.

INTERROGATION OF AARON HOUSER   The end result of Aaron Houser's interrogation strayed from that of Michael Crowe and Joshua Treadway. Why? It could be that his dad stepped in with a cautious approach and Aaron Houser's unique disposition of calmness when confronted with others who are agitated. While found "chilling" to police, this disposition may be what kicked in during questioning and kept Aaron from buckling.

After Houser's arrest, Gregg Houser, Aaron's father, contacted police and told them not to talk to his son until he joined him at the station. When detectives asked that Aaron be tested, Gregg agreed, believing that his son had "nothing to hide." Aaron signed a form consenting to take the test but police never advised him of his Miranda rights. This would come back to haunt them later on. Police did not get far with Houser; he never confessed to any involvement in the murder and, "the teen shot out of his chair, angry and upset, when first accused of being involved in the slaying" (Sauer & Wilkens, 1999, May 14, p. A-1). Not accomplishing much, police decided to abort the accusatory approach, instead they asked him to provide them with a hypothetical scenario of how he, Treadway, and Crowe would go about killing Stephanie. Aaron, who enjoyed passing time by "engaging in hypotheticals at school," was happy to oblige with a play-by-play script of how the deed would be accomplished: "I would grab her from the arm, place it behind her back. I would stand behind her, cover her mouth. I would take out the knife. Then I would cut her throat" (p. A-1).

Police viewed this as highly disturbing. One Orange County psychologist described Houser as a "sociopath . . . Charles Mansion with an IQ" (p. A-1). Maybe Aaron Houser was simply a normal, typical young teen with an active imagination that coincided with the interactive video games of the late 90s era and probably similar to those today. It is important to note that regardless of how graphic Aaron's hypothetical fantasy of killing Stephanie Crowe appeared, the autopsy showed no similarities between Houser's fiction and the reality of evidence.

Plans were to try Joshua Treadway first, then Michael Crowe and Aaron Houser together. San Diego Superior Court Judge John M. Thompson tossed Michael Crowe's statement out on the grounds of promises of leniency; Judge Thompson also tossed out Aaron Houser's hypothetical statements, and for violation of *Miranda*. Joshua Treadway's statement from the first 10 hours of interrogation was thrown out due to deprivation of sleep and food; statements made from the first 8 hours of the second interrogation were deemed inadmissible by Judge Thompson because of *Miranda* violations. The 2 remaining hours of interrogation out of 20 were allowed, but only as evidence against Treadway. Fortunately for these three young teenagers, their cases never made it to trial. Ordered by the defense, further DNA testing of clothing worn by transient Richard Tuite concluded that blood found on both of his shirts was the blood of Stephanie Crowe. Police picked Tuite up and questioned him about complaints made by neighbors that he had been roaming the Crowe neighborhood the night of Stephanie's murder. A neighbor saw him peering into the Crowe house from their driveway. Police did not record questioning Tuite but they did take his clothing for testing—the first DNA tests indicated negative for blood from Stephanie Crowe. Tuite had a history with police that included stabbing a woman. After 7 months in Juvenile Hall, Michael Crowe, Joshua Treadway, and Aaron Houser were free to go home.

Suspects interrogated and tried as adults are getting younger

Second, we refer to the case of Christian Ryan Romero, with sentencing still pending as of this writing. Ten years after Michael Crowe, through police-released videos, the public again witnessed an interrogation of a child. Viewers watched as an Arizona boy, 8-year-old Christian Ryan Romero, confessed to murdering his father, Vincent Romero and a family friend, Tim Romans, with a .22 caliber, single-shot rifle on November 5, 2008.

Small-framed Christian, sitting in a large chair, feet dangling unable to reach the floor, with two female detectives sitting within close proximity, announced that he killed his dad: "Cause I already saw him bleeding . . . and I kinda saw him shaking and I think I was holding the gun . . . I think it might have gone off—I don't know." After further probing, accusations, and lying by police, Christian describes his actions: "I went upstairs and then I saw my dad and then I got a gun and then fired it at my dad—he was on the ground and then I reloaded it . . . "(Sawyer, 2008). Romero's confession came after close to an hour of interrogation.

Releasing interrogation tapes within a day or two after Christian's arrest created a media frenzy. Similar to Michael Crowe, every major news station throughout the country played excerpts, with mental health and legal experts expressing their concerns relating to the reliability and voluntariness of Christian's statements. Within 5 days of the murders, Superior Court Judge Michael P. Roca issued a gag order in an attempt to salvage the integrity of this case. Since then it has been difficult to obtain interrogation and hearing transcripts, but from the Transcript of Detained Advisory Hearing and Detention Hearing (2008) and the Motion to Suppress Statements & Request for Voluntariness Hearing (2008) we gain enough insight to see that Christian Romero's Miranda rights were violated directly at the onset of police questioning him.

Sometime between 4:30 and 5:00 p.m., Christian Romero ran to a neighbor's house, telling them that he found his father, Vincent Romero, and Tim Romans dead. The neighbor called 911. Police interviewed neighbors within the surrounding vicinity to include Christian as to what they saw or heard. Throughout the course of time, police received information from Tim Roman's wife that she heard Christian's voice over the phone calling to Tim as she talked with her husband shortly before his death. Police immediately determined that Christian may have lied to them during initial questioning when he said that he found the victims already dead. Police officers quickly began formulating their own scenarios as to how the murders may have occurred, to include Christian as the shooter. In other words, at that time Christian became a suspect. After a briefing involving "10 to 15 law enforcement officers discussing potential options of the case" (Motion to Suppress, 2008, p. 3), police decided to interview Christian again. This time police asked that Christian's family take him to a local health center for what they termed "a forensic interview" (2008, p. 4).

Three members of Christian's family accompanied him for further questioning. According to the motion to suppress document all three members of the family asked to be present during questioning, but police denied these requests. Christian's grandfather asked for legal representation—police also denied this request. Under the pre-conceived idea that Christian may be the shooter, police took him to a small room and began interrogating him. After observing the interrogation videos, Christian's defense argued,

> The officers sat in chairs across from Christian in a triangle posture.
> At no time did any officer advise Christian that he was a suspect in

any crime. At no time prior to questioning Christian, or any other
time for that matter, did the officers advise him of his Miranda
warnings ... At no time did the officers allow him to speak with an
attorney, or advise him that he was not required to answer any of
their questions ... At no time did the officers advise Christian that
he would not be going home with his family after the questioning.
At no time did the officers determine, through testing or otherwise,
whether Christian could understand what they were asking of him.
(Motion to Suppress, 2008, pp. 4–5)

The defense further argued:

The length of the interrogation was approximately one hour.
During that time Christian was not offered water (until the end of
the interrogation) or food, nor given any offers to use the restroom.
One hour for an adult is not unduly long, however for an eight year
old it is. (2008, p. 10)

During questioning, detectives denied suspecting Christian as the shooter
before interrogating him. How could that be? Their suspicion prompted the
second interview. The defense also found numerous lies laced throughout the
entire interrogation process. Police indicated that while they are trained to lie
for adult suspects they were not trained to lie to 8-year-old children. In any
sense, they did lie. In the initial portion of the interrogation, the two detectives questioning Christian tried to develop some rapport with him by
attempting to create an environment of trust between them. The following is
an excerpt from the interrogation with detective Avila questioning Christian:

AVILA:	This is the room that we talk to people. And we make a promise to each other that we're only gonna tell the truth.
CHRISTIAN:	(nods)
AVILA:	Okay?
CHRISTIAN:	'kay.
AVILA:	I have to tell you the truth, I can't lie, Debbie can't lie, and you can't lie to us.
CHRISTIAN:	(nods)
AVILA:	Is that okay?
CHRISTIAN:	Yeah.
AVILA:	We're just gonna tell the truth. Okay.
CHRISTIAN:	(nods)
AVILA:	We're not gonna make anything up, we're just gonna be honest, okay?
CHRISTIAN:	(nods)
AVILA:	Even if it's bad stuff okay, we just need ta [sic], talk the truth, just us, in this room. Is that okay?
CHRISTIAN:	Yeah. (2008, pp. 5–6)

This initial portion of the interrogation was not void of falsities. Detective Avila informed Christian that it was "just" them in that room who would discuss the truth. Could this 8-year-old young child have possibly believed that what he said would have gone no further than that room? Could he have believed that members of law-enforcement would be nothing but honest with him? Of course it is possible. What little child would not look up to police with trusting eyes? Suspects, adults and adolescents alike, even with a history, fall prey to such subtle play on semantics; a naïve, vulnerable child at the age of eight, who may still be losing baby teeth, would definitely believe whatever police told him.

Eventually, questioning became accusatory in nature and lying by police became more conspicuous. For most of the interrogation Christian denied any involvement in the murders. At first, police used a similar approach with Christian as they did with Aaron Houser. They asked Christian for his account as to what might have happened to his dad and Tim. Christian offered the possibility of neighbors down the street from him or someone in a white car. When they could not bring him to the point of incriminating himself, they began accusing him of not being honest with them:

> AVILA: Um, you're sure that you weren't home.
> CHRISTIAN: (nods) Yeah. Yeah.
> AVILA: You're sure.
> CHRISTIAN: Mm-hm.
> AVILA: Okay, because I heard sumthin, that somebody said that, um, somebody was calling yer name and that you weren't answering, at the house.
> CHRISTIAN: Who was calling my name?
> AVILA: Nobody was calling yer name?
> CHRISTIAN: No.
> NECKEL: In the house?
> CHRISTIAN: No. (2008, p. 17)

This line of questioning must have confused Christian. He was told that someone was calling his name at the house but when he responded back with, "Who?" he was not told who that person was. Police kept challenging his insistence that he was not home. When detectives questioned Christian about Tim, asking him how Tim may have gotten on the ground Christian replied: "I think he got shot." Detective Neckel replied, "You think he got shot? Did you maybe shoot im[*sic*] by accident?" Christian responded, "No" (2008, p. 17). Accusations continued, pushing for a confession detective Avila continued:

> But there's times you really gotta tell the truth and this is one 'a those times, okay? Honey, I'm gonna help ya, okay, I'm gonna (unk) in with ya. I'm gonna help ya, okay, we've gotta get, we need ta know, what the truth is. (2008, p. 19)

Still not getting his cooperation, detectives Avila and Neckel intermittently resorted to innuendos:

> AVILA: I need you ta tell us the truth, really, really bad, okay, so, so you don't have ta be in bigger trouble, okay? . . .
>
> AVILA: How bout if we had somebody that told us that you mighta shot em . . .
>
> NICKEL: I'm telling ya, that's what we heard . . . (2008, p. 19)

Avila went on to lie about how many guns were used to shoot the victims. Christian had his own gun, his father taught him how to shoot, therefore he did understand the workings of at least a .22 caliber, single-shot rifle. Avila told Christian that police knew for a fact that the bullets shot were from the same gun. According to the defense, Avila could not have known this at the time of the interrogation. She lied.

Christian's defense raised the question as to whether "Christian was in custody for purposes of Miranda" (2008, p. 8). With the facts that adult family members drove Christian in for questioning, police sequestered him from his family into in a small room, one detective questioning him wore her pistol in full view, and Christian knew family members wanted to sit in with him but they were denied that opportunity, the defense argued:

> He was not handcuffed, but was not told he could stop the inter-
> view at any time. Under these circumstances would a reasonable
> 8-year-old feel as though he/she could get up off the couch and
> walk out the door of the interrogation room without being stopped
> by the officers? No way in hell. (2008, p. 9)

Judge Roca agreed that Christian's rights under *Miranda* were violated. He therefore did not allow the use of Christian's interrogation statements as evidence.

How well would have Christian understood his rights even if they were administered to him? From what we have already discussed from our findings in this chapter, he would not have understood the significance of his rights or his decision to invoke or waive those rights at all. Christian never heard his rights until Judge Roca advised him at the detention hearing. We now give you Judge Roca's version of Miranda warnings for an 8-year-old.

CHRISTIAN'S RIGHT TO SILENCE

> Okay. Mr. Romero, you've had the opportunity to discuss with Mr.
> Brewer the contents of the petition. It is two very serious charges,
> two counts each of premeditated homicide. In addressing these
> cases—these charges, you have a number of important rights. They
> include the right to confront and cross-examine all of the witnesses
> against you, the right to present witnesses and physical evidence
> that's favorable to you, the right to require, that is to force people to
> come forward, if they have favorable testimony, and the right to

testify on your own behalf if you choose or to remain silent if you choose. That right to remain silent extends beyond the issue of anything to be proven, and it pertains to this hearing as well. You have an absolute right to remain silent. What you do say can be used against you in court. (Transcript of Detained Advisory Hearing, 2008, p. 9)

CHRISTIAN'S RIGHT TO AN ATTORNEY

The way that all of these rights are more than an empty promise is by another and equally important right, and that is the right to represented by an attorney. Mr. Brewer is here on your behalf standing in at Ms. Cooper's request. Ms. Cooper is an attorney in Show Low. She has been appointed to represent you throughout the remainder of these proceedings. Mr. Brewer is also an attorney in Show Low and has agreed to appear here specially on your behalf today . . . Okay. Anything you say to him is a secret. Anything you tell him, he cannot tell anyone else unless you authorize it. Okay? His advice to you is his advice with your best interest in mind. He is unalterably and absolutely on your side, and that is how your rights are more than a meaningless promise. Attorneys enforce people's rights, and that's what he is here for. (2008, p. 10)

Judge Roca brilliantly caps off his rendition of Miranda warnings with, "Do you have any questions? If you do, you may want to talk to Mr. Brewer first" (2008, p. 10). We can only speculate as to how much Christian actually understood—our bet would be practically nothing at all.

Although sentencing remains pending, this case has undertaken some changes. In February, 2009, through a plea bargain, the State reduced Christian Romero's charges to one charge of negligent homicide for the death of Tim Romans—they dropped charges related to the death of his father, Vincent Romero. Originally, prosecutors wanted to try Christian as an adult; however, early on in the proceedings they conceded to the fact that experts would declare Christian incompetent to stand trial, and without his confession, the best way to go about closing this case would be to lessen the charges. With charges reduced, the court released Christian to his mother's care under conditions of an extended furlough. According to the Memorandum of Agreement (2009), after admitting to the charge of negligent homicide, the court stipulated that Christian must remain on "Intensive Probation until further order of the Court," until he turns 18 years old (2009, p. 2). Christian spends his days at home under the watchful eyes of his mother and probation officer. How long this lasts will be determined with sentencing. At the time of this writing, sentencing has been continually delayed. Judge Michael Roca has been disqualified as assigned judge due to, what Romero's defense argues, "bias against the juvenile" (Notice of Change of Judge for Cause, 2009, p. 3). Judge Roca randomly decided to reject an already accepted plea and wanted Christian placed in the custody of the Department of Corrections.

So far, young Christian has avoided detainment in Juvenile Hall. It may be quite some time before we gain full access to files and documents that have been kept away from public reach. We do not know all of the facts as to whether or not Christian Ryan Romero committed the act of murder and why—those ifs and whys will eventually come to light. We do know one thing for certain about this case; just as with Michael Crowe, Joshua Treadway, and Aaron Houser, Christian Romero never arrived safely to that guarded threshold of constitutional rights constructed under *Miranda*. Instead, police denied this little boy the sanctity against self-incrimination and his right to an attorney.

Children in the United States will remain under the threatening cloud of Miranda violations through police misconduct as long as police can get away with it. Outside of physical abuse, baleful psychological tactics have remained unchanged throughout time. Police lose sight of age and competence once suspects enter the interrogation room. Only with an attorney present at the onset of questioning can our children be secure under *Miranda*. The majority opinion of *In re Gault* (1967) specifically stipulated that:

> The juvenile needs the assistance of counsel to cope with problems
> of law . . . to make skilled inquiry into the facts, to insist upon
> regularity of the proceedings, and to ascertain whether he has a
> defense and to prepare and submit it. The child "requires" the
> guiding hand of counsel at every step in the proceedings against
> him. (1967, p. 36)

No matter if children are being questioned as victims, for "forensic interviewing," or as witnesses, children should never be confronted with any form of questioning at any time without the presence of an attorney. As we see with the additional cases presented here, even with parents involved the final results are usually disastrous.

Court inconsistencies also add to the threat. What one court deems in violation of *Miranda* another court may interpret differently. In the case of Christian Romero, so far the Superior Court appears to be acting in the best interest of this now 9-year-old child. He spent very little time in detention and may never be placed behind locked doors; the prosecution agreed to reduce charges, released Christian into the custody of his mother, and insisted on psychological care. However, a red flag has been raised with this case. Initially, the State opted to try Christian as an adult on two counts of murder. Christian could have easily been spending the rest of his life in prison. If Christian were tried as an adult this would not be as unusual a case as most may think. Many courts are set-up to try 7-year-olds as adults. According to a recent policy research report from the Lyndon B. Johnson School of Public Affairs at the University of Texas at Austin,

> In 22 states plus the District of Columbia, children as young as 7
> can be prosecuted and tried in adult court, where they would be
> subjected to harsh adult sanctions, including long prison terms,

mandatory sentences, and placement in adult prison. Certain states have transfer policies that increase the likelihood that young children will end up in the adult criminal justice system for their offenses. (Deitch, Barstow, Lukens, & Reyna, 2009, p. xv)

The report goes on to state:

The vast majority of crimes committed by young children are handled in juvenile court, including a large number of serious offenses including murder. But this is not always the case. In fact, every year nearly 80 children aged 13 and younger are judicially transferred to adult court. Between 1985 and 2004, 703 children aged 12 and under, and 961 children aged 13 were judicially transferred to adult court. The total numbers of young children in adult criminal court are actually much higher than this because the data cannot capture the numbers of children sent to the adult system via automatic transfer laws or laws allowing the prosecutor to file cases directly in adult court. (p. xv)

These numbers continue to climb year after year. Are we shifting back to 18th and 19th century mentality where children 7 years of age were tried and sentenced to death just as adults? With statistics such as those above, apparently we are. Since the *Roper v. Simmons* case in 2005, science and technology have played an important role in courts understanding cognitive development in determining culpability. The U.S. Supreme Court determined that the Eighth and Fourteenth Amendments "forbid" imposing the death penalty on offenders who were under the age of 18 when their crimes were committed. Although a great beginning, this decision needs to be taken much further. Imposing adult sentencing for children who commit crimes must also be forbidden. Incarcerating children for life serves as nothing less than a death sentence. A child does not commit a crime for adult reasons. A child commits a crime for childlike reasons and needs to be treated accordingly by police, prosecution, and the courts.

Comprehensibility of *Miranda* Among those with Limited English Speaking and Reading Proficiency

Many suspects are not proficient in the English language. Venkatraman (2006, p 40) summarizes the situation:

Nearly 47 million people, or 18 percent of the U.S. population, speak a language other than English at home. According to the 2000 census, nearly 30 percent of all Spanish speakers, 25 percent of all Asian and Pacific speakers, and 15 percent of Indo-European language speakers classified themselves as 'limited English proficient,' or LEP.

But even these figures do not fully encapsulate the problem, because they do not include illegal immigrants, citizens of foreign countries temporarily visiting in the U.S., or migrant farm-workers who do not report their usual U.S. place of residence or work camp. A large population of individuals who speak, read, and write with limited English proficiency, hereinafter referred to as LEP, or those who do not understand English at all, create language barriers that increase intensity to already existing problems of Miranda comprehensibility.

Bharathi A. Venkatraman, attorney for the Civil Rights Division Coordination and Review Section of the U.S. Department of Justice, Washington, D.C., points out problems stemming from language barriers between LEP populations and police: "Language barriers present challenges to the execution of a variety of law enforcement functions . . . So far many jurisdictions are dealing with these barriers in an ad-hoc fashion" (2006, p. 40). Venkatraman warned that, "Strained communication between officers and LEP persons can compromise the integrity of the judicial process" (2006, p. 41). Briere (1978, pp. 241–242) concluded that the level of the difficulty of the language of the rights compounded with anxiety, fear, and perhaps hostility seriously affect LEP suspects' performance. Language barriers also complicate LEP suspects' ability to comprehend their constitutional rights to silence and counsel, making it imperative for police to include the assistance of translators and interpreters. It is important to keep in mind, however, that the competency of such translators and interpreters can play a pivotal role in the outcome of Miranda proceedings.

Competent or Incompetent Interpreters and Translators

Police confronted with LEP suspects face complex issues when delivering Miranda warnings in oral and written form. Written forms require a transla-tor while verbal issuance requires an interpreter (Curtis, 2006). Both jobs demand high levels of proficiency in both languages. Having basic knowledge of a foreign language usually exposes inadequacies within legal settings. Unfortunately, according to Isabel Framer, former President of Community and Court Interpreters of the Ohio Valley (2000), "lack of knowledge about the field is rampant" (p. 3). There are many instances in which police inter-rogators will use other officers or office clerks with little or basic knowledge of a suspect's native tongue to interpret and translate.

Using individuals with less than adequate skills with the foreign language and legal terms will most likely send the case to appellate courts, ending up in reversals. As a classic example, the case of *Ohio v. Ramirez* (1999) illustrates problems resulting from the use of incompetent translators and interpreters. Police obtained an administrative assistant with limited knowledge of Spanish and "no familiarity with legal terms" to interpret Miranda warnings to the suspect. The defense used an "expert witness whose first language was Spanish," having no experience with legal terms, and the prosecutor found an over-confident expert witness "born in Madrid, Spain, a professor of Spanish at an Ohio college, and highly familiar with the American justice system." All were accepted as qualified translator and interpreters respectively at some point throughout this case (1999, pp. 1067–1068).

Alejandro Ramirez, a 20-year-old Mexican national who could not speak, read, or write a word of English, was taken by police for questioning regarding a murder. The original Miranda warnings administered to Ramirez were rendered "insufficient to adequately apprise Ramirez of his rights" by the appellate court (1999, p. 1065). The non-validity of Ramirez's waiver of rights stems from the fact that no one knows exactly what the police translator did convey to the suspect. The interpreter for the defense indicated that the police translator used the preposition "underneath" in a physical sense when attempting to translate rights "under the law." Ramirez was also informed that he had "the right hand side for the presence of an attorney" instead of his "right to an attorney." The prosecution's expert witness, one with the greatest qualifications, argued that interpreting by the defense expert witness was "overly technical," concluding that what Ramirez was initially read by the police translator could have easily been understood. What is unfortunate here is the fact that the prosecution's translator admitted that she changed the language of the exchange so that it made more sense (1999, p. 1069). This is not acceptable in an adversarial system where what is truly stated carries great weight. The court also indicated that Ramirez did not receive all components of the warnings— the translator for the police literally excluded them. Problems with incorrect terms and deletions or additions to the warnings by interpreters and translators are quite common as Nakane (2007) found in recent research.

Problems with Communication between Suspects, Interpreters, and Police

Determining whether or not suspects are capable of understanding Miranda rights in English through oral and written form is just one segment of issues that must be factored in when dealing with LEP suspects. According to Nakane (2007), when an interpreter or translator is needed, specific factors should be considered:

1. The translator's competence to "decompose the grammatically complex legal text and translate it into the target language" (p. 90). In "face-to-face" settings it can be challenging for translators to accurately replicate what has been written in English into another language.
2. The ability of the interpreter to maintain the legal implications of the warnings. It can be a juggling act for the interpreter to execute a word-for-word phrase that would convey the accurate meaning of the warning and express legal implications as well. If the interpreter is not familiar with legal terms the illocutionary force—its actual strength— can be altered and meaning is then lost.

3. Pragmatic, syntactic and grammatical structures and concepts can be a tough task for an interpreter in order to obtain an accurate translation. Individuals with basic knowledge of a language and little if any legalese can likely be of no benefit to police or suspect and, as indicated in *Ramirez*, cases end up in appellate courts and at times reversed and remanded for further consideration. It creates an unnecessary hurdle and delay within the judicial system.

4. Dynamics of the interpreter can serve as a language and cultural bridge between suspects and police officer. This can be difficult, however, because the interpreter is only responsible for interpreting the Miranda verbal warnings with no elaborating on the part of the interpreter. With the case of *Ramirez*, a language and cultural gap developed as a result of the lack of competence by the interpreter—here is an excerpt:

> Interpreter: O.K. Alejandro? Here are your rights [underneath] the law.
> Ramirez: Mmm-hmm.
> Interpreter: Ah, you have the right that something . . . that you . . . ah . . . can use against yourself in a court of law. You have [absolutely] on the [right hand side] to stay in silence, if you prefer. You have the right hand side to an attorney . . .
> Ramirez: Hmm?
> Interpreter: And also you have the [right hand side] for the presence of an attorney here with you during the questions and also if you can't pay for an attorney, it is possible for having an attorney, O.K.? Without paying before the questions, O.K.? Do you understand all of your rights [underneath the law]?
> Ramirez: Mmm-hmm.
> Interpreter: O.K. Good. He says he does understand his rights as I have read them.
> Police Officer: Does . . . he knows that, ah, he doesn't have to . . . have to talk . . .
> Interpreter: That's correct
> Police Officer: Did you ask him? Does he want to make a statement without a lawyer?
> (*Ohio v. Ramirez*, 1999, pp. 1067–1068)

At this point in Mirandizing, the interpreter asks Ramirez if he wants to "talk a little tiny bit" without an attorney or with one present. Ramirez's response was "unintelligible." The interpreter confirmed to the police officer that Ramirez was willing to speak without an attorney present.

As the opinion noted in this case, the apprising was insufficient with "convoluted" questions presented to the appellant (*Ohio v. Ramirez*, 1999,

p. 1068). The police officer, not understanding Spanish, had no clue that Ramirez was never apprised of his right to an attorney free of charge. The interpreter may have tried to relay that component to the suspect but did a poor job of doing so. Also, Ramirez was never warned that if he did choose to speak, what he said could be held against him in a court of law. The police officer could only trust that the interpreter was competent to interpret the verbal warnings given by him over to the suspect.

In the situation of interpreting verbal warnings, Nakane (2007) addressed specific elements that affect the outcome of interpretation:

(1) Turn construction: "When the interrogator hands over a turn to the interpreter can make a critical difference in the quality of interpreted warnings" (2007, p. 94). Nakane found that delivering the warnings with frequent handovers to the interpreter allows for more accurate interpreting. Advising suspects that they have a right to remain silent and that anything said could be held against them in a court of law works better together as one turn and having the right to an attorney and affording one next in turn, etc. If a police officer would advise with a combination of right to silence and right to counsel, this could cause a breakdown in interpreting and illocutionary forces (adequately expressing the level of importance of these rights by the interpreter).

(2) Turn boundaries: The location of turn boundaries affects difficulty in interpreting warnings (2007, p. 102). If a police officer advises suspects by breaking up the flow of thought, this could prove problematic for the interpreter and suspects. For example, advising on the right to silence as one turn then combining the components that anything said could be used against suspects in a court of law and the right to an attorney for the second turn would make it difficult for the interpreter to structure the complexity into the foreign language in order to make sense out of it. With some languages sentence structure is different or even opposite of English. The Japanese language branches left, which is reverse from English. According to Nakane, "subordinate clauses appear before the main clause, and the predicate usually appears at the end of a sentence" (2007, p. 102). Without fluency in both languages it could be highly difficult for an interpreter to accurately and effectively issue Miranda warnings to many LEP suspects.

Deaf and Hearing Impaired Suspects with Limited English Proficiency

We find it imperative to include vulnerable suspects rarely included in *Miranda* research: deaf and hearing-impaired suspects. When confronted with the ordeals of the legal system, deaf suspects face difficulties with the

English language similar to foreign-speaking suspects with English as their second language. According to Dubow, Greer and Strauss (1992, p. 177):

> A great number of deaf adults would find the language of this [Miranda] warning strange and incomprehensible because of the many idioms used in it. True, each word in and of itself is simple but when two or more are put together in a special sense, they can be totally unintelligible to a deaf individual because many deaf adults give each word narrow or literal meaning.

Unique problems arise when questioning deaf suspects, especially when advising them of their Miranda rights and assessing competence to waive those rights (Vernon, Raifman, Greenberg, & Monteiro, 2001, p. 45). Similar to LEP suspects, an interpreter is needed for communication between suspects and police. Similar to mentally retarded suspects, many deaf suspects suffer reading and writing deficiencies. While many deaf persons have normal IQ levels, some deaf criminals have been found to "experience marked linguistic deficits, and have an increased probability of brain damage and mental disorders" (Vernon et al., 2001, p. 46).

Challenges When Administering Miranda Warnings to Deaf Suspects

Police have only three options when administering Miranda warnings to deaf suspects: written form, lipreading, or American Sign Language (ASL). Unfortunately, all three methods have their shortcomings. For many deaf suspects, the written Miranda form would not be an option. Prelingually deaf people, those born deaf or lost hearing before age 3, have never had the chance to hear and understand the spoken language. Vernon et al. (2001) found that 30% of prelingually deaf people read at or below 2nd grade reading level and "leave school functionally illiterate," 60% could read at or below a 5th grade level, and 5% could read at 10th grade level. Rogers, Hazelwood, Sewell, and Shuman (2008, p. 78) established that suspects need at least an 8th grade education to understand right to an attorney and continuing rights. Briere (1978 p. 241) found that 50% of 8th eighth grade students experience difficulty with reading comprehension of Miranda's language. This tells us that 95% of prelingually deaf people would have problems comprehending Miranda warnings in their simplest, written form. Lipreading does not sufficiently help the majority of deaf suspects. Lipreaders "comprehend only about 5% of what is spoken." Besides, 40% to 60% of English sounds are "invisible or look like some other sound" (Vernon, Raifman & Greenberg, 1996, p. 123; Vernon et al., 2001, p. 47). A dilemma exists within the realm of interpreting for deaf suspects: All deaf suspects receiving Miranda warnings would need certified ASL interpreters and even though ASL accommodates most deaf suspects, it still has its limitations.

Limitations of ASL

Away from the common usage within daily life such as "work, recreation, body functions, emotions, food, sexual behavior, etc.," ASL has no signs for legal terms or words used in legal context such as "rights," a term that permeates throughout Miranda's components. For literate and educated deaf suspects, the term could be conveyed via fingerspelling (manual alphabet), but for the illiterate, undereducated deaf suspect, this would not be an option (Vernon et al., 1996, p. 123). ASL syntax organization and vocabulary presents itself as if it were another dialect of English. It is common among the educated deaf to use ASL and fingerspelling, thus making it easier to communicate when there is no sign for a particular word. Some educated deaf will invent new signs for "special words" as they converse. This can produce problems between even certified interpreters and educated suspects understanding each other. It also has no relevance to the 30% prelingually deaf who are functionally illiterate. While these suspects communicate adequately in routine daily living, they are "markedly limited or unable to make an informed, knowing decision about waiving their Miranda rights . . ." (Vernon et al., 2001, p. 47).

Challenges Interpreters, Police, and Deaf Suspects Face

Interpreters using ASL interpret continuously as the officer speaks and this can lead to many errors and omissions (Vernon et al., 2001, p. 51). Furthermore, police do not know what is actually being interpreted. Deaf suspects also place high reliance on sight in order to communicate. Along with ASL, suspects concentrate on facial expressions and body language to help discern the demeanor of different speakers—as to whether they are agreeable or angry, for example.

With so much at risk when it comes to the highly vulnerable circumstances that deaf suspects face when taken into custody, interpreters' ability with ASL and legal terminology should be fully scrutinized before placing anyone in the position to interpret. Police have a difficult time finding interpreters certified for legal interpreting. Because of the "regional, ethnic, and idiosyncratic" variations, ASL is not so easy to master (Vernon et al., 2001, p. 52).

When hearing interpreters have problems with adequately translating, "relay interpreters" are called in to assist. Relay interpreters are deaf themselves and familiar with the variety of signs used by different suspects. They work between the suspect and hearing interpreter by relaying difficult signs used by suspects over to the hearing interpreters as well as relaying back to suspects by rephrasing what the hearing interpreter is signing (Vernon et al., 2001, pp. 52-53). Here we have a possible scenario of a suspect being questioned with police present, a hearing interpreter, a relay interpreter, and if all things are done properly, an attorney will be present as well. Even with all of these participants, a video recording will be imperative for judging waiver validation should the suspect sign one. The police officer cannot be sure if his or her statements are accurately interpreted, the attorney most likely doesn't know anything about ASL, and the two interpreters are working together— one can hear, the other is deaf. Video recording would give those assessing validity of a waiver a birds-eye view of the circumstances surrounding Miranda issuance and questioning.

Challenges with Waiver of Rights

A need not to appear "different"—a problem also with mentally challenged persons—is often present in deaf people. Vernon and his colleagues have described the problem:

> Conversely, deaf people often perceive the police officer as an authority figure of great power and control. They are anxious to accommodate such a person in order to minimize the time in interrogation. When the officer places a printed Miranda form in front of the deaf suspect or has an interpreter sign the warnings, the deaf person will initial and sign that she/he understands.
> (Vernon et al., 1996, p. 128)

Police mistakenly hold the opinion that, because of the presence of an interpreter and the provision of written warnings, deaf suspects understand Miranda's language, thus validating their waiver of rights. Just like many other suspects, when deaf suspects find themselves in precarious situations, intimidating circumstances will aggravate already existing cognitive and intellectual deficiencies. Deaf suspects' nodding yes or signing yes as though they understand may only be a "non-directive response" in order to deal with their confusion (Vernon et al., 1996, p. 129). The case of *Michigan v. McBride*, (2006), a *per curiam* decision, illustrates such a problem.

Mary Ann McBride, deaf and mute, arrested and charged with murder, successfully had inculpatory statements suppressed by the Michigan Court of Appeals and waiver of rights judged invalid on the grounds that McBride did not understand her Miranda rights, therefore unable to intelligently waive those rights. This case illustrates the chaos that can arise during questioning of deaf suspects. Videotapes gave full account of the circumstances surrounding the appellate court's decisions regarding adequate Mirandizing and validity of McBride's waiver of rights.

According to videotapes, McBride's interpreter's back faced the video camera (*People v. McBride, 2006*, p. 1). This did not allow viewers to assess her interpreting abilities. According to Vernon et al. (2001, p. 51), signs from interpreters and suspects must be captured on video to include hands, arms, and faces. "Facial expression and body language are important components of communication that are critical in deaf communication." When the police asked McBride if she could read or write, the video indicated that she responded with a "shrug" and no actual signing as to yes or no. Her interpreter relayed this as an affirmative response (*Michigan v. McBride*, 2006, p. 2). McBride signed to her interpreter inquiring as to needing a lawyer wherein the police officer responded with, "Well, you have a right to have one" (*Michigan v. McBride*, 2006, p. 3). The videotape also showed that police administered Miranda warnings but omitted McBride's right to an attorney before and during questioning and that an attorney could be appointed without cost. When asked if she understood her rights, McBride never responded one way or the other. As the detective read McBride her Miranda rights he placed the written form in front of her. In spite of the fact that McBride could not read the form and watch her interpreter at the same time, the detective had her sign the form, never indicating that the form was to serve as McBride's waiver of rights (*Michigan v. McBride*, 2006, p. 4).

The appellate court ruled on the basis of the videotape and the fact that no one bothered to inquire into McBride's level of education or comprehensibility before being interviewed (*Michigan v. McBride*, 2006, p. 11). In most cases, interpreters will investigate this in order to effectively interpret between suspects and police. In this case, the interpreter failed to do her job. McBride however, did not have the luxury of having her confession suppressed for long. Her case went to the Michigan Supreme Court, who reversed the lower appellate court's ruling and admitted McBride's confession as evidence. The Michigan Supreme Court believed that "the totality of the circumstances surrounding the interrogation reflects that the defendant knowingly, intelligently, and voluntarily waived her Miranda rights" (*Michigan v. McBride*, 2008). Higher court justices with greater insight into the complexity between the deaf and language may have rendered their opinion in favor of the defendant and agreed with the lower court's decision. Unfortunately, without the necessary education, such insight will remain absent behind the judicial bench.

Mentally Handicapped and Mentally Ill Suspects' Ability to Comprehend Miranda Warnings

Another group for whom the comprehension of Miranda rights is suspect includes those who are emotionally disturbed and mentally challenged. Rogers, Harrison, Hazelwood, and Sewell (2007, p. 401) have estimated that 695,000 mentally disordered offenders are arrested and Mirandized in the United States each year.

Viljoen, Roesch, and Zapf (2007) caution as to the critical role that police and lawyers play in the detection of "potential legal impairment, and referring defendants for further evaluation" (p. 500). Criticism has been raised that both police and lawyers fall far short in their abilities to identify mentally disordered suspects and their impaired abilities to understand the warnings of interrogation; in many cases lawyers simply "overestimate" suspects' abilities to comprehend, even among young suspects (p.500). For mentally challenged suspects, receiving warnings with reading comprehension requirements above 3rd grade would not result in an intelligent decision to invoke or waive rights (Fulero & Everington, 1995, p. 535). Such suspects would need at least a 7th grade reading level to comprehend the simplest warning (Rogers, Harrison, Hazelwood, & Sewell, 2007; Fulero & Everington, 1995). According to Briere (1978, p. 241), 50% of 8th grade students would have difficulty comprehending Miranda's language—the mentally deficient have little chance of understanding Miranda warnings.

Cognitive and Emotional Capacities

In most cases, "Miranda warnings are often read fast and with little room for explanation, the police usually require a one-word answer to each of them" when checking for suspects' understanding (Weiss, 2003, p. 455). Suspects receiving a long version of Miranda warnings must understand and decide upon each of the rights given them. With all of this to mentally process, suspects are then asked to either invoke or "voluntarily, knowingly, and intelligently" waive these rights while considering consequences that lie ahead from their decision (*Miranda v. Arizona*, 1966, p. 444). This can be a tough challenge for most suspects—it can be disastrous for those mentally handicapped and mentally ill, especially under the influence of the "antagonistic forces" of police (*Miranda v. Arizona*, 1966, p. 461).

Resistance

When all suspects find themselves held for questioning by police, whose sole motive is to extract a confession, cognitive and emotional agility will determine how well they hold-up under fire. Suspects must quickly assess the situation to determine their course of action within an atmosphere of multiple stressors. Police hurl statements, comments, and accusations, attempting to throw suspects off guard in order to maintain control in hopes of obtaining either a confession or at least an incriminating statement. How well can mentally retarded and mentally ill suspects cognitively and emotionally resist obdurate interrogators by invoking their rights to silence and counsel in order to make "intelligent" decisions? Many researchers find resistance unattainable.

Leo (2008) indicated that, "virtually all suspects waive their Miranda rights, or are legally constructed to have waived them." If that is the case, mentally deficient suspects must offer no or little resistance to police. Considering their abilities, the likelihood of waiving rights and confessing, even falsely confessing, would be high. Similar to juvenile suspects, individuals who are mentally deficient are compliant and eager to please, especially to those in authority. Mentally handicapped suspects display acquiescence by answering yes to any question posed, whether the question is relevant or makes any sense at all. This can be because they don't understand but want to please, or they understand but won't challenge authority. They are highly suggestible and easy to manipulate and confuse. Such suspects have poor conceptual and communication abilities and lack in cognition to reasonably judge and adequately respond to a given situation. They cannot grasp the concept of possible future consequences from waiving rights—they can only deal with the present (Leo, 2008, pp. 233–234). Mentally ill suspects may comply with police in waiving rights even if they recognize that negative consequences may follow. Follette, Davis, and Leo (2007) found confessions can be true or false in these cases. With an aim to please, mentally retarded suspects will work hard to give police what they want to hear "regardless of the facts" (2007, p.45). Some courts will disregard suspects' mental state when judging on the validity of a waiver while other courts will take into account such mental issues.

In *Colorado v. Connelly* (1986), Francis Connelly traveled from Boston to Denver, approached an off-duty Denver police officer, and confessed to the murder of Mary Ann Junta that he had supposedly committed a year earlier. Connelly received Miranda warnings twice, at the time of his initial confession to the officer and later before questioning by detectives. Connelly stated that he understood his rights and also informed police that he had been a patient in various mental hospitals. Connelly even showed police the physical location where the confessed murder took place. Police believed that Connelly fully understood "the nature of his acts" (1986, p. 157). The morning after his confession, Connelly became "visibly disoriented . . . giving confused answers to questions" (1986, p. 161). He also stated that "the voice of God" had told him to go to Denver and confess and if he didn't confess, he was instructed to commit suicide. After a psychological evaluation, a psychiatrist testified that Connelly suffered from chronic schizophrenia and was in a chronic state "experiencing command hallucinations" even at the time of his confession (1986, p. 161). On the basis of the psychiatrist's testimony that Connelly's condition interfered with his "volitional abilities; that is, his ability to make free and rational choices," the Colorado trial court suppressed Connelly's statements, finding them to be involuntary. Colorado appealed to the U.S. Supreme Court, who reversed the lower court's ruling.

The majority ruled that the absence of any "government coercion" in obtaining a confession made the waiver by Connelly valid. Chief Justice Rehnquist firmly argued that *Miranda's* protection goes no further than protection from "government coercion,"—Connelly's perception of a reluctant waiver through a demand by the "voice of God" is not covered under the United States Constitution (1986, p. 171). In dissent, Justice Brennan pointed out critical items that were not factored in by the majority ruling: Not only was Connelly delusional and incompetent to stand trial, he also had a history of "thought withdrawal and insertion" (1986, p. 174). Due to the fact that Connelly had not taken his anti-psychotic medication for at least 6 months prior to confessing, the court's psychiatrist indicated that Connelly "was unable to make free and rational choices due to auditory hallucinations"

(1986, p. 175). It had been determined by the psychiatrist that Connelly probably knew his rights were read to him but the information was irrelevant because of the command hallucination to confess or commit suicide (1986, p. 175).

Justice Brennan raised a few extraordinary points that the majority never took issue with: Absolutely no physical evidence linked Connelly to the confessed crime, police made no positive identification that an unidentified victim was in fact Mary Ann Junta, and no evidence existed that a crime actually occurred at Connelly's alleged location. Justice Brennan adamantly argued that there was "not a shred of competent evidence in this record linking the defendant to the charge of homicide. There was only Mr. Connelly's confession" (1986, p. 183).

In the case of *Illinois v. Braggs* (2003), the appellate court found that suspect Mary Braggs' mental retardation required consideration for judging waiver validation. Braggs, with an IQ of 54 (2003, p. 4), was questioned six times about a double murder, confessed to the crime, was tried, and convicted. On appeal, Braggs argued for suppression of her confession because she did not understand her rights under *Miranda*. Police and clinical psychologists confirmed Braggs' inability to communicate and lack of response to questions regarding the understanding of Miranda warnings. Considering Braggs' mental deficiencies, psychologists also determined that Braggs would never be fit to stand trial. Psychologists recognized that Braggs could not comprehend more than a one-step command (2003, p. 5). Informing her that she has the right to silence and that anything she said would be used against her in a court of law would go far beyond her comprehension capabilities. Justices in this case found that Mary Braggs did not have the capacity to waive her rights knowingly and intelligently. Also, considering the numerous sessions of questioning along with testimony from police as to her mental competency, the court found that "police knowingly exploited defendant's mental retardation," coercing a confession (2003, p. 5).

Research by Weiss (2003) has found that mentally handicapped suspects routinely do not understand Miranda warnings, rendering the language "meaningless." Concepts could not be formed in order to make a decision knowingly and intelligently. Mentally ill suspects struggle with disorganization of thought processes and are impaired in executive functioning and attention (Redlich, 2004). These impairments and deficits contribute significantly to comprehensibility of *Miranda's* warnings of rights. Unfortunately, finding a way to deal with problems of comprehensibility among mentally challenged and mentally ill suspects can be a difficult task. It would take additional training for police in the area of mental health and psychology but this would go against the procedural nature as to how police are trained to obtain confessions.

Police, suspects, attorneys, interpreters, and judges struggle with Miranda warnings as they are delivered today. Problems will continue due to lack of education on the part of legal and judicial professionals in the area of comprehensibility. Education stemming from the wide array of research on cognitive capabilities and comprehensibility among vulnerable suspects will benefit everyone. Also, police, even if they recognize problems with comprehension among suspects, will not stray from their training to extract a confession no matter what it takes. A change in police training can be a huge step in the direction of leveling the legal field toward a more balanced system of *Mirandizing* all suspects.

6

Supreme Court Decisions Since *Miranda*

> We have explicitly recognized that Miranda warnings are not
> required simply because the questioning takes place in the
> station house, or because the questioned person is one whom
> the police suspect.
>
> —(*California v. Beheler*, 1983, p. 125)

In the 40 plus years since the *Miranda* decision, the United States Supreme
Court has issued more than 70 decisions relevant to the application of the
Miranda warnings. The general effect of these has been to maintain the
requirement of the warnings, but not to broaden their application and rather,
to restrict them. Some supporters of defendants' rights believe the restrictions
have gone so far as to emasculate the warnings. One critic goes so far as to
state, "The Supreme Court has spent the intervening three decades disinherit-
ing *Miranda* as the bastard child of the Fifth Amendment" (Moreno, 2005,
p. 400).

This chapter describes and evaluates decisions that reflect these patterns,
specifically challenges that gave the Court the opportunity to broaden the
application, only to have it choose not to, as well as challenges that gave the
Court the opportunity to restrict *Miranda's* breadth. These restrictions are
numerous; Moreno (2005) has listed the variety:

> Statements obtained in violation of *Miranda* can be presented to a
> grand jury (*United States v. Calandra*, 1974). These statements can
> be used by the prosecutor at trial if the violation was for public
> safety reasons (*New York v. Quarles*, 1984) or if the statements were
> used to impeach (*Harris v. New York*, 1971; *Oregon v. Hass*, 1975).
> Derivative evidence obtained through *Miranda* violations is also
> admissible (*United States v. Patane*, 2004). Police officers who
> disregard *Miranda* do not face mandatory criminal or civil
> sanctions. (*Chavez v. Martinez*, 2003, p. 397)

But first we examine the reasons why this general pattern of decisions has occurred.

The Composition of the Supreme Court

Within 10 years of the *Miranda* decision, four of the five justices who were in its majority were gone from the bench, while two of the four dissenters remained. The replacements for Chief Justice Warren and Justices Fortas, Black, and Douglas were appointed by Republican Presidents, and tended to favor the government over defendants' rights. Warren Burger replaced Earl Warren as Chief Justice in 1969 and served until 1986. Eras in Supreme Court history are labeled by the name of the Court's Chief Justice—"the Warren Court," "the Roberts Court"—and Chief Justice Burger's tenure saw a significant erosion in the breadth of application of Miranda warnings.

This trend was reflected not only in the actual decisions, but also in which cases the Court chose to decide. For example, for the years from 1973 to 1977, the Court granted *certiorari* to only one of the 35 appeals from defendants who claimed that their Miranda rights had been ignored. But during that same time period, the Court granted *certiorari* to 13 of the 25 cases in which the government claimed that a lower court had restricted the police in their *Miranda*-related interrogations (Stone, 1978).

With regard to its actual decisions in the first seven years after Warren Burger became Chief Justice, the Court ruled on 11 cases involving the scope and application of *Miranda*; in 10 of these the Court "interpreted *Miranda* so as not to exclude the challenged evidence" (Stone, 1978, p. 100). (In the remaining case, the Court avoided making a ruling specific to the *Miranda* law.) In these formative years of the Burger Court, "despite the relative frequency and complexity of these decisions, neither Justice White or Stewart, both of whom dissented in *Miranda*, nor any of the four justices appointed by Richard Nixon, has found it necessary to cast even a single vote to exclude evidence because of a violation of *Miranda*" (Stone, 1978, p. 101). This pattern continued during William Rehnquist's term as Chief Justice, from 1986 to 2005, with one notable exception, the *Dickerson* case described later in this chapter. Chief Justice Roberts' first four terms have seen only limited interest in the *Miranda* ruling.

The Decision Whether to Broaden *Miranda* Rights

In 1986, the Supreme Court had the opportunity to broaden the application of the Miranda warnings for those suspects who were about to be interrogated. It chose not to.

Brian "Butch" Burbine was arrested on June 29, 1977 in Cranston, Rhode Island, for burglary and the brutal murder of Mary Jo Hickey in March of that year. The vicious crime had gone unsolved for 3 months, despite media calls for a swift arrest (the crime had been the topic of a local television special). When approached by a police officer at his residence, Burbine refused to waive his Miranda rights. At that point the detective spoke to the other suspects in the burglary, each of whom implicated Burbine in the victim's murder. About 7 p.m., three police officers from the Providence, Rhode Island, police department arrived at the Cranston police office for the purpose of questioning Burbine.

Meanwhile, Burbine's sister telephoned the Public Defender's office to obtain legal assistance for her brother; at that time, about 7:45 p.m., she did not know that her brother was a murder suspect but was aware that he had been charged with breaking and entering. The attorney she asked for who had previously been in contact with Burbine was not available, but another Assistant Public Defender, Allegra Munson, was commandeered to represent him. At 8:15 p.m. Ms. Munson called the Cranston police station; the conversation was described as the following:

A male voice responded with the word "Detectives." Ms. Munson identified herself and asked if Brian Burbine was being held; the person responded affirmatively. Ms. Munson explained to the person that Burbine was represented by attorney [Richard] Casparian who was not available; she further stated that she would act as Burbine's legal counsel in the event that the police intended to place him in a lineup or question him. The unidentified person told Ms. Munson that the police would not be questioning Burbine or putting him in a lineup and that they were through with him for the night. Ms. Munson was not informed that the Providence Police were at the Cranston police station or that Burbine was a suspect in Mary's murder. (*Moran v. Burbine*, 1986, p. 418)

Burbine was not informed by the police of his sister's efforts to provide him counsel or of the attorney's phone inquiry. Thus the police committed two separate lies: a lie of commission to the attorney and a lie of omission to Burbine.

Meanwhile, less than an hour after the phone call, the police took Burbine to an interrogation room and conducted the first in a series of interrogations. Prior to each session, he signed a printed form waiving his rights to an attorney. Apparently, according to the state, at least three times during the evening Burbine was left in a room where he had access to a telephone but did not make any calls. Eventually, that evening, he admitted to murdering Mary Jo Hickey.

Prior to his trial, Burbine's attorney sought to suppress his confession, but the trial judge denied the motion, concluding that while it was true that Ms. Munson phoned the detective bureau, "there was no . . . conspiracy or collusion on the part of the Cranston Police Department to secrete this defendant from his attorney" (*Moran v. Burbine*, 1986, p. 419). Further, stated the judge, the constitutional right to request an attorney belonged solely to the defendant, and because the defendant never asked for an attorney, the telephone call had no relevance to the admissibility of his confession.

The jury at Burbine's trial found him guilty of murder in the first degree, and so he appealed to the Supreme Court of Rhode Island. That court affirmed the trial judge's decision, stating that the right to the presence of counsel belongs solely to the accused and may not be asserted by "benign third parties, whether or not they happened to be attorneys" (*Moran v. Burbine*, 1986, p. 420).

But Burbine had more success when he appealed to the Court of Appeals for the First Circuit. That court reversed the decisions of the lower courts, concluding that the conduct of the police had fatally tainted Burbine's "otherwise valid" waiver of his Fifth Amendment privilege against self-incrimination and the right to counsel. The court reasoned that by failing to inform Burbine that an attorney had called and that the attorney had been assured that no questioning would take place until the next day, the police had deprived Burbine of information crucial to his ability to waive his rights knowingly and intelligently. It even went further, concluding that the refusal to tell Burbine showed "deliberate and reckless irresponsibility" (*Moran v. Burbine*, 1986, p. 420). The First Circuit then concluded that Burbine should be retried, without the admissibility of the confession. Hence, the State of Rhode Island appealed the decisions to the U.S. Supreme Court ("Moran" was the Superintendent of the Rhode Island Department of Corrections).

Why did the Supreme Court grant *Certiorari*?

In 1986, only two justices remained from the *Miranda* decision twenty years before—one who supported *Miranda* (Brennan) and one who did not (White). Of the other seven justices, only one had been appointed by a Democratic president (Marshall). Had Warren and the others who supported the original decisions still been on the Court, it's uncertain whether they would have agreed to take on the case. Warren, for example, might have been content to let the First Circuit's decision stand because it reflected his values. For Warren, fairness superseded all other considerations in deciding legal questions.

The Supreme Court of course receives many more appeals than it can decide. In 1986, the Court received about 5,000 appeals and decided only 180 of them. Why did it decide to consider this appeal? To grant *certiorari*, at least four of the nine justices must vote affirmatively. The votes of the individual justices are ordinarily not reported (on occasion, a justice may be so outraged by the decision that he or she writes a dissent from the decision to grant, or not grant, *certiorari*). So all we know is that at least four justices agreed that the Court should consider the correctness of the First Circuit's reversal. We can speculate that several justices felt that that decision was wrong and hence, sought to rectify it.

Certainly there are many reasons for granting *certiorari*. If two or more of the 13 circuit courts render conflicting conclusions on the same issue, the

Supreme Court may feel pressure to be the arbiter. Conflicts between states (often over water rights) go directly to the Supreme Court for resolution. Cases in which a legislature (state or federal) has passed a law that seems to violate the Constitution receive attention. Does the Court take a case simply because the lower court's decision was wrong? The justices deny they do. Fred Vinson, while Chief Justice, wrote, "The Supreme Court is not, and never has been, primarily concerned with the correction of errors in lower court decisions" (1961, p. 55). But it is a fact that, of the cases for which the Supreme Court grants *certiorari*, it reverses the decision of the lower court between 70% and 75% of the time (Wrightsman, 2006). We believe that most of the conservative majority of the justices felt that the action by the First Circuit in the Burbine case, which chastised the police, was an impediment to effective law enforcement and should not remain as the final word.

Given that, what was the reason behind the majority's decision in *Moran v. Burbine*? Justice Sandra Day O'Connor, in writing the majority opinion, noted that Burbine's appeal did not dispute the fact that the police administered the required warnings, made sure he understood his rights, and obtained a waiver from him in writing. At no time did he request a lawyer. There is no suggestion that the police resorted to physical or psychological pressure to elicit his confession. Should his confession have been suppressed just because the police did not inform him of the attorney's phone call? No, wrote Justice O'Connor, "events occurring outside the presence of the suspect and entirely unknown to him surely can have no bearing on the capacity to comprehend and knowingly relinquish a constitutional right" (*Moran v. Burbine*, 1986, p. 423). She acknowledged that "no doubt the additional information would have been useful to [Burbine], perhaps even it might have affected his decision to confess. But we have never read the Constitution to require that the police supply a suspect with a flow of information to help him to calibrate his self-interest in deciding whether to speak or stand by his rights" (p. 423).

The Court was critical of the First Circuit's opinion that the police showed "deliberate and reckless irresponsibility" by failing to inform Burbine of the phone call; only when such an action "deprives a defendant of knowledge essential to his ability to understand the nature of his rights and the consequences of abandoning them" (p. 425) is it relevant to the validity of a waiver of Miranda rights, wrote Justice O'Connor.

But, say liberals, what is wrong with insisting that, given the phone call, the police tell Burbine of the phone call? Requiring that, wrote Justice O'Connor "would represent a significant extension of our precedents" (p. 425). If police are less than forthright in their dealings with an attorney, does the Fifth Amendment require a reversal of a conviction? Here is an instance where advocates of the due process model and supporters of the crime control model interpret the Fifth Amendment differently. Justice O'Connor, in failing to "extend" Miranda rights, concluded that the Court's opinion "strikes the proper balance between society's legitimate law enforcement interests and the protection of the defendant's Fifth Amendment rights [and] we decline the invitation to further extend *Miranda's* reach" (p. 425). While she acknowledged that, "we share [Burbine's] distaste for the deliberate misleading of an officer of the court" (p. 425), she concluded that the rationale in *Miranda* does not forbid police deceptions of an attorney.

Justice O'Connor reflected a "distaste" for the police actions. Attorneys for Burbine argued that the conduct of the police was so offensive that they deprived him of the fundamental fairness guaranteed by the Due Process Clause of the Fourteenth Amendment. But Justice O'Connor and the majority of the justices were not willing to go that far, writing that "the challenged conduct falls far short of the kind of misbehavior that so shocks the sensibilities of civilized society" (pp. 434–435).

Chapter 4 described how, when the justices in 1966 were constructing the Miranda procedures, they considered requiring the actual presence of a lawyer but chose not to. In describing that decision, Justice O'Connor's interpretation was "the Court found that a suspect's Fifth Amendment rights could be adequately protected by less intrusive means" (p. 426). Police questioning, often an essential part of the investigatory process, could continue in its traditional form, the Court held, "but only if the suspect clearly understood that, at any time, he could bring the proceeding to a halt, or short of that, call in an attorney to give advice and monitor the conduct of his interrogators" (p. 427-428). She went on to draw the conclusion that "full compensation of the rights to remain silent and request an attorney are sufficient to dispel whatever coercion is inherent in the interrogation process" (p. 428), an idealistic observation that ignores the problems described in Chapters 5 and 7.

Five other justices signed on to Justice O'Connor's opinion (Chief Justice Burger and Justices White, Blackmun, Powell, and Rehnquist). But three justices dissented; Justice Stevens filed a dissenting opinion, which Justices Brennan and Marshall joined. Justice Stevens' dissent argued for the broader interpretation of the goals of *Miranda* and in so doing concluded that the majority's opinion was a violation of the *Miranda* decision. It quoted from the *Miranda* decision—

> any evidence that the accused was threatened, tricked, or cajoled
> into a waiver will, of course, show that the defendant did not
> voluntarily waive his privilege. The requirement of warnings and
> waiver of rights is a fundamental [sic] with respect to the Fifth
> Amendment privilege and not simply a preliminary ritual to existing
> methods of interrogation. (*Miranda v. Arizona*, 1966, p. 476)

Is an error of omission as significant as an error of commission when it comes to evaluating the treatment of a suspect by the police? Justice Stevens in effect said "yes." He wrote:

> In my opinion there can be no constitutional distinction . . .
> between a deceptive misstatement and the concealment by the
> police of the critical fact that an attorney retained by the accused or
> his family has offered assistance either by telephone or in person.
> (p. 454)

He concluded that, "*Miranda* . . . clearly establishes that both kinds of deception vitiate the suspect's waiver of his right to counsel" (p. 455). Later in his dissent, he wrote, "In my view, as a matter of law, the police deception of Munson was tantamount to deception of Burbine himself. It constituted a violation of Burbine's right to have an attorney present during the questioning that began shortly thereafter" (p. 464).

The difference between Justice O'Connor's opinion for the Court and Justice Stevens' dissent epitomized the distinction between advocacy of crime control and of due process. Justice O'Connor was concerned about procedures that would inhibit the detection and prosecution of crimes; she wrote that,

> The Miranda warnings' objective is not to mold police conduct for its own sake. Nothing in the Constitution vests in us the authority to mandate a code of behavior for state officials wholly unconnected to any federal right or privilege. The purpose of the Miranda warnings instead is to dissipate the compulsion inherent in custodial interrogation and, in so doing, guard against abridgement of the suspect's Fifth Amendment rights. (p. 426)

In contrast, Justice Stevens' dissent serves as a clear example of a concern for due process. He reminds us that the *Miranda* decision placed the burden of proving the validity of a waiver of constitutional rights is always on the government, and a deliberate deception of a defendant—regardless of the defendant's guilt—is a violation of due process. While Justice O'Connor was concerned about impediments to police effectiveness, Justice Stevens documented examples of police interfering with the relationship between an attorney and his or her client;

> In Oklahoma, police led a lawyer to several locations while they interrogated the suspect; in Oregon, police moved the suspect to a new location when they learned that his lawyer was on the way; in Illinois, authorities failed to tell a suspect that his lawyer had arrived at the jail and asked to see him; in Massachusetts, police did not tell suspects that their lawyers were at or near the police station. (p. 442)

Our society subscribes to two goals, the prosecution of crimes and the protection of suspects' rights, and we seek a balance between the two. Inevitably, the human arbiters of these conflicting values often side with one over the other. In recent years the Court has chosen to side with the police and the prosecution.

How much can the Police Alter the Wording of the *Miranda* Rights?

Chapter 5 recounted how the Court has allowed for the variation in the wording and length of statements that inform suspects of their Miranda rights. The Supreme Court has, in effect, upheld these variations in wordings; in

California v. Prysock (1981) it overturned a lower-court opinion that police should give the warnings using the precise language of the *Miranda* opinion. The Supreme Court, in this decision, stated that, "*Miranda* itself indicated that no talismanic incantation was required to satisfy its strictures" (p. 359). But what if the wording is—at least in the eyes of some—so altered that it limits the suspect's rights significantly? Is this kind of alteration acceptable? The case of *Duckworth v. Eagan*, decided in 1989, answered this question. Once again, it was a case for which the lower court had ruled in favor of the defendant, thus apparently spurring the conservatives on the Court to give it another look by granting it *certiorari*.

The Facts of the Case

Gary Eagan was a suspect in the stabbing of a woman who—he later confessed—had refused to have sex with him. Prior to the confession, he had been given his Miranda warnings, but they included the provision that a lawyer would be appointed "if and when you go to court." It was that variation that caused the Court of Appeals for the Seventh Circuit to rule that such advice did not comply with the requirements of the original *Miranda* decision. But the Supreme Court disagreed, with Chief Justice Rehnquist writing the opinion for the 5-person majority. It should be acknowledged that the facts of the interrogation present a complex picture. Eagan first had contact with Chicago police officers but they concluded that the crime had been committed on the other side of the Indiana state line. So, on May 17, 1982, Eagan was turned over to the Hammond, Indiana, police. About 11 a.m. that day, the Hammond police questioned him but first read him a waiver form and had him sign it. Since this case rests on the legitimacy of the wording of the waiver, it is useful to reprint it in full:

> Before we ask you any questions, you must understand your rights. You have the right to remain silent. Anything you say can be used against you in court. You have a right to talk to a lawyer for advice before we ask you any questions, and to have him with you during questioning. You have this right to the advice and presence of a lawyer even if you cannot afford to hire one. We have no way of giving you a lawyer, but one will be appointed for you, if you wish, if and when you go to court. If you wish to answer questions now without a lawyer present, you have the right to stop answering at any time. You also have the right to stop answering at any time until you've talked to a lawyer. (*Duckworth v. Eagan*, 1989, p. 199)

After Eagan signed the form, he claimed that he had been with the woman earlier on the night of the crime, but they had been attacked by several men in a van who abducted the woman. Eagan was then placed in a cell at the Hammond police headquarters. Some 24 hours later, in the late afternoon of May 18, he was again questioned; again he was given his Miranda rights but this time the "if and when you go to court" phrase was not included. The statement instead simply said, "If I do not have an attorney, one will be provided for me" (p. 200). Eagan signed this waiver agreement and confessed to the stabbing. He led officers to the Lake Michigan beach where they recovered the knife used in the stabbing and several items of clothing.

At his trial, Eagan's confession was admitted into testimony despite his attorney's objections. He was found guilty of attempted murder and sentenced to 35 years in prison.

The Majority Opinion of the Supreme Court

The appeals court for the Seventh Circuit, in a divided opinion, had found that the inclusion of "if and when you go to court" in the first warning to be "constitutionally defective because it denies an accused indigent a clear and unequivocal warning of the right to be appointed counsel before any interrogation" and "link[s] an indigent's right to counsel before interrogation to a future event" (p. 201). That court's majority thus concluded that "as a result of the first warning [the respondent, Eagan] arguably believed that he could not secure a lawyer during interrogation" and that the second warning "did not explicitly correct this misinformation" (p. 201).

But, as noted, the Supreme Court's opinion concluded that, "We have never insisted that Miranda warnings be given in the exact form described in that decision" (p. 203) and stated that "We think the initial warnings given to respondent touched all the bases required by *Miranda*" (p. 204). The opinion stated that the "if and when you go to court" advice simply anticipated a frequent question from suspects after they waive their Miranda rights: "When will I get an attorney?" Thus, in a quite brief opinion, did the majority of the Supreme Court dispose of Eagan's appeal.

The Dissent

Justice Thurgood Marshall wrote a strongly-worded dissent, joined by Justices Brennan, Blackmun, and Stevens, in which he concluded that the majority had reached its result "by seriously mischaracterizing" the *Miranda* decision (p. 215). He wrote:

> A warning qualified by an "if and when you go to court" caveat . . . leads the suspect to believe that a lawyer will not be provided until some indeterminate time in the future after questioning. I refuse to acquiesce in the continuing debasement of this historic precedent. (p. 216)

Justice Marshall went on to sarcastically evaluate the majority opinion:

> In lawyer like fashion, the Chief Justice parses the initial warnings given Eagan and finds that the most plausible interpretation is that Eagan would not be questioned until a lawyer was appointed when

he later appeared in court. What gets wholly overlooked in the Chief Justice's analysis is that the recipients of police warnings are often frightened suspects unfettered in the law, not lawyers or judges or others schooled in interpreting legal or semantic nuance. Such suspects can hardly be expected to interpret, in as facile a manner as the Chief Justice, "the pretzel-like warnings here— intertwining, contradictory, and ambiguous as they are" . . . The majority thus refuses to recognize that "the warning of a right to counsel would be hollow if not couched in terms that would convey to the indigent—the person most often subjected to interroga- tion—the knowledge that he too has the right to have counsel present" (*Miranda v. Arizona*, 1966, p. 473). Even if the typical suspect could draw the inference that the majority does—that questioning will not commence until a lawyer is provided at a later court appearance—a warning qualified by an "if and when" caveat still fails to give a suspect any indication when he will be taken to court. Upon hearing the warnings given in this case, a suspect would likely conclude that no lawyer would be provided until trial. In common parlance, "going to court" is synonymous with "going to trial." Furthermore, the negative implication of the caveat is that, if the suspect is never taken to court, he "is not entitled to an attorney at all." An unwitting suspect harboring uncertainty on this score is precisely the sort of person who may feel compelled to talk "voluntarily" to the police, without the presence of counsel, in an effort to extract himself from his predicament. (pp. 217–218)

Justice Marshall's dissent observed that the majority opinion stated that the procedure by the Indiana police "accurately described the procedure for the appointment of counsel in Indiana" (p. 204), but for him, that was not sufficient to justify it. He wrote:

If a suspect does not understand that a lawyer will be made available within a reasonable period of time after he has been taken into custody and advised of his rights, the suspect may decide to talk to the police for that reason alone. The threat of an indefinite deferral of interrogation, in a system like Indiana's, thus constitutes an effective means by which the police can pressure a suspect to speak without the presence of counsel. Sanctioning such police practices simply because the warnings given do not misrepresent state law does nothing more than let the state-law tail wag the federal constitutional dog. (p. 220)

He also pointed out the obvious; the questionable phrase could easily be eliminated. Justice Marshall wrote:

It poses no great burden on law enforcement officers to eradicate the confusion stemming from the "if and when" caveat. Deleting the sentence containing the offending language is all that needs to be done. Purged of this language, the warning tells the suspect in a straightforward fashion that he has the right to the presence of a lawyer before and during the questioning, and that a lawyer will be appointed if he cannot afford one. The suspect is given no reason to believe that the appointment of an attorney may come after interrogation. (p. 221)

The cases of *Moran v. Burbine* and *Duckworth v. Eagan* have several similarities. At the circuit court level, both cases had been seen as ones in which police actions (or inactions) had violated the spirit of the original *Miranda* decision. But the United States Supreme Court chose to reconsider both decisions and found the circuit court's ruling to be in error. In both cases, the conservative members of the Court controlled the opinion. (Interestingly, in the *Moran v. Burbine* case, decided in 1986, Justice Blackmun sided with the majority, but in *Duckworth v. Eagan*, three years later, he sided with the dissenters, just one indication of his movement toward a more liberal ideology during the 1980s.)

More importantly, the rationale by the majority in both cases reflected the value of crime control—specifically giving more leeway to the police—and the rationale of the minority reflected due process—specifically sympathizing with the defendant's situation. Would these distinctions apply in a different type of case, one in which the defendant is uncertain about wanting an attorney?

What If the Suspect Makes an Ambiguous Response?

In 1981, in *Edwards v. Arizona*, the Supreme Court had held that law-enforcement officers must immediately cease questioning of a suspect who has clearly expressed a desire to have legal counsel during questioning. But what if the suspect is vague and ambiguous when he or she responds to the warnings? In 1994, in *Davis v. United States*, the Court provided its answer.

Davis was a naval seaman charged with the murder of another sailor after a game of pool at a club on a naval base. When he was interrogated by the Naval Investigative Service, Davis was provided his rights. He initially waived his rights to remain silent and to counsel, both orally and in writing. But about one and a half hours into the interrogation Davis said, "Maybe I should talk to a lawyer." The response by the military interrogators at this point was to try to determine what he meant. An agent testified,

> We made it very clear that we're not here to violate his rights, that if he wants a lawyer, then we will stop any kind of questioning with him, that we weren't going to pursue the matter unless we have it clarified: is he asking for a lawyer or is he just making a comment about a lawyer, and he said, "No, I'm not asking for a lawyer," and then he continued on, and said, "No, I don't want a lawyer." (*Davis v. United States*, 1994, p. 455)

After a short break the interrogator continued for another hour, at which point Davis said, "I think I want a lawyer before I say anything else" (p. 455). At that point questioning ended. Davis was convicted of unpremeditated murder, and sentenced to life in a military prison.

When Davis appealed, the United States Court of Military Appeals affirmed the admissibility of the contents of the interrogation but recognized that state and federal courts have had conflicting reactions to a suspect's ambiguous or equivocal responses; that court wrote:

> Some jurisdictions have held that any mention of counsel, however ambiguous, is sufficient to require that all questioning cease. Others have attempted to define a threshold standard of clarity for invoking the rights to counsel and have held that comments falling short of the threshold do not invoke the right to counsel. Some jurisdictions . . . have held that all interrogation about the offense must immediately cease whenever a suspect mentions counsel, but they allow interrogators to ask narrow questions designed to clarify the earlier statement and the [suspect's] desires respecting counsel. (p. 456)

Hence, the Supreme Court granted *certiorari*. And it should be noted that in its previous responses to the general question posed here, the reaction of the Supreme Court has been complex. Yes, *Edwards v. Arizona* determined that if a suspect requests counsel at any time during the interrogation, he or she is not subject to further questioning until a lawyer has been made available or the suspect has reinstated conversation. In *Michigan v. Harvey* (1990), the Court gave a reason, "to prevent police from badgering a defendant into waiving his previously asserted *Miranda* rights" (1990, p. 350). But the Court has said that this aspect of *Miranda* "is not itself required by the Fifth Amendment's prohibition on coerced confessions, but is instead justified only by reference to its prophylactic purpose" (*Connecticut v. Barrett*, 1987, p. 528).

Thus, in 1994 the Court could have gone either way. "Maybe I should talk to a lawyer" could suffice to end the interrogation or it could not. The Supreme Court resolved the question by ruling that the suspect "must unambiguously request counsel" (p. 459), thus it rejected Davis's appeal to have his confession made inadmissible. Justice O'Connor wrote, "He must articulate his desire to have counsel present sufficiently clearly that a reasonable police officer in the circumstances would understand the statement to be a request for an attorney" (p. 459). Writing for the Court, Justice O'Connor saw the petitioner's brief in this case as an "invitation to extend *Edwards* and require law-enforcement officers to cease questioning immediately upon the making of an ambiguous or equivocal reference to an attorney" (p. 459). To permit an ambiguous statement to terminate questioning would create an obstacle to "legitimate police investigative activity" (p. 460).

Interestingly, Justice O'Connor's opinion cites the *Miranda* decision itself to justify the Court's decision. She wrote: "We also noted that if a suspect is 'indecisive in his request for counsel' the officers need not always cease questioning. See [*Miranda v. Arizona*] at [page] 485" (*Davis v. United States*, 1994, p. 460). But the citation is from a section of the *Miranda* decision that quotes what, at that time, were the FBI's guidelines for handling an interrogation. In *Miranda*, the Court noted that the procedures of the FBI were consistent with the ones it was advocating.

It is important to point out that the opinion of the Court in *Davis v. United States* places the burden on the defendant, not on the police, to determine whether a request for legal assistance has been made. Justice O'Connor wrote:

> If we were to require questioning to cease if a suspect makes a statement that *might* be a request for an attorney, [the] clarity and ease of application would be lost. Police officers would be forced to make difficult judgment calls about whether the suspect in fact wants a lawyer even though he has not said so, with the threat of suppression if they guess wrong. (p. 461, italics in original)

The Supreme Court was unanimous in its bottom-line judgment in the case of *Davis v. United States*, but Justice David Souter wrote a concurring opinion (joined by Justices Blackmun, Stevens, and Ginsburg) that expressed caution. He noted that suspects "would seem to be an odd group to single out for the Court's demand of heightened linguistic care" (p. 469). As Chapter 5 showed, many of them lack a confident command of the English language, they are relatively uneducated, and "many more will be sufficiently intimidated by the interrogation process or overwhelmed by the uncertainty of their predicament that the ability to speak assertively will abandon them" (pp. 469–470). (In his concurrence Justice Souter included a footnote referring to social-science evidence "that individuals who feel intimidated or powerless are more likely to speak in equivocal or nonstandard terms when no ambiguity or equivocation is meant" [p. 470]).

Given his concerns, why did Justice Souter (and his co-signers) agree to endorse the majority opinion? He wrote, "I am not persuaded by petitioner's [Davis'] contention that even ambiguous statements require an end to all police questioning" (p. 475). He expected that law enforcement officials would follow "good police practice" and, given an ambiguous request, confine their questions "to verifying whether the individual meant to ask for a lawyer" (p. 476). But as we will illustrate in Chapter 7, that is not always so.

Does "A Right to Remain Silent" Apply When No Charges are Filed?

As Chapter 1 argued, almost everybody who grew up with a television set knows that the right to remain silent is a part of a criminal suspect's rights. The eminent law professor Alan Dershowitz says, "It's probably the best known phrase to emanate from our Constitution" (2008, p. xvii). But Dershowitz argues that you don't always have the right to remain silent—you don't if you don't go to trial. Basing his concerns on the decision in the case of *Chavez v. Martinez* (2003), he concluded,

> All you have is the right to *exclude* fruits of compelled self-incrimination at your criminal trial—*if* you ever have a criminal trial. If the objective of the interrogation is to produce intelligence information rather than evidence to be used against you in your criminal trial—an increasingly common objective in the age of terrorism—you may not have any rights at all. (2008, p. xix)

So Dershowitz is saying that, based on this little-known case, if you are not charged and are thus not a criminal defendant, you do not have the right to remain silent. Is his interpretation too extreme? Just what did the justices decide in *Chavez v. Martinez*? Although the case received little attention, both the facts and the decision in the case are provocative.

The Facts of the Case

On November 25, 1997, two Oxnard, California, police officers were investigating a possible drug sale. While they were questioning a suspect, a farm worker named Oliverio Martinez approached on a bicycle. It was dark. They ordered Martinez to stop, dismount, spread his legs, and place his hands behind his back. He complied, and one of the officers patted him down, discovering a knife in Martinez's waistband. An altercation resulted. Martinez and the police officer disagree over what initiated the altercation; the officers claimed that Martinez ran away from them and they tackled him while in pursuit; Martinez maintained that he never attempted to flee and that one of the police officers tackled him, without warning.

The next action is also disputed. The officers claimed that Martinez drew a gun from the holster of one of the police; he denied this. At any rate, the police officer shouted, "He's got a gun," leading the other police officer to fire her gun at Martinez five times, hitting him in the face, legs, and back, and causing him to be permanently blinded and paralyzed from the waist down. He was then placed under arrest.

The petitioner in the eventual appeal to the Supreme Court, Ben Chavez, a patrol sergeant, arrived on the scene a few minutes later, along with paramedics. Officer Chavez accompanied Martinez in the ambulance on the way to the hospital and questioned him both in the ambulance and in the emergency room. The following is an English translation of parts of the tape-recorded interaction, in Spanish, that occurred at the hospital. During this questioning, both Chavez and Martinez expected that Martinez would die.

> Chavez: What happened? Oliverio, tell me what happened
> Martinez: I don't know.
> Chavez: I don't know what happened?
> Martinez: Ay! I am dying. Ay! What are you doing to me?
>   (Unintelligible scream).

Chavez:	What happened, sir?
Martinez:	My foot hurts . . .
Chavez:	Olivera, sir, what happened?
Martinez:	I am choking.
Chavez:	Tell me what happened.
Martinez:	I don't know.
Chavez:	"I don't know"
Martinez:	My leg hurts
Chavez:	I don't know what happened (sic).
Martinez:	It hurts.
Chavez:	Hey, hey look.
Martinez:	I am choking.
Chavez:	Can you hear? Look, listen, I am Benjamin Chavez, with the police in Oxnard, look.
Martinez:	I am dying, please.
Chavez:	OK, yes, tell me what happened. If you are going to die, tell me what happened. Look I need to tell (sic) what happened.
Martinez:	I don't know.
Chavez:	You don't know. I don't know what happened. Did you talk to the police?
Martinez:	Yes.
Chavez:	What happened with the police?
Martinez:	We fought.
Chavez:	Huh? What happened with the police?
Martinez:	The police shot me.
Chavez:	Why?
Martinez:	Because I was fighting with them.
Chavez:	Oh, why were you fighting with the police?
Martinez:	I am dying. . .
Chavez:	OK, yes you are dying, but tell me why you are fighting with the police?
Martinez:	Doctor, please, I want air, I am dying
Chavez:	OK, OK, I want to know if you pointed the gun [to yourself] at the police.
Martinez:	Yes.
Chavez:	Yes, and you pointed it [to yourself]? [sic] at the police pointed the gun? [sic] Huh?
Martinez:	I am dying, please . . .
Chavez:	OK, listen, listen, I want to know what happened, OK?
Martinez:	I want them to treat me.
Chavez:	OK, they are do it [sic], look when you took out the gun from the tape [sic] of the police . . .
Martinez:	I am dying . . .

Chavez:	OK, look, I want to know if you took out [sic] the gun of the police?
Martinez:	I am not telling you anything until they treat me.
Chavez:	Look, tell me what happened, I want to know, look well don't you want the police [sic] know what happened to you?
Martinez:	Uggggh! My belly hurts . . .
Chavez:	Nothing, why did you run [sic] from the police?
Martinez:	I don't want to say anything more.
Chavez:	No?
Martinez:	I want them to treat me, it hurts a lot, please.
Chavez:	You don't want to tell [sic] what happened with you over there?
Martinez:	I don't want to die, I don't want to die.
Chavez:	Well, if you are going to die tell me what happened, and right now you think you are going to die?
Martinez:	No.
Chavez:	No, do you think you are going to die?
Martinez:	My belly hurts, please treat me.
Chavez:	Sir?
Martinez:	If you treat me I will tell you everything, if not, no.
Chavez:	Sir, I want to know if you think you are going to die right now?
Martinez:	I think so.
Chavez:	You think so? OK. Look, the doctors are going to help you with all they can, OK? That they can do.
Martinez:	Get moving, I am dying, can't you see? Come on.
Chavez:	Ah, huh, right now they are giving you medication.
	(*Chavez v. Martinez*, 2003, pp. 784–786)

During all of the questioning, his blindness made it impossible for Martinez to distinguish Chavez from the medical people. He assumed that treatment was being withheld until he complied. He begged the officer to desist and provide treatment for him. Later in the questioning Martinez admitted that he took the gun from the officer's holster and pointed it at the police. At no point during the interrogation was Martinez given his Miranda warnings. Martinez did not die, although he remains blinded and partially paralyzed. He was never charged with a crime and his responses were never used against him in any criminal prosecution. But he filed a civil suit against the police, claiming that Chavez's actions violated his Fifth Amendment right not to be "compelled in any criminal case to be a witness against himself" (*Chavez v. Martinez*, 2003, p. 765) as well as his Fourteenth Amendment due process right to be free of coercive questioning.

The police officer claimed that qualified immunity prohibited him from being sued, but the district court judge disagreed. The police officer then appealed to the Ninth Circuit court, but that appellate body agreed with the district judge, concluding that Chavez's actions deprived Martinez of his Fifth and Fourteenth Amendment rights. The Ninth Circuit, in regard to the issue that came to the forefront as a result of the Supreme Court's subsequent opinion, was quite explicit. "A police officer violates the Fourteenth Amendment when he obtains a confession by coercive conduct, regardless of whether the confession is subsequently used at trial" (*Chavez v. Martinez*, 2003, p. 766).

So the Supreme Court had to decide whether a police officer is entitled to qualified immunity and whether, in this situation, the officer's conduct (the Court opinion came to call it "alleged conduct" [p. 766]) violated a constitutional right. In short, the Court decided that Oliverio Martinez's allegations failed "to state a violation of his constitutional rights" (p. 766). The decision for the Court was authored by Justice Clarence Thomas, but the case generated a fractured result—six different opinions from the nine justices—and only Chief Justice Rehnquist signed on to Justice Thomas's full opinion without qualification. Three of the justices (Stevens, Kennedy, and Ginsburg) would have affirmed the decision of the Ninth Circuit. Regardless, Justice Thomas's opinion stands as the opinion of the Court.

Justice Thomas's rationale was the following: the Fifth Amendment requires that "no person . . . should be compelled *in any criminal case* to be a *witness* against himself" (p. 766, italics added). He wrote:

> We fail to see how, based on the text of the Fifth Amendment, Martinez can allege a violation of this right, since Martinez was never prosecuted for a crime, let alone compelled to be a witness against himself in a criminal case . . . In our view, a "criminal case" at the very least requires the initiation of legal proceedings . . . it is enough to say that police questioning does not constitute a "case" any more than a private investigator's precomplaint activities constitute a "civil case. (p. 767)

Thus, it was ruled that it is not until statements from an interrogation are used in a trial that a constitutional violation could occur.

A reader of the above excerpts from Officer Chavez's questioning may be tempted to describe them as "inhumane" and "shocking." Justice Thomas disagreed; he wrote:

> We cannot agree with Martinez's characterization of Chavez's behavior as "egregious" or "conscience shocking" . . . Here, there is no evidence that Chavez acted with a purpose to harm Martinez by intentionally interfering with his medical treatment. Medical personnel were able to treat Martinez throughout the interview . . . Nor is there evidence that Chavez's conduct exacerbated Martinez's injuries or prolonged his stay in the hospital. (pp. 774–775)

The last sentence in the section of Justice Thomas's opinion reflects his bias in favor of crime control over due process; he wrote:

> Moreover, the need to investigate whether there had been police misconduct constituted a justifiable government interest given the

risk that key evidence would have been lost if Martinez had died without the authorities ever hearing his side of the story. (p. 775)

What does it take to "shock the conscience of the Court"? The decision left that question unanswered. However, it seems clear that, to quote Justice Ginsburg's dissent, Martinez's answers were not "the product of his free and rational choice" and that such an interrogation was "the functional equivalent of an attempt to obtain an involuntary confession from a prisoner by torturous methods" (p. 801).

Why Doesn't the Court Dispense with *Miranda* Warnings Entirely?

The four previous cases each resulted in a decision by the Supreme Court that diluted the impact of the original *Miranda* decision. What would the Court do if it was given a chance to dispense with *Miranda* entirely? That opportunity arose in the year 2000 when the Court granted *certiorari* to the case of *Dickerson v. United States*.

The facts of the case are quite straightforward: Charles Dickerson was charged with several bank robberies in Virginia in which he used a gun. When he was captured and interrogated by the FBI, he was not given his Miranda warnings; during the interrogation he confessed. At trial he moved to suppress the confession, which the judge granted. All this seems quite what we would expect. Why, then, did the case appear before the Supreme Court, with Dickerson as the petitioner?

The government appealed the decision to suppress his confession to the Fourth Circuit Court of Appeals, using a little-known federal law which in effect would have emasculated *Miranda* if it had been followed. This leads us to an amazing story: A law was adopted by Congress back in 1968: Public Law 18 U.S.C. 3501. Soon after, experts noted its potential effect on a *Miranda* requirement (Burt, 1969), but it was virtually ignored by law-enforcement agencies during the next 20 years. Cassell wrote, "After 1975, 3501 appeared to have simply slipped the collective consciousness of federal prosecutors" (1999b, p. 200). This law, passed in response to Richard Nixon's call for a return to "law and order," made the admissibility of confessions such as Dickerson's turn solely on whether they were made voluntarily. The Fourth Circuit, in a divided vote, made a blockbuster ruling on February 8, 1999, concluding that the *Miranda* decision was not a constitutional holding and "therefore Congress could by statute have the final say on the question of admissibility" (*Dickerson v. United States*, 2000, p. 432). The Circuit Court thus ruled that Dickerson's confession was admissible.

Because it was believed that Congress could not overrule the *Miranda* decision without passing a constitutional amendment, U.S.C. 3501 was rarely used by federal prosecutors (White, 2001b). In fact, according to Paul Cassell in an article published in 1999, the Department of Justice "has prohibited its prosecutors from defending the statute in cases like *Dickerson*, and has asserted that the statute is unconstitutional" (1999b, p. 178). The Attorney General of the United States, Janet Reno, even filed a brief supporting Dickerson's appeal to the United States Supreme Court.

While federal prosecutors might have "forgotten" Public Law 3501, the Supreme Court had not. In fact, in a concurring opinion in the *Davis v. United States* case previously described in this chapter, Justice Scalia berated the United States government for ignoring the law; he wrote: "with limited exceptions the provision has been studiously avoided by every administration, not only in this Court but in the lower courts, since its enactment more than 25 years ago" (*Davis v. United States*, 1993, pp. 463–464). Furthermore, he wrote, "I will no longer be open to the argument that this Court should continue to ignore the commands of Public Law 3501 simply because the Executive declines to insist that we observe them" (p. 464).

With Justice Scalia throwing down the gauntlet, with a conservative Chief Justice in charge, and with seven appointees of Republican Presidents on the bench, it appeared that the Court might use the *Dickerson* appeal as a vehicle to return to a voluntariness standard and dispense with the requirement of warning suspects. Court watchers and pundits contemplated—even anticipated—a world without *Miranda* (Moreno, 2005).

The actual vote on the case, announced at the end of the Court's term in June 2000, was a surprise: 7 to 2 to uphold *Miranda*, with the majority opinion written by Chief Justice Rehnquist. Why this outcome? Two themes emerge in the opinion of the Court; one is that the erosions of the Miranda warnings instituted by the Court over the past 30 years made it a more acceptable procedure; the other was Rehnquist's concern about the tendency of Congress to make laws that reflect its interpretation of what the Constitution says (Greenhouse, 2000).

On the first of these points, Chief Justice Rehnquist wrote:

> We don't think there is . . . justification for overruling *Miranda*. *Miranda* has become imbedded in routine police practice to the point where the warnings have become part of our national culture . . . our subsequent cases have reduced the impact of the *Miranda* rule on legitimate law enforcement while reaffirming the decision's core ruling that unwarned statements may not be used as evidence in the prosecutor's case in chief. (p. 443)

Interestingly, Chief Justice Rehnquist wrote that the Court (then, in 2000) would not "agree with *Miranda's* reasoning and resulting rule [if it] were . . . addressing the issue in the first instance" (p. 443). But, he concluded, "principles of *stare decisis* weigh heavily against overruling it now" (p. 443).

On the second point, the Chief Justice wrote:

> This Court has supervisory authority over the federal courts, and we may use that authority to prescribe rules of evidence and procedure that are binding in those tribunals . . . Congress may not legislatively

supersede our decisions interpreting and applying the Constitution. (p. 437)

In his summary, he added, "We conclude that *Miranda* announced a constitutional rule that Congress may not supersede legislatively" (2000, p. 444). These are important statements because conservatives have argued that no basis for the *Miranda* decision exists in the Constitution. In his opinion for the Court, Chief Justice Rehnquist acknowledged the ambiguity, writing:

> This case therefore turns on whether the *Miranda* Court announced a constitutional rule or merely exercised its supervisory authority to regulate evidence in the absence of congressional direction. Recognizing this point, the Court of Appeals surveyed *Miranda* and its progeny to determine the constitutional status of the *Miranda* decision. Relying on the fact that we have created several exceptions to *Miranda's* warnings requirement and that we have repeatedly referred to the Miranda warnings as "prophylactic" and "not themselves rights protected by the Constitution," the Court of Appeals concluded that the protections announced in *Miranda* are not constitutionally required. We disagree with the Court of Appeal's conclusion, although we conceded that there is language in some of our opinions that supports the view taken by that court. But first and foremost of the factors on the other side—that *Miranda* is a constitutional decision—is that both *Miranda* and two of its companion cases applied the rule to proceedings in state courts—to wit, Arizona, California, and New York. Since that time, we have consistently applied *Miranda's* rule to prosecutions arising in state courts. It is beyond dispute that we do not hold a supervisory power over the courts of the several States. With respect to proceedings in state courts, our authority is limited to enforcing the commands of the United States Constitution. (*Dickerson v. United States*, 2000, p. 437, citations omitted)

The Chief Justice further argued that the authors of the *Miranda* opinion "thought it was announcing a constitutional rule" (p. 438). But clearly Chief Justice Rehnquist's justification for keeping *Miranda* did not satisfy its critics. They pointed out that even while a Supreme Court decision can rule on the constitutionality of an act of Congress, the Court lacks the authority to promote "prophylactic rules"—essentially safeguards. Thus *Miranda's* rules could be overridden by a federal statute. Justice Scalia's dissent—described as "vitriolic" by one observer (Moreno, 2005, p. 401)—noted that the majority opinion did not address this issue. He summarized as follows:

> Today's judgment converts *Miranda* from a milestone of judicial overreaching into the very Cheops' Pyramid (or perhaps the Sphinx would be a better analogue) of judicial arrogance. In imposing its

Court-made code upon the United States, the original opinion at least *asserted* that it was demanded by the Constitution. Today's decision does not pretend that it is—and yet *still* asserts the right to impose it against the will of the people's representatives in Congress ... Far from believing that *stare decisis* compels this result, I believe we cannot allow to remain on the books even a celebrated decision—*especially* a celebrated decision—that has come to stand for the proposition that the Supreme Court has power to impose extra constitutional constraints upon Congress and the States. This is not the system that was established by the Framers, or that would be established by any sane supporter of government by the people. I dissent from today's decision, and, until [Public Law] 3501 is repealed, will continue to apply it in all cases where there has been a sustainable finding that the defendant's confession was voluntary. (p. 465, italics in original)

But only Justice Thomas signed on to Justice Scalia's dissent. Other justices who had written opinions or concurrences that supported the erosion of *Miranda*—O'Connor and Souter for example—sided with the majority in upholding the waiver rights.

Where Do we Stand Today?

The *Dickerson* decision reiterated that any legislation proposed as an alternative to *Miranda* would have to provide an assurance that suspects were informed of their right to remain silent and made aware of options in exercising that right (White, 2001b). While supporters of defendant's rights were relieved on learning that the Court had decided not to abandon *Miranda* entirely, they had little cause for celebration when they examined the basis for the Court's opinion.

Chief Justice Rehnquist wrote, with approval, how recent decisions, such as those described in this chapter, had reduced the impact of the *Miranda* rule. And the second basis for the decision seemed to reflect more a "turf battle" with Congress than anything else, as the opinion made clear that the Supreme Court was the ultimate arbiter of the Constitution. While William Rehnquist was Chief Justice, the Court frequently took aim at legislation passed by Congress. From 1995 to 2005, the Court invalidated all or part of more than 30 laws passed by Congress, including laws that had widespread public support because they put constraints on such matters as child pornography, violence toward women, and possession of guns near school buildings.

The present Supreme Court, as it completed its 2008-2009 term, remained committed to permitting erosions of the Miranda rights. It reflects this bias not only in the decisions it makes on cases for which it has granted *certiorari* but also its decisions about those appeals that it rejects. As the introduction to this chapter indicated, most of the appeals which it chooses not to hear (thus leaving as binding the decision by the lower court) have been brought by criminal defendants whose claims of *Miranda* violations have been rejected. Two recent cases decided by circuit courts serve as examples. In the first of these (*Anderson v. Terhune*, 2006), the defendant James Anderson, after provocation from a detective about his involvement in a murder, replied, "I don't want to talk about it anymore" (2006, p. 4). At this point the detective accused Anderson of drug use, he replied, "I plead the Fifth" (p. 5). But the interrogation continued and after three and a half hours, Anderson confessed. Challenging the admissibility of the confession at trial, his lawyers were unsuccessful; the trial judge concluded that "I plead the Fifth" was insufficient to qualify as a wish to remain silent, and Anderson was convicted. The Ninth Circuit Court of Appeals, despite its reputation as the most liberal circuit, deferred to the judgment of the trial judge and upheld the conviction. But the judges on the three-judge panel were split (the judge in the minority noted it was obvious that the detective knew what Anderson meant).

The second case (*Van Hook v. Anderson*, 2007) reflects even more egregious behavior by the police. Robert Van Hook was suspected of murder; upon his arrest he said he wanted a lawyer. Before one arrived, a detective told Van Hook that he had talked to Van Hook's mother by phone and she believed that Van Hook wanted to talk. After questioning resumed, Van Hook confessed to the murder. His appeal, after his conviction and sentence to death, was heard by the Sixth Circuit Court of Appeals. In a sharply decided 8 to 7 *en banc* decision, it ruled that no violation of *Miranda* had occurred. The judges in the minority offered three dissenting opinions; one of them noted that no evidence existed that the Ohio detective had actually spoken to Van Hook's mother; there is no mention of the call in 776 pages of police records and notes. Is this a police ploy to avoid the "bright line" rule of *Edwards v. Arizona* (1981) that police cannot resume questioning until the suspect "himself" initiates discussion? Other circuits have approved the resumption of questioning after a relative or friend has alerted the police that the suspect wants to talk. Despite the questionable police behavior and the disagreement among circuits, the Supreme Court denied *certiorari* to both these cases.

Thus, in summary, the application of *Miranda*, as interpreted by the Court, is not what its authors intended. In the words of a recent reviewer,

> The Supreme Court's jurisprudence interpreting *Miranda*, viewed
> in its entirety, consists of a long series of decisions that have
> gradually chipped away the protection that Miranda warnings were
> intended to provide and has encouraged deliberate attempts to
> circumvent the warnings requirement. (Thompson, 2006, p. 647)

It is these "deliberate attempts to circumvent" that are the topic of Chapter 7.

7

Police Reactions to the *Miranda* Requirements

To discuss police questioning without knowing what such questioning is really like is playing Hamlet without the ghost.
—(Yale Kamisar, 1980, p. 1)

We have already described the initial reaction of law-enforcement officials to the requirement that they inform suspects of their rights. The purpose of this chapter is to describe how police training and tactics have evolved over the last 40 years in their efforts to obtain confessions.

The Goal of Interrogations

Despite what police might say, the purpose of an interrogation is to get a confession. An admission of guilt from a suspect not only radically increases the probability of a conviction, thus improving the police clearance rate, but it releases the police from the responsibility of looking for other suspects for the crime of concern. Furthermore, the confession—or follow-up inquiries—may provide information that permits the police to clear other, previously unsolved, crimes.

Police know the rules about what is legal during an interrogation. As will be described in this chapter, there are ample training manuals and workshops staffed by lawyers and law-enforcement officials who are fully informed about not only the *Miranda* decision but those court decisions subsequent to *Miranda*. No police officer wants to see a confession that he or she elicited thrown out by a judge or panel of judges. So the challenge becomes to test the limits of the law in obtaining an admission of guilt.

Training Manuals

Several manuals designed to instruct police in the art of interrogation exist, including *Fundamentals of Criminal Investigation* by O'Hara and O'Hara, a seventh edition of which was published in 2003, and *The Confession: Interrogation and Criminal Profiles for Police Officers* by Macdonald and Michaud (1987). But the most prominent of these is *Criminal Interrogation and Confessions*, first authored by Inbau and Reid in 1962 (and revised a year after *Miranda* in order to include procedures to deal with the mandated warnings). In the year 2001 it appeared in its fourth edition, with two additional authors, Buckley and Jayne. It was the 1962 edition of this book that was extensively cited by the Supreme Court in the *Miranda* decision (on pages 449-453 of the opinion).

The *Miranda* opinion quotes the following from the first edition of the O'Hara and O'Hara manual:

> If at all practicable, the interrogations should take place in the investigator's office or at least in a room of his choice. The subject should be deprived of every psychological advantage. The atmosphere suggests the invincibility of the forces of the law. (*Miranda v. Arizona*, 1966, pp. 449–450)

Other manuals reflect this theme that the suspect is removed of all outside resources, placed in a room where he feels he has no "escape." Furthermore, the interrogator often becomes relentless, as evidenced in this excerpt from the O'Hara and O'Hara manual, again quoted by the authors of the *Miranda* decision:

> Investigator will encounter many situations where the sheer weight of his personality will be the deciding factor. Where emotional appeals and tricks are employed to no avail, he must rely on an oppressive atmosphere of dogged persistence. He must interrogate steadily and without relent, leaving the subject no prospect of surcease. He must dominate his subject and overwhelm him with his inexorable will to obtain the truth. He should interrogate for a spell of several hours pausing only for the suspect's necessities in acknowledgment of the need to avoid a charge of duress that can be technically substantiated. In a serious case, interrogations may continue for days, with the required intervals for food and sleep, but with no respite from the atmosphere of domination. It is possible in this way to induce the subject to talk without resorting to duress or coercion. The method should be used only when the guilt of the suspect appears highly probable. (*Miranda v. Arizona*, 1966, p. 451)

The authors of the *Miranda* decision doubtless cited this advice from the manual in order to reinforce their differing view of just what is "duress" or "coercion." They went on to spell out some of the tactics used by the police;

one is called minimalization. Here the police reconceptualize for the suspect the attributional implications of his or her crime by diminishing its seriousness or by providing a face-saving external attribution of blame. The interrogator might, for example, suggest to the suspect that there are extenuating circumstances in his or her actions, providing such excusing conditions as self-defense, passion, or simple negligence. Or the blame might be shifted onto a specific person such as the victim or an accomplice.

Inbau and Reid (1962) offered the following example of how such attributional manipulation has been successfully used as bait: A middle-aged man, accused of having made sexual advances toward a 10-year-old girl was told that, "this girl is well-developed for her age. She probably learned a lot about sex from boys. She may have deliberately tried to excite you to see what you would do."

The *Miranda* opinion cites the following example from the Inbau and Reid manual (1962, p. 40) as an example of minimization:

> Joe, you probably didn't go out looking for this fellow with the
> purpose of shooting him. My guess is, however, that you expected
> something from him that's why you carried a gun—for your own
> protection. You knew him for what he was, no good. Then when
> you met him he probably started using foul, abusive language and
> he gave some indication that he was about to pull a gun on you, and
> that's when you had to save your own life. That's about it, isn't it,
> Joe? (*Miranda v. Arizona*, 1966, pp 451-452)

Another deceptive tactic described in the *Miranda* opinion, by now familiar to viewers of crime shows, is the "good-cop, bad-cop" procedure, described as follows:

> In this technique, two agents are employed. Mutt, the relentless
> investigator, knows the subject is guilty and is not going to waste
> any time. He's sent a dozen men away for this crime and he's going
> to send the subject away for the full term. Jeff, on the other hand, is
> obviously a kind-hearted man. He has a family himself. He has a
> brother who was involved in a little scrape like this. He disapproves
> of Mutt and his actions and will arrange to get him off the case if
> the subject will cooperate. He can't hold Mutt off for very long.
> The subject would be wise to make a quick decision. (*Miranda v.
> Arizona*, 1966, p. 452)

Sometimes the police use the "bad-cop" alone to induce a confession; that is, they try to frighten the suspect into confessing. One way to accomplish this is by exaggerating the seriousness of the offense and magnitude of the charges; hence this is called "maximization," in contrast to the "minimization" strategy described above. For example, in theft or embezzlement cases, the reported loss—and hence the consequences for a convicted defendant—could be increased. Another variation of the scare tactic is for the interrogator to presume to have a firm belief about the defendant's culpability based on independent "factual" evidence. The police manuals are replete with specific suggestions about how to use what is referred to as the "knowledge-bluff" trick. The interrogator could thus pretend to have strong circumstantial evidence (for example the suspect's fingerprints at the scene of the crime) or even have a police officer pose as an eyewitness and identify the suspect in a rigged lineup.

The Martin Tankleff case, described in Chapter 4, provides an egregious example. On September 7, 1988, Martin Tankleff, a 17-year-old high-school senior living with his parents, placed a 911 call at 6:11 a.m., reporting that he had discovered his father in his home office "gushing blood from the back of his neck" (Firstman & Salpeter, 2008, p. 10). According to his account it was only after his 911 call that he went to his parents' bedroom (in a distant part of the large house) and found his mother's body on the floor, on the far side of the bed. An ambulance and a police car arrive soon after; the police have young Tankleff, dressed in a t-shirt and shorts and barefoot, wait on the driveway. When homicide detective Jim McCready arrives on the scene about 7:40, he examines the crime scene and then questions Marty Tankleff. Immediately he is suspicious of the young man's story, Marty is too matter of fact, he's showing no tears (Firstman & Salpeter, 2008). The presence of blood in some parts of the house and its absence in other parts don't jibe with Marty's account. Marty has already told the detectives and neighbors, "I know who did it. It was Jerry Steuerman" (Firstman & Salpeter, 2008, p. 12). Steuerman, Seymour Tankleff's business partner, was the last to leave the poker game at the Tankleff home at about 3:00 a.m. that day. He was in debt to Seymour Tankleff to the tune of about $500,000. But Detective McCready thought Marty kept bringing up Steuerman's name too much, he was "trying a little too hard to point the finger elsewhere" (Firstman & Salpeter, 2008, p. 21). So he takes Marty to police headquarters and begins to question him around 8 a.m. By that time Marty knows his mother is dead and his father is in a coma and close to dying.

The questioning becomes increasingly confrontational:

Police officer:	Marty, what happens to the money? Say your father doesn't make it. Who would inherit the estate?
Tankleff:	I would.
Police:	What about your sister?
Tankleff:	She doesn't get that much.
Police:	Why is that?
Tankleff:	My mother wanted it that way.
Police:	And what would happen if your parents were dead and Jerry Steuerman was out of the picture—what would happen then?
Tankleff:	I guess then I would get everything?

Police:	You know Marty, you don't seem very upset about all this. Your mother's dead, your father's in bad shape. And we haven't seen you cry all day. Not a tear.
Tankleff:	I guess I was all cried out before you came.
Police Officer McCready:	After I spoke to you in my car, I went back inside and looked at the phones in the kitchen. And there was no blood on them. How do you explain that, Marty? A situation like this, you get blood in your fingernails, you get it in the crevices of your fingers. You told us you cried your heart out before the cops arrived. When you cry, you wipe your eyes, you dab your nose. I don't see any blood on your face. I don't see your eyes all red from crying. You said you never went all the way into your mother's room. You never touched her.
Tankleff:	That's right.
Police Officer McCready:	Marty, I don't believe that. Do you know why I can't believe that? Because your hair was in your mother's hand. How did it get there, Marty? You don't know? You keep saying you didn't take a shower this morning. We did a humidity test Marty. We know you took a shower this morning.
Tankleff:	I didn't—I swear. (Firstman & Salpeter, 2008)

As if these two lies were not enough (none of Marty's hair was in his mother's hand, and no "humidity test" had been done—and a later examination of the shower trap found no blood), McCready continued in his persistent questioning. After three hours of this, McCready left the interrogation room to answer a phone call in the next room, leaving Tankleff and another police officer in the interrogation room. Through an open door, Tankleff heard him say: "Homicide, McCready. Yeah, John, it's Jimmy. Yeah? No kidding, he came out of it? Okay, great. Thanks a million" (Firstman & Salpeter, 2008, p. 34).

McCready returned to the interrogation room and stood over Marty: "That was the detective I talked to earlier at the hospital. They pumped your father full of adrenalin, he's out of his coma and he's conscious. He said you did this. He said you beat him and stabbed him."

Tankleff:	I can't believe that.
McCready:	They taped the whole thing. We'll play it for you if you want.
Tankleff:	But it's not true.
McCready:	Why would he say that if it's not true?
Tankleff:	I don't know, maybe because I'm the last person he saw . . . Could I have blacked out and done it?

(Firstman & Salpeter, 2008, pp. 34–35)

In actuality, Seymour Tankleff never regained consciousness and died 24 days later.

According to police records it was at 11:54 a.m., about the time of the final lie, that Marty Tankleff was given his Miranda rights, although he has no memory of waiving them (Tankleff, 2009). At any rate, the police wrote out a confession, written in the first-person, but actually written by Detective McCready, not Tankleff. On the first page there is a recitation of each *Miranda* right, and a space for Marty to initial. He never did so, nor did he sign the "confession" written by the police.

In its *Miranda* decision the Court recognized that the manuals recommended the eliciting of a confession may rely on trickery. After describing a number of tactics described by O'Hara and O'Hara and by Inbau and Reid, the *Miranda* decision concluded that, "the very fact of custodial interrogation exacts a heavy toll on individual liberty and trades on the weakness of individuals" (*Miranda v. Arizona*, 1966, p. 455). But current training manuals persist in advocating the use of trickery and even in ignoring invocations of *Miranda* (Weisselberg, 1998). For example, the "question first" tactic used in the Seibert case described in Chapter 1 has been advocated in police manuals for several states, including Illinois, New Mexico, and California (Thompson, 2006).

Training Programs

Beginning in 1974, John E. Reid, one of the authors of the most prominent training manual, began offering seminars for police and security personnel. The program, which became titled John E. Reid and Associates, based in Chicago, has trained more than 300,000 police and security professionals, mostly in 3-day workshops emphasizing techniques of interviewing and interrogation (Buckley, 2007). The training program has come to be known as the "Reid technique" and includes a number of assumptions and procedures.

For example, throughout this book we have referred to police "interrogations." The proponents of the Reid Technique make a distinction between an interview by the police and an interrogation. In a speech, Joseph Buckley (2007), current director of the Reid Institute, described the interview as typically lasting 30 to 45 minutes; in it, the police officer asks three types of questions: non-threatening ones that seek biographical and employment information and make casual conversation, investigative ones that ask suspects to tell their story, and behavior-provoking questions, such as "What if you had done it? How would you have done it?" (Buckley, 2007). An interview is non-accusatory; its purposes seemingly are to gather information and build rapport with a suspect. The suspect's responses to the interview are then evaluated by the police detective; specifically, he or she makes a judgment about the suspect's likelihood of being the perpetrator. This judgment is based on the suspect's responses to questioning during the interview. As the latest edition of the Inbau and Reid manual puts it, "conducting a non-accusatory interview of the suspect is indispensable with respect to identifying whether the suspect is, in fact, likely to be guilty" (2001, p. 9).

Let us say that a police detective follows the Inbau and Reid admonitions and does a non-accusatory interview first. How often does the police officer conclude that the suspect did *not* commit the crime? The manual by Reid and his associates does not provide an answer to this question; in truth, any answer would be only an estimate. But what is relevant here is that the manual does not even consider this question; instead, the focus is on collecting information in the interview that links the suspect to the crime. In actuality, it is our impression that in most interviews, the police detective has already formed an impression that the interviewee is the culprit, just as Detective McCready did. And often it is based on limited information, hunches, and stereotypes about how guilty and innocent persons differ when under scrutiny.

During such interviews, it is typical that suspects deny their culpability; often they offer reasons why they did not commit the crime. Thus the question arises: How capable are police in detecting lying by suspects?

Detecting Deception

The most recent edition of the Inbau and Reid manual devotes five chapters and more than 100 pages to how the interview procedure may facilitate the detection of deception. Open-ended questions—for example, "Please tell me everything you know about the fire at your business"—are encouraged, as they provide a more extended response. The manual suggests the following as indications of deception:

1. Varying levels of detail: "The investigator should be suspicious that an account may be deceptive if it contains a great deal of detail leading up to the main incident but the description of the main incident lacks this level of detail" (2001, p. 108).
2. Perfect chronology within the account: "An account that goes from A to Z without ever skipping back in time is somewhat suspicious" (2001, p. 108).

3. The absence of thoughts or emotions. It is the view of Inbau and Reid that fabricated accounts are focused entirely on behaviors, "these reported behaviors occur in isolation from the normal process of experiencing thoughts or emotions" (2001, p. 108).
4. Phrases indicating a time gap. These, for the authors, indicate that the suspect has consciously deleted information from his or her account.

Inbau and his associates also focus on non-verbal behaviors. They acknowledge that there isn't any behavior that always indicates lying. But they go on to make assertions that imply clear-cut behavioral differences between truthful and deceptive suspects. Consider, for example, posture. They write:

> The truthful subject's posture will be upright in the chair and he will align his body with the interviewer so as to assure direct communication. During important statements, the truthful subject may lean toward the interviewer to emphasize the statement. A deceptive subject may slouch in the chair and appear somewhat distant and disinterested in the interviewing process. One of the most telling behaviors of deception relating to posture is one that is static. In this instance the subject assumes an initial posture during the interview and remains essentially in the same posture throughout the course of the interview. (2001, p. 144)

Or consider eye contact. They write, "Generally speaking, a suspect who does not make direct eye contact is probably withholding information" (2001, p. 151). (However, they do recognize that cultural customs and physical problems can affect eye contact.) Their reliance on eye contact is held despite overwhelming evidence that liars do not avert eye contact in an interrogation any more than truth-tellers do, nor do they "fidget, sweat, or slump in a chair any more often" (Carey, 2009, p. D1).

How well can Police Detect Deception?

Critics of police interrogations focus on the assumption that police can distinguish between those suspects who are lying and those who are telling the truth. Because they see themselves as crime specialists, police detectives tend to believe that their investigative and factual judgments are superior to those of non-specialists (Leo, 2008). A survey of 631 police investigators found that they claimed they could detect lying at a 77% rate of accuracy (Kassin et al., 2007). In fact, Detective Jim McCready, interviewed on national television years after his role in the Tankleff investigation, bragged about his instinct for knowing when someone was lying to him; "Oh, I'm better than a polygraph," he said (Firstman & Salpeter, 2008, p. 19). According to John E. Reid and Associates, police detectives trained in the Reid procedure can distinguish truth-telling from lying 85% of the time. Can they?

Research has consistently shown that people in general are no better than chance in their ability to detect deception (DePaulo, 1994; Vrij, 2008).

Furthermore, as Meissner and Kassin (2004) have summarized, training programs create only small and inconsistent improvements (Bull, 1989; Porter, Woodworth, & Birt, 2000; Vrij, 1994), and police detectives and others with on-the-job experience do only slightly better than chance, or worse (Bull, 1989; DePaulo, 1994; Ekman, O'Sullivan, & Frank, 1999).

A program of research by Meissner and Kassin (2002, 2004) presents sobering and surprising results on the matter of the accuracy of police in the detection of deception. For example, Kassin, Meissner, and Norwick (2005) compared the levels of accuracy of police officers and lay people in a task that is very similar to what police detectives do in real life. They recruited and paid inmates in a Massachusetts prison to give, on videotape, a full confession regarding the crime for which they were serving a prison term *and* to concoct a false confession to a crime that another inmate had committed. Thus the materials that they presented to respondents (police detectives and college students) were videotapes of 10 different inmates, each of whom confessed to a crime. Five of these were true and five were false. The task for respondents was simply to indicate, for each confession, whether it was true or false. The overall level of accuracy by respondents was 53.9%, not significantly different from guessing (a sheer coin flip would have produced a 50% accuracy rate). But students were significantly better than these police investigators, with accuracy rates of 58.9% and 43.3% respectively. Despite the failure of the police officers to do better than chance, they were more confident than the students that their judgments were accurate (an average of 7.35 on a scale of 1-10, compared with the student's average of 6.21). Analyses of responses indicated that the police more often judged the confession to be true, whether it was or not. Police officers apparently enter the interrogation room with a presumption of guilt that "activates a process of cognitive confirmation" (Meissner & Kassin, 2004, p. 93). These results confirmed previous research analyzed in a meta analysis by Meissner and Kassin (2002) which found that investigators, compared to naive respondents, showed a proclivity to judge suspects as deceptive rather than truthful.

Training Police to Bypass *Miranda*

As Weisselberg (2008) has noted, present-day police interrogators are better trained than their 1960s counterparts. They have available a number of training manuals, as previously described. New members of the police force attend a training academy operated by a local or state agency. In-service training is routine. Those officers who become investigators or detectives usually have attended advanced training sessions. A recent nationwide survey of police administrators found that two-thirds of the respondents indicated that "most" or "some" officers in their department had received training in the "Reid method" (Zalman & Smith, 2007).

Just as police training has become more frequent and systematic since the time that the *Miranda* decision was written, so too do we have better information about which interrogation tactics are widely used in the United States, and as Weisselberg has observed, "they are many of the same tactics discussed by the justices" (2008, p. 1537). For the authors of *Miranda*, isolation was one of the most significant aspects of interrogation, and it remains so today.

The Timing of the Miranda Warnings

One of this book's authors recently observed a videotape of an interrogation in a nearby state. The suspect had been accused of rape; it was a "she-said, he-said" situation. Two college students who had met at the swimming pool at their apartment complex had retreated to his apartment as a thunderstorm threatened the pool's occupants. One thing led to another, but was the sexual activity consensual?

The police officer who questioned the suspect seemed solicitous of his feelings; he began by saying to the young man, "There are two sides to every story, I want to hear your side. You can tell me your side now, or if you want an attorney to be present, we can put you in jail until we can get one for you." Given this choice, the young man began to tell his side of the story. Only later was he Mirandized.

The *Miranda* decision assumed that the warnings would be given and waivers obtained prior to the start of questioning. Is this assumption true today? Weisselberg's answer is "Not always." For example, he notes: "Officers sometimes use 'softening up' tactics—such as conditioning suspects to waive their rights or describing the evidence against them and making their situation appear hopeless—before giving warnings or obtaining waivers" (2008, p. 1519).

The decision in *Missouri v. Seibert*, described in Chapter 1, outlined a "two-step" Miranda warning done intentionally to produce a legally-admissible confession. But the Supreme Court's ruling left open the opportunity for police officers to engage in conversation prior to Mirandizing the suspect. Mosteller (2007) has divided the "softening up" practices into two types; the first is a mild version that includes tactics such as the establishment of rapport, done in the hopes of lessening the likelihood that the suspect will invoke his or her Miranda rights. Lower federal courts have been tolerant of such procedures; one such court wrote, "There is nothing inherently wrong with efforts to create a favorable climate for confession" (*Hawkins v. Lynaugh*, 1988, p. 1140).

But the second type, described by Mosteller as "bold but honest" and "more challenging" (2007, p. 1261), confronts the suspects with the evidence against them before giving warnings and obtaining waivers. For example, in *United States v. Washington* (2006), FBI agents described the charges and told the suspect about his opportunity to cooperate; then they gave him his Miranda warnings. The suspect said that he was willing to listen without an attorney present and then made self-incriminating statements. The 9th Circuit Court approved of this procedure.

Three other cases that were appealed in 2005 and 2006 portray the police still confronting the suspect before giving him the opportunity to waive his rights. These were the following:

1. In *United States v. Peterson* (2005), police officers took 50 minutes to describe the evidence against the defendant and told him to remain silent every time he tried to speak. Then they got him to waive his Miranda rights.

2. In *Hairston v. United States* (2006), the police detective showed the suspect a videotape (with no audio) of another suspect and then asked Hairston if he wanted to tell his side of the story. After Hairston said "yes" the officer administered the Miranda warnings and obtained a waiver.

3. In *United States v. Gonzalez-Lauzan* (2006), the police extended the length of evidence description, taking 2 hours and 30 minutes to do so. After Gonzalez-Lauzan said, "Okay, you got me," they gave him his warnings and obtained his waiver.

In each of these cases the federal court approved of the procedure, concluding that it was within the objectives of *Miranda* and did not intrude on the suspect's rights to make a rational choice about waiving his rights.

Observations of interrogations

On rare occasions, social scientists have observed police interrogations. To what degree do they find that such "softening up" procedures are used?

Leo (1996a; 1996c) observed interrogations by three police departments and described several strategies used to obtain Miranda waivers. One was similar to the experience observed by one of the authors and described earlier; the police tell the suspect that "there are two sides to every story and that they will only be able to hear the suspect's side of the story if he waives his rights and chooses to speak to them" (1996c, p. 661). Another procedure was to try to minimize the significance of the Miranda waivers by blending the warnings into the conversation or emphasizing that the warnings are only a formality; for example, "here's something I have to do; let's get it out of the way." A third procedure gives the suspect an incentive for waiving his or her rights; the suspect is told "that the purpose of the interrogation is to inform the suspect of the existing evidence against him and what is going to happen to him, but that the detective can only do so if the suspect waives his rights" (Leo, 1996c, p. 664).

A more recent article by Leo and White (1999) gave a more detailed description of these strategies. The researchers found that frequently police detectives would strive to develop what appeared to be a non-adversarial relationship with the suspect, so that the latter would see the officer as a neutral problem solver who was trying to work things out. Juvenile suspects are often the recipients of such tactics; Chapter 5 described some of the problems adolescents have in comprehending Miranda warnings. As noted in that chapter, Barry Feld (2006) observed a number of such tactics. Sometimes the warnings and waivers were characterized as formalities, or bureaucratic rituals, that had to be completed before the officer could speak to the suspect. In many of the cases (56%) police asked questions prior to giving Miranda warnings, some-times to build rapport with the juvenile suspect. Feld found that "in about one-fifth (17%) of cases, officers described their roles as neutral parties, or objective fact finders trying to determine what happened, rather than as adversaries" (2006, p. 258).

The tendency of innocent suspects to waive their Miranda rights

At this point an important question arises: just which type of suspect is more likely to waive his or her rights: the guilty suspect or the innocent one? Available data are consistent and perhaps surprising: innocent suspects are more likely to waive their rights. Leo (1996) found that four of five suspects waived their rights and that people who had no prior felony record were far more likely to waive their rights than were those with criminal justice experi-ence. Kassin and Norwick (2004) created an opportunity for some respon-dents to commit a mock crime (stealing a $100 bill from a drawer in a nearby classroom), while other respondents merely opened and shut an empty drawer without theft. Then each respondent, whether innocent or guilty, was questioned by an officious man acting as a police detective. Each respondent was asked whether he or she, in effect, waived their Miranda rights. (They were asked to choose between "I am willing to make a statement and answer questions at this time" or "I am *not* willing to make a statement or answer questions at this time"). Overall, 42 to 72 suspects (58%) signed the waiver option, but the difference in response rates in the two types of respondent was striking; 81% of the innocent suspects waived their rights while only 36% of the guilty suspects did. Many of the innocent suspects (72%) gave as their reasons for waiving their rights "I did nothing wrong" or "I didn't have any-thing to hide" (Kassin & Norwick, 2004, p. 216). As the authors observed, "These results indicate that people have a naïve faith in the power of their own innocence to set them free" (Kassin & Norwick, 2004, p. 218).

The current status of the timing of the Miranda warnings

Weisselberg (2008) has provided the most systematic review of the position of current police training programs and manuals with regard to when police should give the Miranda warnings. A telecourse cautions that one common error on the part of police is to give Miranda warnings too early and conse-quently lose a chance to obtain a statement (Weisselberg, 2008, p. 1559). A number of training manuals not only advocate preliminary rapport-build-ing questions but also suggest providing the suspects information about the crime under investigation.

At this point, according to the manuals, do the police go too far? In other words, when does chit-chat stop and interrogation begin? A California district attorney's office has stated that prior to seeking a waiver:

Officers will sometimes explain to the suspect the nature of the
crime he is believed to have committed, and even summarize the
evidence of his guilt. This seems to be a permissible practice so long
as the officer's explanation was brief, accurate, and dispassionate.
(Weisselberg, 2008, p. 1559)

While procedures vary from department to department, it does appear
that at least in some, the provision of a Miranda waiver has been delayed until
after a confrontation or interrogation has begun. Weisselberg's summary is
the following:

We do not today have a clean separation between administration of
Miranda warnings and the use of interrogation tactics, at least not
in the way the *Miranda* Court envisioned. Observational studies
and my review of training materials provide significant evidence
that the warnings and waiver regime has been moved at least
partway into the interrogation process, contrary to the "time out"
from the pressures of interrogation the Court imagined. Officers
may use pre-Miranda conversation to build rapport, which is
important to obtaining a Miranda waiver and—eventually—a
statement. Officers may also downplay the significance of the
warning or portray it as a bureaucratic step to be satisfied before a
conversation may occur. There is also evidence that police often
describe some of the evidence against suspects before seeking
waivers. A few cases have approved extreme versions of this tactic.
(2008, p.1562)

Questioning After a Suspect Invokes his or her Right to Remain Silent

The authors of the opinion were quite explicit that questioning could not
begin unless the suspect had waived his or her rights to silence or to an attorney. In fact, they wrote that suspects could show their preferences "in any
manner." As Chapter 6 noted, in the 1994 decision of *Davis v. United Sates*,
the Supreme Court equivocated from that explicit position. Recall that Davis
had initially waived his rights orally and in writing, but in the midst of the
interrogation, he said, "Maybe I should talk to a lawyer." The Naval
Investigative Service interrogators inquired, and Davis then said he did not
want a lawyer. Later in the interrogation he made a clear-cut request for an
attorney and questioning ceased. After he had been convicted, he appealed,
claiming that the interrogation should have stopped after he made the ambiguous remark about needing a lawyer. The Supreme Court ruled that this
statement was "not an unambiguous or unequivocal request for counsel [and
hence] the officers have no obligation to stop questioning him" (*Davis v.
United States*, 1994, p. 459).

This decision did not refer to a right to remain silent upon the reading of the Miranda rights, but as Weisselberg has observed, "many jurisdictions have now extended *Davis* to the initial waiver state" (2008, p. 1579). At least eight federal circuit courts out of the 13 have applied *Davis* to initial waivers and at least seven of these courts have applied it to the right to remain silent. Similarly, the highest courts of 19 states have applied *Davis* at the initial waiver stage and the highest courts of 13 states have extended *Davis* to the invocation of the right to remain silent during an ongoing interrogation. Weisselberg's thorough survey found no "decision of a state high court or federal appellate court refusing to extend *Davis* to the right to remain silent" (2008, p. 1580).

The following are some examples of comments made by suspects which appellate courts have found not to be sufficiently unambiguous under the *Davis* standard:

"I think it's about time for me to stop talking."
"I'm not saying shit to you anymore, man. You, nothing personal man, but I don't like you. You're scaring the living shit out of me ... That's it. I shut up."
"Get the f—out of my face. I don't have nothing to say. I refuse to sign [the answer form]."
"I think I would like to talk to a lawyer."
"Do you think I need a lawyer?"
"I can't afford a lawyer but is there any way I can get one?"
(Weisselberg, 2008, pp. 1580–1581, italics omitted)

Police training programs are well aware of these interpretations of the *Davis* decision. A California directive tells police "a person's invocation of the Miranda right to have an attorney present or to speak to an attorney can only be invoked by a clear and express request for an attorney" (Weisselberg, 2008, p. 1583).

As the *Davis* decision came to be interpreted in lower courts, the distinction between express and implied waivers of rights became more salient. Express waivers reflect an explicit set of questions to the suspect; for example, do you understand each of the rights explained to you? Do you want to talk about this case or not? Do you want a lawyer or not? Express waivers also include clear-cut answers of yes and no to the above questions. An implied waiver is defined for police recruits, in California at least, as occurring when a suspect "acknowledges understanding the warnings and exhibits conduct indicating waiver of the rights" (Weisselberg, 2008, p. 1584). While an express waiver is preferred by the police, implied waivers are better than no waivers at all, and they are increasingly surviving challenges in court. Interestingly, the current Miranda card used in California states each of the four rights and after each asks "Do you understand?" There is no question specifically asking "Do you want to talk or not?" Or "Do you want a lawyer or not?"

Weisselberg's reaction to the above changes is sobering:

The evidence now seems contrary to the *Miranda* Court's belief that warnings and waivers would create an unpressured "time-out" prior to questioning, and that suspects would have to articulate waivers clearly before questioning could begin. We also can no longer indulge in the assumption that questioning will take place only with suspects who have decided that they are willing to speak, or that suspects are easily able to stop questioning once it has begun. (2008, p. 1588)

8

The Future of the *Miranda* Ruling

> Once interrogators recite the fourfold warning and obtain a
> waiver, *Miranda* is irrelevant to both the process and the
> outcome of the subsequent interrogation.
> —(Richard Leo, 2008, p. 281)

The foregoing chapters have, we believe, demonstrated that at present the
Miranda ruling does not have the impact that its authors intended. Thus, the
question is: should efforts be made to recapture its impact or should the issue
be simply left alone?

To a large degree, law-enforcement officials have come to terms with the
Miranda requirement. They are aware of the judicial decisions that have nar-
rowed its impact, and they have adjusted their interrogative techniques to
maintain at least grudging acknowledgment of the requirement. It is, instead,
the defenders of defendants' rights who have despaired about *Miranda*.

Evaluations of the Current Status of *Miranda*

Charles Weisselberg

Charles Weisselberg, whose articles have been extensively cited in this book, is
one example. His thorough review even contends that,

> The system of warnings and waivers that the Court presented as a
> solution in *Miranda* is now detrimental to our criminal justice
> system. It is bad enough that *Miranda's* vaunted safeguards appear
> not to afford meaningful protection to suspects. But it turns out
> that following *Miranda's* hollow ritual often forecloses a searching
> inquiry into the voluntariness of a statement. Further, it has frozen
> legislative and other efforts to regulate police interrogation
> practices. (2008, p. 1523)

Our earlier chapters, organized around limitations in operationalizing the *Miranda* decision, are in keeping with what Weisselberg identified as four assumptions made by the *Miranda* authors about how the warnings and waivers would operate to protect suspects' Fifth Amendment rights. We now review these and offer Weisselberg's critique of their current operational status:

The decision to limit the requirement of warnings and waivers to custody situations

Our Chapter 4 described the ambiguity of the term "custody"; the original *Miranda* decision focused on custody because the justices felt that the "inherently coercive" nature of interrogations occurred in custodial situations. But Weisselberg doubts, as we do, whether the inherently compelling pressures of being arrested and questioned are limited to the station house.

The comprehensibility of the *Miranda* warnings

Our Chapter 5 has reviewed empirical work that shows the difficulty members of special groups—adolescents, the mentally challenged, non-English speakers, and the deaf—have in understanding their rights. Weisselberg writes, "There can be no legitimate justification for a warning and waiver regime unless we administer warnings in a way that the suspects understand" (2008, p. 1590). His review of the empirical literature is similar to ours, and his conclusion is the same: the assumption of the Court does not fare well.

The Supreme Court's subsequent decisions that have limited the application of the rights and waivers

Here Weisselberg is quite explicit: "the effectiveness of *Miranda's* regime has been greatly reduced by practices that the Supreme Court has tolerated if not openly encouraged. In *Davis*, the majority recognized that many suspects might not be able to articulate their rights with sufficient precision, but the Court adopted its rule nevertheless" (2008, p. 1591). We described the *Davis v. United States* (1994) decision in Chapter 6 as one of the most salient examples of the Court's erosion of *Miranda*, and in Chapter 7, relying on Weisselberg's analysis, we reviewed how the lower courts have extended the impact of the decision in the *Davis* case by approving of implied waiver practices. Weisselberg's view is: "The net result is to shift the burden to suspects to invoke their rights affirmatively at the outset of interrogation, and to do so with a very high degree of precision" (2008, p. 1591).

The police reaction to the *Miranda* requirements

The Court assumed a separation between the rights-and-waiver procedure and the interrogation. The problem has always been that the sheer fact of arrest, with its handcuffing, searching, and placement in a police car or cell, supplies some pressures, and the question, raised by Justice White in his *Miranda* dissent, is legitimate: How can we assume that waivers are not tainted by those same pressures? The Court's decision was to recognize this fact but to conclude—or at least, to hope—that the warnings and waivers would be given and obtained in an atmosphere that was free of additional pressures. This is difficult to achieve, and the current practices of the police, including the softening-up tactics described in Chapter 7, make it nearly impossible. Weisselberg recognizes the dilemma:

> Officers need to do their jobs. We cannot forbid all pre-warning communications between officers and suspects, nor should we want to, but we must understand that even 'mild' softening-up tactics can reduce the efficacy of a system or warnings and waivers. (2008, p. 1591)

Weisselberg's summary is sobering:

> So how well do *Miranda's* safeguards fare overall? I believe that we have a *Miranda* rule that is somewhat limited in reach, which sometimes locates warnings and waivers within the heart of a highly-structured interrogation process, provides admonitions that many suspects do not understand, and appears not to afford many suspects a meaningful way to assert their Fifth Amendment rights. As a prophylactic device to protect suspects' privilege against self-incrimination, I believe *Miranda* is largely dead. (2008, p. 1592)

Richard Leo

Richard Leo's evaluation of the current impact of *Miranda* is equally disturbing to supporters of due process because Leo, like Weisselberg, has devoted his professional career to efforts to support the rights of the accused. In his recent book (Leo, 2008), he summarizes the impact around four types of participants in the legal system:

Suspects

As noted earlier, the overwhelming majority of custodial suspects (78% to 96% in various studies) waive their rights (whether knowingly or unknowingly). Leo quotes Malone's take: "Miranda warnings have little or no effect on a suspect's propensity to talk . . . Next to the warning label on cigarette packs, *Miranda* is the most widely ignored piece of official advice in our society" (1986, p. 368).

Police

Leo is succinct: "Police have successfully adapted to *Miranda* in the last four decades" (2008, p. 281). Describing *Miranda* in the words of one observer of police tactics as a "manageable annoyance," Leo identifies the irony reflected in the constant discrepancy between the goals of the Warren Court and the current practices.

> Following an initial adjustment period, [the police] have learned to comply with *Miranda*—or at least how to create the appearance of complying—and still elicit a high percentage of incriminating admissions and confessions . . . .Because police have learned how to "work" *Miranda* to their advantage—i.e., to issue Miranda (or avoid having to issue) warnings in ways that will result in legally accepted waivers—*Miranda* exerts minimal restraint on police interrogation, contrary to the intentions and beliefs of the Warren Court as well as its many contemporary liberal and progressive supporters . . . . All of this is, arguably, exactly the opposite of the Warren Court's intentions when it created the *Miranda* rules. If the goal of *Miranda* was to reduce the kinds of interrogation techniques and custodial pressures that create station house compulsion and coercion, then it appears to have failed miserably. The reading of rights and the taking of waivers has seemingly become an empty ritual. (2008, p. 281)

Leo even suggests that the police have skillfully turned *Miranda* into a tool of law enforcement, "a public relations coup" (p. 281) that never would have been foreseen by the Warren Court. He wrote, "*Miranda* has mostly helped, not hurt, law enforcement . . . it has shifted courts' analysis from the voluntariness of a confession to the voluntariness of a *Miranda* waiver" (p. 281).

Prosecutors

Keeping with the shift in reactions, prosecutors now "overwhelmingly support *Miranda*" (Leo, 2008, p. 282). A prosecutor's goal is to get convictions, and having had defendants waive their rights aids in plea bargaining and getting incriminating statements admitted for trial. Also, prosecutors are aware that when defendants have claimed they confessed falsely, judges and jurors are less likely to believe them if they have waived their Miranda rights.

Trial judges

Observers agree that, in Leo's words, "*Miranda* has eased the lot of trial judges" (2008, p. 282). White wrote: "A finding that the police have properly informed the suspect of his Miranda rights thus often has the effect of minimizing the scrutiny afforded interrogation practices following the Miranda waiver" (2001a, p. 1220). Other observers even conclude that as long as the judge knows that the Miranda warnings have been given, many of them have ignored police misconduct. Once a "swearing contest" arises, judges usually side with the police officer's version, as we saw in the decision in *Lego v. Twomey*, especially if the defendant has waived his or her rights.

While Leo does not choose to "mourn" the passing of *Miranda* as Weisselberg did, his overall evaluation of the impact of *Miranda* is similar:

> *Miranda's* contemporary impact thus appears rather limited. Once feared to be sand in the machinery of criminal justice, *Miranda* has now become part of the machine. Police, prosecutors, and courts have all adapted to and diluted *Miranda*, using it to advance their own objections rather than to enforce the privilege against self-incrimination or the right to counsel (Kamisar, 1996). *Miranda* imposes few, if any, serious costs on them or the criminal justice system as a whole. It does not impede law enforcement. It also offers few benefits to its intended recipients. Rather than eliminating compulsion inside the interrogation room, it has motivated police to develop more subtle and sophisticated interrogation strategies. How police "work" *Miranda* makes a mockery of the notion that a suspect is effectively apprised of his rights and has a continuous opportunity to exercise them. (Leo, 2008, p. 283)

Is *Miranda* Worth Saving?

Both Weisselberg and Leo believe that *Miranda* has become an obstacle to the protection of defendants' rights, and the remedy is to discard it and substitute tests of voluntariness and reliability of confessions. These are worthwhile considerations, but the focus of this chapter is on the problem that caused the Court to develop the Miranda rights.

Coercive interrogations are undesirable not only because they challenge the value of fairness, but because they lead to false confessions which, in turn, lead to false convictions. Advocates of the crime-control model and the due-process model may disagree about whether suspects deserve to be treated "fairly," but anyone—regardless of his or her values—should be concerned if people are falsely convicted. The Innocence Project, with its analysis of the DNA of convicted persons, has made the public aware that errors do occur, and that some of those defendants who were convicted on the basis of their confessions are innocent. We still have false confessions 40 years after *Miranda*.

Thus our goal, in discussing possible reforms, is to emphasize innovations that are effective, first in reducing the number of false confessions, and second in reducing the number of convictions of innocent persons, for which a false confession was the primary determinant.

Ways to Reduce False Confessions

People have difficulty believing that persons would admit to police that they have committed acts that they did not do. In trial after trial, jurors have convicted a defendant based on his or her confession, even when the physical evidence disputes his or her confession.

Why do false confessions occur? The simple answer reflects Kurt Lewin's formula that behavior, i.e., the giving of a false confession, is a function of the person and the environment. Some persons are susceptible to making false admissions; because of delusions or guilt they may spontaneously and falsely claim they committed a crime. But most of those susceptible to making false confessions are highly suggestible.

Interrogative Suggestibility

Interrogative suggestibility is defined by Gisli Gudjonsson as "the extent to which within a closed social interaction, people come to accept messages communicated during formal questioning, as the result of which their subsequent behavioral response is affected" (1991, p. 280). Five interrelated components are part of the concept:

1. A closed social interaction between the interrogator and the interviewee.
2. A questioning procedure that involves two or more participants.
3. A suggestive stimulus.
4. Acceptance of the suggestive stimulus.
5. A behavioral response to indicate whether or not the suggestion is accepted (Gudjonsson, 1991).

Interrogative suggestibility, according to Gudjonsson (1987, 1991), differs from other types of suggestibility in four ways: the above-mentioned closed nature of the social interaction, the questions dealing with past experiences and recollections, the inclusion of a component of uncertainty, and its stressful situation with important consequences for the person being interviewed. In this situation, the interrogator can manipulate three aspects—uncertainty, interpersonal trust, and expectation—to alter the person's susceptibility to suggestions. But characteristics of the interviewee also affect the process; as an instance, the type of coping strategy used during the interview affects his or her level of suggestibility. Gudjonsson has provided an example:

> Avoidance coping is likely to facilitate a suggestible response
> whereby people give answers that to them seem plausible and
> consistent with the external clues provided, rather than only giving
> definite answers to questions they clearly remember. In contrast,
> a nonsuggestible coping strategy involves the critical analysis of the
> situation and a facilitative problem-solving action. (1991, p. 282)

Furthermore, people who are suspicious are less suggestible than those with a trusting cognitive set; those with poor memories and low intelligence are generally more suggestible; and low self-esteem, lack of assertiveness, and anxiety affect suggestibility.

Gudjonsson (1984b) has developed two forms of a suggestibility scale in order to assess respondents' responses to leading questions and negative feedback. The Gudjonsson Suggestibility Scale (GSS) uses a narrative paragraph describing a fictitious mugging, which is read to the respondent. The respondent is then asked to recall all that he or she can remember about the story. After a delay of about 50 minutes, the respondent is asked 20 specific questions, 15 of which are subtly misleading. After answering these, the person is informed that he or she has made a number of mistakes (even if no errors have been made), and thus it is necessary to ask each question once more. The person is instructed to try to be more accurate than before. Any change in answers from the previous trial is labeled a "shift"; the extent to which people give in to the misleading questions is scored as a "yield." "Yield" and "shift" are added together to create a "total suggestibility" score (Gudjonsson, 1991). Interestingly, these two measures are not highly correlated and load on different factors (Gudjonsson, 1984b).

It is possible to manipulate the expectations of respondents prior to interrogation in order to reduce or enhance suggestibility as measured by the suggestibility scale (Gudjonsson & Hilton, 1989; Hansdottir, Thorsteinsson, Kristindottir, & Ragnarsson, 1990). Furthermore, interrogative suggestibility has been found to be significantly related to the coping strategy that respondents report using during the test (Gudjonsson, 1988). Those respondents who were most suggestible tended to use an avoidance coping strategy during the interrogation. Gudjonsson (1991) observes this to mean that,

> They failed to be able to evaluate each question critically and give
> answers that to them seemed plausible and consistent with the
> external cues provided. Non-suggestible subjects, on the other
> hand, were able to adopt a critical analysis of the situation which
> facilitated the accuracy of their answers. (p. 285)

Interrogative suggestibility appears to be mediated by anxiety. Scores on the GSS are correlated with state anxiety as measured by the Spielberger State-Trait Anxiety Inventory. Respondents who gave in most to the interrogative pressures were those who rated themselves as being most anxious at the time (Gudjonsson, 1988).

The ultimate validity of the proposal that individual differences in interrogative suggestibility affect behavior during questioning is to have a test of actual criminal suspects. Three studies have made a comparison between two groups of such suspects; those who were able to resist police interrogation pressures in spite of some salient evidence against them, and those who made a self-incriminating confession that they subsequently retracted. The first study (Gudjonsson, 1984a) compared the suggestibility scores of 12 alleged false confessors and 8 resisters; the latter group was found to be significantly more intelligent and less suggestible than the alleged false confessors. In a similar study using a larger sample, Gudjonsson (1991) compared 100 alleged false confessors with 104 other criminal defendants charged with similar offenses.

(All had been referred to psychologists for evaluation.) The mean ages for the two groups were 29 and 34, respectively. The average IQ of the alleged false confessors was 80.0, significantly less than the average of 91.4 for the comparison group. The alleged false confessors scored significantly higher on measures of suggestibility, compliance, and acquiescence. The third study compared the suggestibility scores of 20 resisters and 20 alleged false confessors who were matched for age, gender, intelligence level, memory recall capacity, and the seriousness of the offense (Gudjonsson, 1991). The two groups differed quite clearly in suggestibility. "The ability of the suspect to cope with interrogative pressure is more important than his or her tendency to give in to leading questions per se," concluded Gudjonsson (1991, p. 286).

Perhaps the most impressive demonstration was Gudjonsson's analysis of the responses of alleged Irish Republican Army terrorists in the 1970s. In the fall of 1974 the IRA placed bombs in two public houses in Guildford and Birmingham, England. Five people were killed in one bombing; 21 in the other; more than 150 were injured. Four Irishmen were arrested for one bombing; six for the other. After intense questioning, all four men questioned in the Guildford bombing and four of the six men questioned in the Birmingham bombing made written confessions, although all recanted their confessions at trial, claiming that their confessions had been beaten out of them (Mullin, 1989). One, Paddy Hill, claimed that he had been kicked, punched on the side of the head, and kneed in the thigh. "We're going to get a statement out of you or kick you to death" was the threat that he later reported (Mullin, 1989, p. 100). These claims by the defendants were disregarded by the jury which found all the Irishmen guilty; they were sentenced to life in prison.

One of the Irishmen, Gerry Conlon of the Guildford Four, was the object of a movie, *In the Name of the Father*. Both sets of men served close to 15 years in prison before their confessions were overturned because the English courts acknowledged that the police had coerced the defendants to confess by subjecting them to psychological and physical pressure (Gudjonsson, 2003).

Gudjonsson was able to later interview and administer his suggestibility scale to one member of the Guildford Four and each of the Birmingham Six. The most dramatic finding from the responses of the Birmingham Six was the difference in test scores between the two defendants who did not confess and the four who did. Those two who didn't make written confessions "scored exceptionally low on tests of suggestibility and compliance" (Gudjonsson, 1992, p. 275). And this was 13 years after the crime.

Counteracting the Effects of Interrogative Suggestibility

In England and Wales the Police and Criminal Evidence Act of 1986 requires an appropriate adult be present when the police are interrogating a vulnerable suspect. "Vulnerable" would include juveniles as well as suspects known to be mentally ill or mentally challenged. Empirical work described in Chapter 5 and elsewhere (Drizin & Colgan, 2004; Fulero & Everington, 2004; Redlich, Silverman, Chen, & Steiner, 2004) demonstrates that many suspects are not able to comprehend their Miranda rights.

When the justices, back in 1966, considered remedies for the abuses of police interrogations, one that they considered was the requirement that an attorney be present. The Sixth Amendment permits the right to counsel. But in its *Miranda* decision the Court essentially "abandoned [requiring this] as a solution to pre-indictment interrogation" (Leo & Thomas, 1998, p. 37) and instead substituted the Fifth Amendment's right to avoid answering questions. Interestingly, back in 1959, in the decision in *Spano v. New York*, several justices had suggested that an arrested suspect should have an attorney present at pretrial questioning. What if the Court were to adopt this requirement?

Two objections would immediately be made. First, it would be said that most suspects who are arrested are guilty and many of them are willing to confess without prompting. So why not have an attorney meet with each privately, and if the suspect understands his or her rights and indicates a desire to confess, the attorney withdraws. Second, this requirement would place a burden on overworked public defenders and other defense attorneys. But suspects have a right to attorneys at lineups, a time-consuming activity for the defense counsel.

As noted in the last section, persons of limited mental ability have been found to display higher degrees of interrogative suggestibility (Gudjonsson & Clare, 1995; Everington & Fulero, 1999). Not only are they susceptible to verbal questions, but there are many nonverbal aspects of an interrogation that reflect coercion and thus influence especially the responses of the mentally challenged (Gudjonsson, 1984a). Fortunately, there are instruments that have been developed to determine the degree to which a suspect understands his or her Miranda rights. Chief among these are Grisso's (1998) four scales, originally developed for use with juvenile suspects, but applicable to other types of vulnerable suspects. Grisso's primary measure is the Comprehension of Miranda Rights Scale (CMR), which has the examiner read each of the four main Miranda rights to the suspect, while the suspect is shown the right in printed form. The suspect is then asked to tell the examiner what it says "in your own words." For each of the four rights, the suspect's response is scored as adequate, questionable, or inadequate, according to detailed scoring criteria.

A second measure developed by Grisso, the Comprehension of Miranda Rights Recognition Scale (CMR-R), does not require the suspect to explain the right but instead determines whether the suspect understands the rights. For each of the rights, the examiner offers other statements that mean either the same thing or something different. The suspect indicates either "same" or "different" for three statements for each of the four Miranda rights.

The third measure, Comprehension of Miranda Vocabulary (CMV), is a vocabulary test that uses six words taken from the wording in the original

Miranda decision. Suspects are asked to define each word. The fourth instrument, Function of Rights in Interrogation (FRI), seeks to assess the suspects' understanding of the relevance of the Miranda warnings within the legal process. Four vignettes, along with drawings, are presented, and the suspect is asked questions to determine his or her understanding of the adversary nature of the encounter with the police and the advocacy role of the attorney.

The Grisso instrument has been administered to thousands of suspects who have confessed to crimes, and psychologists have testified at trials about the defendant's failure to comprehend the warnings (see Frumkin, 2008, for examples). But the scales developed by Grisso, originally created almost 30 years ago, need updating and re-norming, and such efforts are underway by several investigators, including Bruce Frumkin and a group spearheaded by Naomi Goldstein at Drexel University (Zelle et al., 2008).

Situational Determinants of False Confessions: The Problem of Police Deception

For a suspect to confess falsely, his or her level of suggestibility may not be enough. As documented earlier in this book, police use a multitude of techniques to encourage a suspect to confess. The original *Miranda* decision decried the use of trickery but it still remains a basic tool in the interrogator's kit. The latest device, as reported by Saul Kassin (2007), is for police to tell suspects that they have the suspect's DNA and they know it will exonerate the suspect, so the suspect confesses. Such bluffs are quite effective in causing innocent suspects to confess (Perillo & Kassin, 2009). Back in the 1950s, even before *Miranda*, the Supreme Court in two cases (*Leyra v. Denno*, 1954, and *Spano v. New York*, 1959) expressed its disapproval of the use of deception and manipulation of emotions in order to elicit a confession. While observers have suggested that the rationale for the Court's overturning the convictions in these two cases may have stemmed from other aspects (Grano, 1993; Hancock, 1996), still, as White has observed, those cases "could provide a starting point for identifying improper police practices" (2001b, p. 47). And it should be recognized that even some of the conservatives who have been on the Court recently have expressed concern; for example, Justice O'Connor's opinion in *Crane v. Kentucky* (to be described later in this chapter) recognized the possibility of a confession being coerced. In the majority opinion in a frequently-cited case, while Chief Justice, William Rehnquist acknowledged that "certain interrogation techniques, either in isolation or as applied to the unique characteristics of a particular suspect, are so offensive to a civilized system of justice that they must be condemned" (*Colorado v. Connelly*, 1986, p. 163).

Chapter 1 described how the Court had restricted the use of the "two-step" Miranda warning, a deceptive technique used by the police to get a confession before giving suspects their rights. It takes only four of the justices to grant *certiorari* to an appeal. If cert is granted to a case in which a defendant has been convicted after being lied to by the police, it is possible that Justice Kennedy, currently the justice least entrenched in an ideology, might side with the four relative liberals. For example, in the 2006–2007 term, even though in the 5-to-4 decisions Justice Kennedy sided with the conservatives two-thirds of the time, he sided with the liberals in all five of the cases that involved appeals from defendants on death row.

Ways to Challenge False Confessions at Trial

As already stated, when a confession is introduced at trial, it is usually a powerful incentive for a jury to convict the defendant. But there are several ways in which the trial procedures can be used to show the jury that either the defendant was coerced into waiving his or her Miranda rights or that the defendant confessed under undue pressure.

Use of an Expert Witness

At a trial, evidence that the defendant has confessed has a powerful influence on the verdict of the jury, even though the defendant has taken the stand to recant the confession (Leo, 1996b, Wrightsman & Kassin, 1993). Costanzo and Leo (2007) listed four ways in which an expert witness can aid a jury:

1. By describing the psychological research literature indicating the possibility—and estimated prevalence of—police-induced false confessions.
2. By demonstrating the impact of particular interrogation methods (removal of support, minimization, apparent sympathy, suggested benefits of confessing, etc.) on the result of confessing falsely.
3. By identifying qualities within the suspect that increase the risk of false confession (suggestibility, youth, mental limitations, naiveté, etc.)
4. By questioning the fit between the suspect's "story" and the actual facts of the crime.

In its decision in the case of *Crane v. Kentucky* (1986) the Supreme Court opened the door to the admissibility of expert testimony in cases with a disputed confession. In this case, the facts of the crime and the subsequent investigation are all-too-familiar to those of us concerned with the abundance of false confessions. During the robbery of a liquor store in Louisville, Kentucky, a clerk was killed. The absence of physical evidence stifled the police in their search for a suspect. But a week after the murder, Major Crane, age 16, was arrested in connection with an unrelated robbery, that of a filling station. After a long interrogation, Crane confessed to committing several robberies and the shooting of a police officer. He initially denied any participation in the murder of the liquor-store clerk, but eventually confessed to that crime as well. He later recanted his confession.

In a preliminary hearing, the judge ruled the confession to be voluntary and so when Crane's defense attorney sought to introduce evidence at the trial about the coercive nature of the interrogation, the request was denied. The ruling came in the face of much ambiguity about the validity of the confession, which was not taped (Fulero, 2004). As Costanzo and Leo tell us: "Mr. Crane [claimed that he] had been held in a small, windowless room, interrogators denied his repeated requests to telephone his mother, he was interrogated for several hours, as many as six police officers in the interrogation room at the same time, and the police officers behaved in an intimidating manner" (2007, p. 83). Many of the details of this robbery that were given by Crane were inconsistent with the facts of the case; for example, he said it occurred during the day, when in fact it occurred at 10:40 p.m. He said he took money from the cash register when in fact none was taken (Fulero, 2004).

When Crane appealed, the Kentucky Supreme Court ruled that the trial judge did not err in excluding testimony on the above matters. There are, in fact, many arguments that prosecutors have used to argue against allowing an expert witness to testify in such a situation: "the findings are not scientific;" "it invades the province of the jury;" "the points the expert would make can be covered in cross examination;" "the knowledge is already possessed by the layperson" (Fulero, 2007). But the United States Supreme Court disagreed and ordered a new trial. (The decision was authored by Justice O'Connor, was only six pages long, and was unanimous.) The Court held that "certain interrogation techniques, either in isolation, or as applied to the unique characteristics of a particular suspect, are so offensive for a civilized system of justice that they must be condemned under the Due Process Clause of the Fourteenth Amendment" (*Crane v. Kentucky*, 1986, p. 684). Recognizing the power of confession evidence on jurors' verdicts, Justice O'Connor's opinion for the Court went on to say:

> A defendant's case may stand or fall on his ability to convince the
> jury that the manner in which the confession was obtained casts
> doubt on its credibility . . . Stripped of the power to describe to the
> jury the circumstances that prompted his confession, the defendant
> is effectively disabled from answering the one question every.
> rational juror needs answered: If the defendant is innocent, why did
> he previously admit his guilt? (*Crane v. Kentucky*, 1986, p. 688)

Thus the Supreme Court said that the state may not exclude "competent, reliable evidence bearing on the credibility of a confession when such evidence is central to the defendant's claim of innocence" (p. 683). But it left unresolved what form the evidence could take (Fulero, 2004).

Videotaping Interrogations

Another type of reform that can affect confession evidence once it is introduced at trial is to present a videotape of the entire interrogation. Jurors can see how and when (and even *if*) the Miranda rights were presented to the defendant; they can also see the degree to which the defendant "knowingly" waived his or her rights.

In the last 20 years, jurisdictions have slowly moved toward a requirement that police interrogations be videotaped. If such a videotape exists, either side may introduce it into evidence. The prosecution often considers it valuable evidence, as it shows the defendant confessing. But we are aware of trials in which the jury has witnessed a defendant being tricked into waiving his or her rights or into confessing, causing the outraged jury to find the defendant not guilty.

Currently, eight states now require videotaping of part or all of the interrogations in cases for at least certain types of crimes; these are Minnesota, Alaska, Illinois, Maine, New Mexico, New Jersey, Wisconsin, and North Carolina. (Also it is required in the District of Columbia.) Texas is considering it. Missouri's legislature passed such a law in mid-2009. Many other states are grappling with how to present what happens during interrogations in order to minimize the effect of a false or unreliable confession (Lassiter & Geers, 2004). In several states, the state supreme courts have stopped short of requiring it, but have issued vigorous opinions that, at the least, permit juries to be informed about implications of their absence: these include New Hampshire, Iowa, and Massachusetts (Kassin et al., 2009). In England, the law requires all interrogations to be taped. A national survey estimated that one-third of all large police departments in the United States do some videotaping of interrogations (Kassin, 1997). But requirements and procedures vary from state to state. Illinois limits the requirement only to murder cases. Often only the confession will be videotaped, preventing the jury from seeing what led up to it. A ruling in Massachusetts has set forward a procedure which seems to facilitate the procedure fulfilling its purpose. The Supreme Court of Massachusetts ruled that when the prosecution introduces evidence of a defendant's confession or statement of a custodial interrogation or an interrogation conducted at a place of detention and there is not at least an audio-tape of the complete interrogation, the defendant is entitled, upon request, to a jury instruction advising that the state's highest court prefers that such interrogations be recorded wherever practicable, and cautioning the jurors that, because of the absence of any recording of the interrogation in the case before them, they should weigh evidence of the defendant's alleged statement with great caution and care (*Commonwealth v. DeGiambattista*, 2004).

The federal government has lagged behind these states in making reforms. The FBI still does not videotape confessions or interrogations. However, this is likely to change; we anticipate a directive from the White House to begin doing so, considering that President Obama, while a state senator in Illinois, led the effort to adopt videotaping in that state.

The vast majority of state regulations do not go into the details of how the videotaping should be done, however, and psychological research has consistently found that what at first appears to be a favorable development may lead to judgments that obstruct the intended effect. For example, the camera angle can make a difference in evaluations. When interrogations are videotaped, typically the camera is directed at the suspect (Geller, 1992; Kassin, 1997). Judgments of the voluntariness of videotaped confessions have been found to be affected by the camera angle (Lassiter & Irvine, 1986; Lassiter & Geers, 2004; Lassiter, 2007). In an initial study in a program of research by Lassiter, respondents watched a tape of an interrogation of an alleged shoplifter from one of three angles; for a third of the respondents, the interrogator was visibly salient; for a third, only the suspect was; and for a third, both participants were. Judgments of coercion were lowest when the suspect was salient, highest when the interrogator was salient, and intermediate when the two were equally visible (Lassiter & Irvine, 1986). This program of research thus produced results that are consistent with the previously described tests of correspondent inference theory (Chapter 4), which deals with the decision to infer whether a person's actions reflect (or "correspond to") an internal characteristic. That is, a camera focused on the suspect increases the attribution by observers that the suspect's response was determined by his or her internal predisposition rather than by any coercive nature of the situation.

The camera-perspective effect is a robust one; the bias extends across various types of crimes, both violent and non-violent (Lassiter, Slaw, Briggs, & Scanlan, 1992). Its effect when videotapes are used is stronger than when audiotapes or transcripts are used (Lassiter & Geers, 2004). Jury deliberations do not diminish the effect, nor does a forewarning to jurors that the camera's perspective might affect their judgments. An instruction from the judge did not diminish the effect (Lassiter et al., 2002). In fact, judges are also susceptible to the effect (Lassiter & Geers, 2004).

Presenting jurors with a videotape of an interrogation in which the waiver of Miranda rights was elicited by browbeating or tricking the suspect can affect a jury's verdict. In a series of experiments, Kassin and Wrightsman (1981) evaluated the effect of different types of instructions from the judge upon jurors' verdicts when a suspect had been coerced into confessing. Instructions that told the jurors to ignore a confession that they felt was coerced had no effect on their judgments of the voluntariness of the confession or on their verdicts, nor did an emphasis on the unreliability of such confessions. But when the jurors were reminded of the unfairness of the procedure, that instruction influenced their judgments of the voluntariness of the confession (though their verdicts remained unaltered).

If jurors watch a videotape of an interrogation in which the Miranda warnings were manhandled, their reactions to a claim that the confession was voluntary may be shaken, and the testimony of an expert witness may be enough to cause them to question the defendant's guilt, especially if no other inculpatory evidence is presented. The research findings of Lassiter and his colleagues make it clear that the advantages of videotaping, especially providing the jurors a more detailed and vivid record of the interrogation, can be achieved if the camera focuses equally on the suspect and the interrogator. Already New Zealand has made it a national policy that all videotaping of interrogations use the equal-focus perspective.

Suggested Reforms

The APLS White Paper

The American Psychology-Law Society is an organization composed of 4,000 social scientists and lawyers concerned with the application of social-science knowledge to the legal system. In early 2009 the Board of Directors of the organization adopted a "white paper" statement which reviewed research on police interrogations and made recommendations for reforms (Kassin et al., 2009). Its very first recommendation is the following: "Without equivocation, our most essential recommendation is to lift the veil of secrecy from the interrogation process in favor of the principle of transparency. Specifically, *all custodial interviews and interrogations of felony suspects should be videotaped in their entirety and with an equal focus on suspects and interrogators*" (Kassin et al., 2009, p. 67, italics in original).

A second concern of the APLS white paper is the treatment of vulnerable suspects. Similar to our earlier recommendation, it urges the mandatory presence of an attorney when vulnerable suspects are Mirandized and interrogated. The review notes that some states permit the presence of a parent, guardian, or other interested adult when a juvenile is questioned. But often the presence of *this type of person* does not increase the tendency for a juvenile suspect to assert his or her constitutional rights, because these adults frequently urge the adolescent to cooperate with the police (Grisso & Ring, 1979; Oberlander, Goldstein, & Goldstein, 2003). Therefore, a professional advocate, preferably an attorney, trained to serve in this role, is recommended (Gudjonsson, 2003; Kassin et al., 2009).

Corroboration of a Confession

A more radical reform, but a reasonable one, is to require corroboration of a confession. The principle has a long history—but an ignored effect—in Supreme Court decisions. In 1954, in *Opper v. United States*, the Court observed that an uncorroborated confession is not enough to convict:

> The doubt persists that the zeal of the agencies of prosecution to protect the peace, the self-interest of the accomplice, the maliciousness of an enemy or the aberration or weakness of the accused under the strain of suspicion may tinge or warp the facts of the confession. (1954, pp. 89–90)

In another ruling in 1954, the Court amplified this position:

> The general rule that an accused may not be convicted on his own uncorroborated confession has previously been recognized by this Court and has been consistently applied in the lower federal courts and in the overwhelming majority of state courts. Its purpose is to prevent "errors in convictions based upon untrue confessions alone;"

its foundation lies in a long history of judicial experience with confessions and in the realization that sound law enforcement requires police interrogations which extend beyond the words of the accused. Confessions may be unreliable because they are coerced or induced, and although separate doctrines excluded involuntary confessions from consideration by the jury, further caution is warranted because the accused may be unable to establish the involuntary nature of his statements. Moreover, though a statement may not be "involuntary" within the meaning of this exclusionary rule, still its reliability may be suspect if it is extracted from one who is under pressure of a police investigation—whose words may reflect the strain and confusion attending his predica- ment rather than a clear reflection of his past. Finally, the experi- ence of the courts, the police and the medical profession recounts a number of false confessions voluntarily made. These are the considerations which justify a restriction on the power of the jury to convict, for this experience with confessions is not shared by the average juror. (*Smith v. United States*, 1954, pp. 152–153, citations omitted)

The question arises: How much corroboration is enough? The *Smith v. United States* (1954) decision offers the following answer:

There has been considerable debate concerning the question of corroboration necessary to substantiate the existence of the crime charged. It is agreed that the corroborative evidence does not have to prove the offense beyond a reasonable doubt, or even by a preponderance, as long as there is substantial independent evidence that the offense has been committed, and the evidence as a whole proves beyond a reasonable doubt that defendant is guilty. In addition to differing views on the substantiality of specific independent evidence, the debate has centered largely about two questions: (1) whether corroboration is necessary for all elements of the offense established by admissions alone, and (2) whether it is sufficient if the corroboration merely fortifies the truth of the confession, without independently establishing the crime charged. We answer both in the affirmative. All elements of the offense must be established by independent evidence or corroborated admissions, but one available mode of corroboration is for the independent evidence to bolster the confession itself and thereby prove the offense "through" the statement of the accused. (1954, p. 156)

These viewpoints receive support in the contemporary view of Weisselberg, described in the next section.

A Return to Voluntariness

Both Weisselberg and Leo, as noted, see little reason to maintain *Miranda*. What do they offer in its place? Weisselberg (2008) anticipates a return to a voluntariness doctrine; he writes:

> There is at least a chance that we could see a voluntariness standard that looks carefully at the dynamics of police interrogation and asks whether a confession was elicited by offensive police conduct. We might see a standard that places greater reliability of a confession by looking at, among other things, the fit between the real facts of the offense and those contained in the suspect's post-admission narrative. Given the few constraints on interrogation tactics after a Miranda waiver is obtained, that type of standard might do more to address concerns about false confessions. We would lose *Miranda's* "bright lines" and courts would have to make many more individualized assessments of the voluntariness of a statement. But this surely is the right outcome. (2008, p. 1599)

Leo offers another substitute; his emphasis is on the reliability of a confession. Can the confession be corroborated by other evidence? Do the statements made in the confession agree with the known facts of the crime? He notes that several state courts and federal district courts have developed a "trustworthiness standard." Under such a standard, before the state may introduce a confession, it "must introduce substantial independent evidence which would tend to establish the trustworthiness of the [confession]" (*Opper v. United States*, 1954, p. 93). Thus, the judge acts as a gatekeeper in determining whether the confession is admitted into evidence. Factors the judge could use to determine the confession's reliability could include "the spontaneity of the statement, the absence of deception, trick, the threats or promises to obtain the statement, the defendant's positive physical and mental condition, including age, education, and experience, and the presence of an attorney when the statement is given" (*State v. Mauchly*, 2003, p. 488).

One can debate the degree of difference between Weisselberg's voluntariness and Leo's reliability, but both use the same criteria to determine whether a confession should be admissible at trial. We endorse their suggestions, but we ask: Is there still a place for *Miranda*?

The Future of *Miranda*

The goals of the authors of the *Miranda* decision were the following: to inform suspects of their rights to remain silent and to have the assistance of counsel, thus dispelling the coercive environment of the interrogation room, and to empower suspects whether to waive or invoke their rights (Thompson, 2006).

The foregoing chapters have shown how and why these goals have not been achieved. Can they be achieved in the future? No set of procedures can prevent all false confessions, but the reforms described in this chapter can have an impact on a significant number of interrogation-induced false confessions. The presence of a professional advocate who makes sure that suspects are informed of their rights immediately and double-checks that a waiver is done knowingly and intelligently can curtail some of the abuses of the system. Videotaping the entire procedure may restrain the police and certainly will inform the jury of the degree of actual voluntariness in the confession. With the implementation of these reforms, the original goals of *Miranda* may yet be salvaged.

References

Anderson v. Terhune, U.S. App. Lexis 27558 (9th Cir. Nov. 5, 2006).

Arizona v. Fulminante, 111 S.Ct. 1246 (1991).

Ashcraft v. Tennessee, 322 U.S. 193 (1944).

Baker, L. (1983). *Miranda: Crime, law and politics.* New York: Atheneum.

Barthel, J. (1976). *A death in Canaan.* New York: E. P. Dutton.

Bedau, H. A., & Radelet, M. L. (1987). Miscarriages of justice in potentially capital cases. *Stanford Law Review, 41,* 21–79.

Betts v. Brady, 316 U.S. 455 (1942).

Black, H. L., Jr. (1995). Hugo Black. In C. Cushman (Ed.), *The Supreme Court justices: Illustrated biographies, 1784-1995* (2nd ed., pp. 376–380). Washington, DC: Congressional Quarterly.

Blackburn v. Alabama, 361 U.S. 199 (1960).

Bouton v. United States, 391 U.S. 123 (1968).

Bram v. United States, 168 U.S. 532 (1897).

Brief of the American Medical Association et al. as Amici Curiae in support of Respondent, Roper v. Simmons, 543 U.S. 551 (2005) (No. 03-633).

Briere, E. J. (1978, September). Limited English speakers and the *Miranda* rights. *TESOL Quarterly, 12*(3), 235–245.

Brown v. Board of Education, 347 U.S. 483 (1954).

Brown v. Mississippi, 297 U.S. 278 (1936).

Buckley, J. P. (2007, September). What is the Reid Technique? Conference on Interrogations and Confessions, University of Texas at El Paso.

Bull, R. (1989). Can training enhance the detection of deception? In J. C. Yuille (Ed.), *Credibility assessment* (pp. 83–99). New York: Kluwer Academic Press/ Plenum Publishers.

Burt, R. A. (1969). Miranda and Title II: A Morganatic marriage? In P. B. Kurland (Ed.), *Supreme Court Review 1969* (pp. 81–139). Chicago: University of Chicago Press.

California v. Beheler, 463 U.S. 1121 (1983).

California v. Dorado, 40 Cal. Rptr.264, 394 P.2nd 952 (1965).

California v. Prysock, 453 U.S. 355 (1981).

Carey, B. (2009, May 12). Judging honesty by words, not fidgets. *New York Times*, pp. D1, D4.

Cassell, P. G. (1996a). All benefits, no costs: The grand illusion of *Miranda* defenders. *Northwestern University Law Review, 90*, 1084–1124.

Cassell, P. G. (1996b). *Miranda's* social costs: An empirical reassessment. *Northwestern University Law Review, 90*, 387–499.

Cassell, P. G. (1998). Protecting the innocent from false confessions and lost confessions—and from *Miranda. Journal of Criminal Law and Criminology, 78*, 497–556.

Cassell, P. G. (1999a). The guilty and the innocent: An examination of the alleged cases of wrongful conviction from false confessions. *Harvard Journal of Law and Public Policy, 22*, 23–603.

Cassell, P. G. (1999b). The statute that time forgot: 18 USC 3501 and the overhauling of *Miranda. Iowa Law Review, 85*, 175–259.

Cassell, P. G., & Fowles, R. (1998). Handcuffing the cops? A thirty-year perspective on *Miranda's* harmful effects on law enforcement. *Stanford Law Review, 50*, 1055–1146.

Cassell, P. G., & Hayman, B. S. (1996). Police interrogation in the 1990s: An empirical study of the effects of *Miranda. UCLA Law Review, 43*, 839–931.

Chambers v. Florida, 309 U.S. 727 (1940).

Chapman v. California, 386 U.S. 18 (1967).

Chavez v. Martinez, 538 U.S. 760 (2003).

Clymer, S. D. (2002). Are police free to disregard *Miranda? Yale Law Journal, 112*, 447–552.

Colorado v. Connelly, 479 U.S. 157 (1986).

Commonwealth of Massachusetts v. DiGiambattista, 442 Mass. 423 (2004).

Connecticut v. Barrett, 479 U.S. 523 (1987).

Connery, D. S. (1977). *Guilty until proven innocent.* New York: Putnam.

Cooper, V. G., & Zapf, P. A. (2007). Psychiatric patients' comprehension of Miranda rights. *Law and Human Behavior, 32*, 390–405.

Cooper, V. G., & Zapf, P. A. (2008, March). Shhh! Miranda (mis)comprehension in the general populace. Paper presented at the meetings of the American Psychology-Law Society, Jacksonville, FL.

Corriero, M. A. (2006). *Judging children as children: A proposal for a juvenile justice system.* Philadelphia: Temple University Press.

Costanzo, M., & Leo, R. A. (2007). Research and expert testimony on interrogations and confessions. In M. Costanzo, D. Krauss, & K. Pedzek (Eds.), *Expert psychological testimony for the courts* (pp. 69–98). Mahwah, NJ: Erlbaum.

Crane v. Kentucky, 476 U.S. 683 (1986).

Cruz v. New York, 481 U.S. 186 (1987).

Culombe v. Connecticut, 367 U.S. 568 (1961).

Curtis, N. (2006, May 15). *Language assistance for law enforcement.* National Association of Judiciary Interpreters and Translators, NAJIT Position Paper. http://www.majit.org/documents/Law%20Enforcement.pdf

Davis v. United States, 512 U.S. 452 (1994).

DeClue, G. (2005). *Interrogations and disputed confessions: A manual for forensic psychological practice.* Sarasota, FL: Professional Resource Press.

Deeley, P. (1971). *Beyond the breaking point.* London: Arthur Backer.

Deitch, M., Barstow, A., Lukens, L., & Reyna, R. (2009). *From timeout to hard time: Young children in the adult criminal justice system.* Austin, TX: The University of Texas at Austin, LBJ School of Public Affairs.

DePaulo, B. (1994). Spotting lies: Can humans learn to do better? *Current Directions in Psychological Science, 3,* 83–86.

Dershowitz, A. M. (2008). *Is there a right to remain silent? Coercive interrogation and the Fifth Amendment after 9/11.* New York: Oxford University Press.

Dickerson v. United States, 120 S.Ct. 2326, 530 U.S. 428 (2000).

Donohoe, J. J., III. (1998). Did *Miranda* diminish police effectiveness? *Stanford Law Review, 50,* 1147–1180.

Dorsciak v. Gladden, 246 Ore. 233, 425 P.2d 177 (1967).

Drizin, S. A., & Colgan, B. A. (2004). Tales from the juvenile confession front. In G. D. Lassiter (Ed.), *Interrogations, confessions, and entrapment* (pp. 127–162). New York: Kluwer Academic/Plenum.

DuBow, S., Geer, S., & Strauss, K. P. (1992). *Legal rights: The guide for deaf and hard of hearing people.* Washington, DC: Gallaudet University Press.

Duckworth v. Eagan, 492 U.S. 195 (1989).

Eddings v. Oklahoma, 455 U.S. 104 (1982).

Edkins, V. A. (2007). Assessing due process and crime control attitudes: Creation and validation of a measure of juror bias. Unpublished Ph.D. dissertation, University of Kansas.

Edkins, V. A., & Wrightsman, L. S. (2004). The psychology of entrapment. In G. D. Lassiter (Ed.), *Interrogations, confessions, and entrapment* (pp. 215–244). New York: Kluwer Academic Press/Plenum.

Edwards v. Arizona, 451 U.S. 477 (1981).

Ekman, P., O'Sullivan, M., & Frank, M. G. (1999). A few can catch a liar. *Psychological Science. 10,* 263–266.

Escobedo v. Illinois, 378 U.S. 478 (1964).

Everington, C., & Fulero, S. (1999). Competence to confess: Measuring understanding and suggestibility of defendants with mental retardation. *Mental Retardation, 37,* 212–220.

Fare v. Michael C., 442 U.S. 707 (1979).

Feld, B. C. (2006). Juveniles' competence to exercise *Miranda* rights: An empirical study of policy and practice. *Minnesota Law Review, 91,* 26–100.

Fellers v. United States, 124 S.Ct. 1019 (2004).

Fikes v. Alabama, 352 U.S. 191 (1957).

Firstman, R., & Salpeter, J. (2008). *A criminal injustice: A true crime, a false confession, and the fight to free Marty Tankleff.* New York: Ballantine.

Follett, W. C., Davis, D., & Leo, R. A. (2007). Mental health status and vulnerability to police interrogation tactics. *Criminal Justice, 22*(3), 42–49.

Formanek, R., Jr. (1985, October 23). Chicago man back in jail after eluding other charges. *Lawrence Journal-World*, p. 30.

Framer, I. (2000, Summer-Fall). Interpreters and their impact on the criminal justice system: The Alejandro Ramirez case. *Newsletter, Community and Court Interpreters of the Ohio Valley I, 1,* 1–7.

Franklin, C. (1970). *The third degree.* London: Robert Hale.

Frontline. (2002). Inside the teen brain. Public Broadcasting System. http://www.pbs.org/wgbh/pages/frontline/shows/teenbrain/interviews/giedd.html.

Frumkin, I. B. (2008, August). New norms for Gudjonsson Suggestibility Scale and Grisso's Miranda tests. Paper presented at the meetings of the American Psychological Association, Boston, MA.

Fulero, S. M. (2004). Expert psychological testimony on the psychology of interrogations and confessions. In G. D. Lassiter (Ed.), *Interrogations, confessions and entrapment* (pp. 247–263). New York: Kluwer Academic/Plenum.

Fulero, S. M. (2007, September). Tales from the front: Expert testimony on the psychology of interrogations and confessions. Conference on Interrogations and Confessions, University of Texas at El Paso.

Fulero, S. M. (2008, August). *Case law of expert testimony regarding Miranda competency and suggestibility.* Paper presented at the meetings of the American Psychological Association, Boston, MA.

Fulero, S. M. (In press). Expert psychological testimony on the psychology of interrogations and confessions: Five years later. In G. D. Lassiter & C. Meissner (Eds.), *Interrogations and confessions: Current research, practices, and policy.* Washington, DC: American Psychological Association.

Fulero, S. M., & Everington, C. (1995). Assessing competency to waive Miranda rights in defendants with mental retardation. *Law and Human Behavior, 19,* 533–543.

Fulero, S. M., & Everington, C. (2004). Mental retardation, competency to waive *Miranda* rights, and false confessions. In G. D. Lassiter (Ed.), *Interrogations, confessions, and entrapment* (pp. 163–179). New York: Kluwer Academic/Plenum Publishers.

Gallegos v. Colorado, 370 U.S. 49 (1962).

Geller, W. A. (1992). *Police videotaping of suspect interrogations and confessions: A preliminary examination of issues and practices.* (A report to the National Institute of Justice.) Washington, DC: U.S. Department of Justice.

Gideon v. Wainwright, 373 U.S. 335 (1963).

Giedd, J. N. (2002). *Inside the teen brain.* Interview by *Frontline*, Public Broadcasting System. http://www.pbs.org/wgbh/pages/frontline/shows/teenbrain/interviews/giedd.html

Graham, F. P. (1970). *The due process revolution: The Warren Court's impact on criminal law.* Rochelle Park, NY: Hayden.

Grano, J. D. (1993). *Confessions, truth, and the law.* Ann Arbor, MI: University of Michigan Press.

Greenhouse, L. (2000, June 28). A turf battle's victim. *New York Times*, pp. A1, A18.

Grisso, T. (1981). *Juveniles' waiver of rights: Legal and psychological competence.* New York: Plenum.

Grisso, T. (1998). *Forensic evaluation of juveniles.* Sarasota, FL: Professional Resources Press.

Grisso, T. (2003). *Evaluating competencies: Forensic assessments and instruments* (2nd ed.). New York: Kluwer Academic/Plenum.

Grisso, T., & Ring, J. (1979). Parents' attitudes toward juveniles' rights in interrogation. *Criminal Justice and Behavior, 6,* 221–226.

Gudjonsson, G. H. (1984a). A new scale of interrogative suggestibility. *Personality and Individual Differences, 5,* 303–314.

Gudjonsson, G. H. (1984b). Interrogative suggestibility: Comparison between "false confessors" and "deniers" in criminal trials. *Medicine, Science, and the Law, 24,* 56–60.

Gudjonsson, G. H. (1987). Historical background to suggestibility: How interrogative suggestibility differs from other types of suggestibility. *Personality and Individual Differences, 8,* 347–355.

Gudjonsson, G. H. (1988). Interrogative suggestibility and its relationship with assertiveness, social-evaluative anxiety, state anxiety, and method of coping. *British Journal of Clinical Psychology, 27,* 159–166.

Gudjonsson, G. H. (1989). Compliance in an interrogative situation: A new scale. *Personality and Individual Differences, 10,* 535–540.

Gudjonsson, G. H. (1991). The application of interrogative suggestibility to police interviewing. In J. P. Schumaker (Ed.), *Human suggestibility: Advances in theory, research and application* (pp. 279–288). London: Routledge.

Gudjonsson, G. H. (1992). *The psychology of interrogations, confessions, and testimony,* New York: Wiley.

Gudjonsson, G. H. (2003). *The psychology of interrogations and confessions: A handbook.* New York: Wiley.

Gudjonsson, G. H., & Clare, I. C. H. (1995). The relationship between confabulation and intellectual ability, memory, interrogative suggestibility, and acquiescence. *Personality and Individual Differences, 19,* 333–338.

Gudjonsson, G. H., & Hilton, M. (1989). The effects of instructional manipulation on interrogative suggestibility. *Social Behaviour, 4,* 189–193.

Hairston v. United States, 905 A.2d 765 (D.C. 2006).

Haley v. Ohio, 332 U.S. 596 (1948).

Hancock, C. (1996). Due process before *Miranda. Tulane Law Review, 70,* 2195–2237.

Hansdottir, I., Thorsteinsson, H. S., Kristinsdottir, H., & Ragnarsson, R. S. (1990). The effects of instructions and anxiety on interrogative suggestibility. *Personality and Individual Differences, 11,* 85–87.

Harris v. New York, 401 U.S. 222 (1971).

Hawkins v. Lynaugh, 844 F.2d 1132 (5th Cir. 1988).

Hopkins, E. Q. (1931). *Our lawless police: A study of unlawful enforcement of the law.* New York: Viking Press.

Hopt v. Territory of Utah, 110 U.S. 524 (1884).

Hutchinson, D. J. (1995). Byron R. White. In C. Cushman (Ed.), *The Supreme Court justices: Illustrated biographies, 1789–1995* (pp. 461–466). Washington, DC: Congressional Quarterly.

In re Gault, 387 U.S. 1 (1967).

Inbau, F. E., & Reid, J. E. (1962). *Criminal interrogation and confessions.* Baltimore, MD: Williams and Wilkins.

Inbau, F. E., Reid, J. E., Buckley, J. P., & Jayne, B. (2001). *Criminal interrogation and confessions* (4th ed.). Gaithersburg, MD: Aspen.

Irons, P., & Guitton, S. (Eds.). (1993). *May it please the Court.* New York: New Press.

Jacobson v. United States, 503 U.S. 540 (1992).

Jackson v. Denno, 378 U.S. 368 (1964).

Johnson v. New Jersey, 384 U.S. 719 (1966).

Jones, E. E., & Harris, V. A. (1967). The attribution of attitudes. *Journal of Experimental Social Psychology, 3,* 1–24.

Jones, E. E., & Nisbett, R. E. (1972). The actor and the observer: Divergent perspectives on the causes of behavior. In E. E. Jones, D. Kanouse, H. H. Kelley, R. E. Nisbett, S. Valins, & B. Weiner (Eds.), *Attribution: Perceiving the causes of behavior* (pp. 79–94). Morristown, NJ: General Learning Press.

Kamisar, Y. (1980). *Police interrogations and confessions: Essays on law and policy.* Ann Arbor: University of Michigan Press.

Kamisar, Y. (1992). Escobedo v. Illinois. In K. Hall (Ed.), *The Oxford companion to the Supreme Court of the United States* (p. 260). New York: Oxford University Press.

Kamisar, Y. (1996, June 10). *Miranda* does not look so awesome now. *Legal Times,* p. A22.

Kassin, S. M. (1997). The psychology of confession evidence. *American Psychologist, 52,* 221–233.

Kassin, S. M. (2007, September). Why innocents confess and why confessions trump their innocence. Conference on Interrogations and Confessions, University of Texas at El Paso.

Kassin, S. M., Drizin, S. A., Grisso, T., Gudjonsson, G. H., Leo, R. A., & Redlich, A. D. (2009). *Police-induced confessions: Risk factors and recommendations.* White paper, American Psychology-Law Society.

Kassin, S. M., Leo, R. A., Meissner, C. A., Richman, K. D., Colwell, L. H., Leach, A. M., & LeFon, D. (2007). Police interviewing and interrogation: A self-report survey of police practices and beliefs. *Law and Human Behavior, 31,* 381–400.

Kassin, S. M., & Fong, C. T. (1999). "I'm innocent!" Effects of training on judgments of truth and deception in the interrogation room. *Law and Human Behavior, 23,* 499–516.

Kassin, S. M., Meissner, C. A., & Norwick, R. J. (2005). "I'd know a false confession if I saw one" A comparison study of college students and police investigators. *Law and Human Behavior, 29,* 211–227.

Kassin, S. M., & Norwick, R. (2004). Why people waive their *Miranda* rights: The power of innocence. *Law and Human Behavior, 28,* 211–221.

Kassin, S. M., & Wrightsman, L. S. (1981). Coerced confessions, judicial instruction, and mock juror verdicts. *Journal of Applied Social Psychology, 11,* 489–506.

Kassin, S. M., & Wrightsman, L. S. (1985). Confession evidence. In S. M. Kassin & L. S. Wrightsman (Eds.), *The psychology of evidence and trial procedures* (pp. 67–94). Newbury Park, CA: Sage.

Kelley, H. H. (1971). *Attribution in social interaction.* Morristown, NJ: General Learning Press.

Kent v. United States, 383 U.S. 541 (1966).

Kleinmuntz, B., & Szucko, J. J. (1984). Lie detection in ancient and modern times: A call for contemporary scientific study. *American Psychologist, 39,* 766–776.

Konecni, V. J., & Ebbesen, E. B. (1986). Courtroom testimony by psychologists in eyewitness identification issues: Critical notes and reflections. *Law and Human Behavior, 10*, 117–126.

Kujovich, G. (1995). Potter Stewart. In C. Cushman (Ed.), *The Supreme Court justices: Illustrated biographies, 1789-1995* (pp. 456–460). Washington, DC: Congressional Quarterly.

Lassiter, G. D. (In press). Videotaping police interrogations: Dos and don'ts. In G. D. Lassiter and C. Meissner (Eds.), *Interrogations and confessions: Research, practices, and policy.* Washington, DC: American Psychological Association.

Lassiter, G. D., Beers, M. J., Geers, A. L., Handley, I. M., Munhall, P. J., & Weiland, P. E. (2002). Further evidence for a robust point-of-view bias in videotaped confessions. *Current Psychology, 21*, 265–288.

Lassiter, C. D., & Geers, A. L. (2004). Bias and accuracy in the evaluation of confession evidence. In C. D. Lassiter (Ed.), *Interrogations, confessions, and entrapment* (pp. 197–234). New York: Kluwer Academic/Plenum Publishers.

Lassiter, G. D., & Irvine, A. A. (1986). Videotaped confessions: The impact of camera point of view on judgments of coercion. *Journal of Applied Social Psychology, 16*, 265–276.

Lassiter, G. D., Slaw, R. D., Briggs, M. A., & Scanlan, C. R. (1992). The potential for bias in videotaped confessions. *Journal of Applied Social Psychology, 22*, 1838–1851.

Lego v. Twomey, 404 U.S. 477 (1972).

Leo, R. A. (1996a). Inside the interrogation room. *Journal of Criminal Law and Criminology, 86*, 266–303.

Leo, R. A. (1996b). *Miranda's* revenge: Police interrogation as a confidence game. *Law and Society Review, 30*, 259–288.

Leo, R. A. (1996c). The impact of *Miranda* revisited. *Journal of Criminal Law and Criminology, 86*, 621–692.

Leo, R. A. (2001a). False confessions: Causes, consequences, and solutions. In S. D. Westervelt & J. A. Humphrey (Eds.), *Wrongfully convicted: Perspectives on failed justice* (pp. 36–54). New Brunswick, NJ: Rutgers University Press.

Leo, R. A. (2008). *Police interrogation and American justice.* Cambridge, MA: Harvard University Press.

Leo, R. A., & Ofshe, R. J. (1998). The consequences of false confessions: Deprivations of liberty and miscarriages of justice in the age of psychological interrogation. *Journal of Criminal Law and Criminology, 88*, 429–496.

Leo, R. A., & Thomas, G. C., III. (1998). *The Miranda debate: Law, justice, and policing.* Boston: Northeastern University Press.

Leo, R. A., & White, W. (1999). Adopting to *Miranda*: Modern interrogations' strategies for dealing with the obstacles posed by *Miranda*. *Minnesota Law Review, 84*, 397–472.

Lewin, N. (1995). John Marshall Harlan. In C. Cushman (Ed.), *The Supreme Court justices: Illustrated biographies, 1789-1995* (2nd ed., pp. 441–445). Washington, DC: Congressional Quarterly.

Leyra v. Denno, 347 U.S. 556 (1954).

Linkletter v. Walker, 381 U.S. 618 (1965).

Lisenba v. California, 314 U.S. 219 (1941).

Lyons v. Oklahoma, 322 U.S. 596 (1944).

Macdonald, J. M., & Michaud, D. L. (1987). *The confession: Interrogation and criminal profiles for police officers.* Denver: Apache.

Malloy v. Hogan, 378 U.S. 1 (1964).

Malone, P. (1986). You have the right to remain silent: *Miranda* after twenty years. *American Scholar, 55,* 367–380.

Mapp v. Ohio, 367 U.S. 643 (1961).

Marks v. United States, 430 U.S. 188 (1976).

Massiah v. United States, 377 U.S. 201 (1964).

McCloskey, M., & Egeth, H. E. (1983). Eyewitness identification: What can a psychologist tell a jury? *American Psychologist, 38,* 550–563.

McCormick, C. T. (1946). Some problems and developments in the admissibility of confessions. *Texas Law Review, 24,* 239–245.

Meissner, C. A., & Kassin, S. M. (2002). "He's guilty!": Investigator bias in judgments of truth and deception. *Law and Human Behavior, 26,* 469–480.

Meissner, C. A., Kassin, S. M. (2004). "You're guilty, so just confess!" Cognitive and behavioral confirmation biases in the interrogation room. In C. D. Lassiter (Ed.), *Interrogations, confessions, and entrapment* (pp. 85–106). New York: Kluwer Academic/Plenum Publishers.

Memorandum of Agreement (Ariz. Super. Ct.) (2009), Case No. JV2008065. http://apps.supremecourt.az.gov/docs/.

Meyer, J. R., & Reppucci, N. D. (2007). Police practices and perceptions regarding juvenile interrogation and interrogative suggestibility. *Behavioral Sciences and the Law, 25(6),* 757– 780.

Michigan v. Harvey, 474 U.S. 344 (1990).

Miranda v. Arizona, 384 U.S. 435 (1966).

Missouri v. Seibert, 124 S.Ct. 2601 (2004).

Montejo v. Louisiana, United States Supreme Court, Case No. 07-1529 (2009).

Moran v. Burbine, 475 U.S. 412 (1986).

Moreno, J. A. (2005). Why the new *Missouri v. Seibert* bad faith police test is a terrible idea. *Arizona Law Review, 47,* 395–418.

Mosteller, R. P. (2007). Police deception before *Miranda* warnings: The case for *per se* prohibition of an entirely unjustified practice at the most critical moment. *Texas Tech Law Review, 39,* 1239–1274.

Motion to Suppress Statements & Request for Voluntariness Hearing, (Ariz. Super. Ct.) (2008), Case No. JV2008-05. http://apps.supremecourt.az.gov/docs/.

Mullin, C. (1989). *Error of judgement: The truth about the Birmingham bombings.* Dublin: Poolbeg.

Nakane, I. (2007). Problems in communicating the suspect's rights in interpreted police interviews. *Applied Linguistics, 281,* 87–112.

New York v. Quarles, 467 U.S. 649 (1984).

Notice of Change of Judge for Cause, (Ariz. Super. Ct.) (2009), Case No. JV2008-05. http://apps.supremecourt.az.gov/docs/.

Oberlander, L., Goldstein, N., & Goldstein, A. (2003). Competence to confess. In I. Weiner & A. Goldstein (Eds.), *Handbook of psychology: Volume 22, Forensic Psychology* (pp. 335–357). New York: Wiley.

Ofshe, R. J., & Leo, R. A. (1997). The social psychology of police interrogation: The theory and classification of true and false confessions. *Studies in Law, Politics, and Society, 16,* 189–251.

O'Hara, C. E., & O'Hara, G. L. (2003). *Fundamentals of criminal investigation* (7th ed.). Springfield, IL: Charles C Thomas.

Opper v. United States, 348 U.S. 84 (1954).

Oregon v. Hass, 420 U.S. 714 (1975).

Oregon v. Mathiason, 429 U.S. 492 (1977).

Packer, H. L. (1964). Two models of the criminal process. *University of Pennsylvania Law Review, 113*, 1–68.

Packer, H. L. (1968). *The limits of the criminal sanction.* Stanford, CA: Stanford University Press.

Paulsen, M. G. (1954). The Fourteenth Amendment and the third degree. *Stanford Law Review, 6*, 411–437.

Paulsen, M. G. (1966). Kent v. United States: The constitutional context of juvenile cases. In P. B. Kurland (Ed.), *Supreme Court Review 1966* (pp. 167–192). Chicago: University of Chicago Press.

Payne v. Arkansas, 356 U.S. 560 (1958).

People v. Braggs. (2003). Docket No. 95350, Illinois Supreme Court. *Modified on denial of rehearing April 15, 2004.* http://www.state.il.us/court/Opinions/ Supreme Court/2004/default.asp.

People v. Hartgraves, 1 Cal. App. 3.d, 117 (1964).

People v. McBride. (2006). COA No. 271579, State of Michigan Court of Appeals, per curiam. http://coa.courts.mi.gov/documents/opinions/final/ coa/20061219_c271579_42_200o.71579.open.coa.pdf.

People v. McBride. (2008). Order, SC: 133142, Michigan Supreme Court. http://courts.michigan.gov/supremecourt/Clerk/11-07/133142/ 133142-Order.pdf.

Perillo, J. T., & Kassin, S. M. (2009, March). To bluff or not to bluff: Stay tuned. Paper presented at the meetings of the American Psychology-Law Society, San Antonio, TX.

Porter, S., Woodworth, M., & Birt, A. R. (2000). Truth, lies, and videotape: An investigation of the ability of federal parole officers to detect deception. *Law and Human Behavior, 24*, 643–658.

Prettyman, B., Jr. (1961). *Death and the Supreme Court.* New York: Harcourt, Brace, and World.

Redlich, A. D. (2004, January). Mental illness, police interrogations, and the potential for false confessions. *Law and Psychiatry, 55*(1), 19–21.

Redlich, A.D., Silverman, M., Chen, J., & Steiner, H. (2004). The police interrogation of children and adolescents. In G. D. Lassiter (Ed.), *Interrogations, confessions, and entrapment* (pp. 107–125). New York: Kluwer Academic/Plenum Publishers.

Redlich, A. D., Silverman, M., & Steiner, H. (2003). Factors affecting pre-adjudicative and adjudicative competence in juveniles and young adults. *Behavioral Sciences and the Law, 21*, 1–17.

Rhode Island v. Ellis, 446 U.S. 291 (1980).

Ring, K. (1971). *Let's get started: An appeal to what's left in psychology.* Unpublished manuscript, University of Connecticut, Storrs, CT.

Rogers v. Richmond, 365 U.S. 534 (1961).

Rogers, R. (2008, August). Wrongs of Miranda rights: Advances in forensic research and psychological expertise. Paper presented at the meetings of the American Psychological Association, Boston, MA.

Rogers, R., Correa, A. A., Hazelwood, L. L., Shuman, D. W., Hoersting, R. C., & Blackwood, H. L. (2009). Spanish translations of *Miranda* warnings and the totality of circumstances. *Law and Human Behavior, 33,* 61–69.

Rogers, R., Harrison, K. S., Hazelwood, L. L., & Sewell, K. W. (2007). Knowing and intelligent: Study of *Miranda* warnings in mentally disordered defendants. *Law and Human Behavior, 31,* 401–418.

Rogers, R., Harrison, K. S., Shuman, D. W., Sewell, K. W., & Hazelwood, L. L. (2007). An analysis of *Miranda* warnings and waivers: Comprehension and coverage. *Law and Human Behavior, 31,* 177–192.

Rogers, R., Hazelwood, L. L., Sewell, K. W., Harrison, K. S., & Shuman, D. W. (2008). The language of *Miranda* warnings in American jurisdictions: A replication and vocabulary analysis. *Law and Human Behavior, 32,* 124–136.

Rogers, R., Hazelwood, L. L., Sewell, K. W., Shuman, D. W., & Blackwood, H. L. (2008) The comprehensibility and content of juvenile *Miranda* warnings. *Psychology, Public Policy, and Law, 14(1),* 63–87.

Roper v. Simmons, 543 U.S. 551 (2005).

Rowland, C. K., & Carp, R. A. (1996). *Politics and judgment in federal district courts.* Lawrence, KS: University Press of Kansas.

Rutledge, D. (2006, October). There is no magic formula, but there are four necessary ingredients. *Police Magazine,* http://www.policemag.com/Articles/2006/10/Point-of-Law.aspx.

Sauer, M., & Wilkens, J. (1999, May 11). Haunting questions: The Stephanie Crowe murder case. Part 1: The night she was killed. *The San Diego Union Tribune,* A-1.

Sauer, M., & Wilkens, J. (1999, May 12). Haunting questions: The Stephanie Crowe murder case. Part 2: The arrest. *The San Diego Union Tribune,* A-1.

Sauer, M., & Wilkens, J. (1999, May 13). Haunting questions: The Stephanie Crowe murder case. Part 3: The knife. *The San Diego Union Tribune,* A-1.

Sauer, M., & Wilkens, J. (1999, May 14). Haunting questions: The Stephanie Crowe murder case. Part 4: More arrests. *The San Diego Union Tribune,* A-1.

Sawyer, D. (News Anchor). (2008, November 19). *Good Morning America* [Television Broadcast]. New York: American Broadcasting Companies, Inc.

Scheck, B., Neufeld, P., & Dwyer, J. (2001). *Actual innocence.* New York: Doubleday.

Schulhofer, S. J. (1996a). *Miranda* and clearance rates. *Northwestern University Law Review, 91,* 278–294.

Schulhofer, S. J. (1996b). *Miranda's* practical effect: Substantial benefits and vanishingly small social costs. *Northwestern University Law Review, 90,* 500–564.

Schulhofer, S. J. (1999, March 1). Miranda now on endangered species list. *National Law Journal,* p. A22.

Schulhofer, S. J. (2006). *Miranda v. Arizona:* A modest but important legacy. In C. S. Steiker (Ed.), *Criminal procedure stories* (pp. 155–179). New York: Foundation Press.

Schwartz, B. (1995). Earl Warren. In C. Cushman (Ed.), *The Supreme Court justices: Illustrated biographies, 1789-1995* (2nd ed., pp. 436–440). Washington, DC: Congressional Quarterly.

Simon, D. (1991). *Homicide: A year on the killing streets.* New York: Ivy Books.

Slobogin, C. (2003). Toward taping. *Ohio State Journal of Criminal Law, 1,* 309–322.

Smith v. Delaware, No. 43, 2006 (Sup. Ct. Del). http://caselaw.lp.findlaw.com/data2/delawarestatecases/43-2006.pdf.

Smith v. United States, 348 U.S. 147 (1954).

Snyder, H. N., & Sickmund, M. (2006). *Juvenile offenders and victims: 2006 National Report.* Washington, DC: U.S. Department of Justice, Office of Justice Programs, Office of Juvenile Justice and Delinquency Prevention, 93–119.

Spano v. New York, 306 U.S. 315 (1959).

Sparf and Hansen v. United States, 156 U.S. 51 (1895).

State v. Mauchley, 67 P.3d 477 (Utah 2003).

State v. Ramirez. (1999). Case No. 97-L-289, Court of Appeals of Ohio, Eleventh Appellate District, Lake County, 135 Ohio App. 3d 89; 732 N.R.2d 1065; 1999 Ohio App. LEXIS 6241, Counsel Corrected November 20, 2000.

Stein v. New York, 346 U.S. 156 (1953).

Stephens, O. H., Jr. (1973). *The Supreme Court and confessions of guilt.* Knoxville: University of Tennessee Press.

Stone, G. R. (1978). The *Miranda* decision in the Burger Court. In P. B. Kurland & G. Casper (Eds.), *Supreme Court Review 1977* (pp. 99–169). Chicago: University of Chicago Press.

Stuart, G. L. (2004). *Miranda: The story of America's right to remain silent.* Tucson: University of Arizona Press.

Tankleff, M. (2009, May 22). Personal communication (transmitted by Saul M. Kassin).

Tanner, S. (Producer). (2007, March 10). *Science of Interrogation* [Television Broadcast]. Washington, DC: National Geographic Channel.

Thomas, G. C., III. (1996). Plain talk about the *Miranda* empirical debate: A "steady-state" theory of confessions. *U.C.L.A. Law Review, 43,* 933–959.

Thomas, G. C., III. (1998). The twenty-first century: A world without *Miranda?* In R. A. Leo & G. C. Thomas, III (Eds.), *The Miranda debate: Law, justice, and policy* (pp. 314–328). Boston: Northeastern University Press.

Thompson v. Keohane, 516 U.S. 99 (1995).

Thompson, S. G. (2006). Evading *Miranda*: How *Seibert* and *Patane* failed to "save" *Miranda. Valparaiso Law Review, 40,* 645–684.

Time Magazine. (1967, August 4). Living with Gault 90(5), p. 68.

Transcript of Detained Advisory Hearing and Detention Hearing. (Ariz. Super. Ct.) (2008). Case # JV2008065. http://apps.supremecourt.az.gov/docs/.

United States v. Bayer, 331 U.S. 532 (1947).

United States v. Calandra, 414 U.S. 338 (1974).

United States v. Gonzalez-Lauzan, 437 F.3d 1128 (11th Cir. 2006).

United States v. Mitchell, 322 U.S. 65 (1944).

United States v. Patane, 124 S.Ct. 2620 (2004).

United States v. Peterson, 414 F.3d 825 (7th Cir. 2005).

United States v. Washington, 462 F.3d 1124 (9th Cir. 2006).

Van Hook v. Anderson, No. 03-4207, 6th Circuit Court of Appeals (2007).

Venkatraman, B. A. (2006). Lost in translation: Limited English proficient population and the police. *The Police Chief.* 73(4), 40–47.

Vernon, M., Raifman, L. J., & Greenberg, S. F. (1996). The *Miranda* warnings and the deaf suspect. *Behavioral Sciences and the Law, 14,* 124–135.

Vernon M., Raifman, L.J., Greenberg, S.F., & Monteiro, B. (2001). Forensic pretrial police interviews of deaf suspects: Avoiding legal pitfalls. *Law and Psychiatry, 24,* 43–59.

Viljoen, J. L., Roesch, R., & Zapf, P. A. (2002). An examination of the relationship between competency to stand trial, competency to waive interrogation rights, and psychopathology. *Law and Human Behavior, 26,* 481–506.

Vinson, F. (1961). Work of the federal courts. In W. F. Murphy & C. H. Pritchett (Eds.), *Courts, judges, and politics* (pp. 54–57). New York: Random House.

Vrij, A. (1994). The impact of information and settings on deception by police detectives. *Journal of Nonverbal Behavior, 18,* 117–132.

Vrij, A. (2008). *Detecting lies and deceit: Pitfalls and opportunities.* New York: Wiley.

Wald, M., Ayres, R., Hess, D. W., Schantz, M., & Whitebread, C. H. (1967). Interrogations in New Haven: The impact of *Miranda. Yale Law Journal, 76,* 1519–1648.

Walker, N. E., Brooks, C. M., & Wrightsman, L. S. (1999). *Children's rights in the United States.* Thousand Oaks, CA: Sage.

Wallace v. Kato, 127 S.Ct. 1091 (2007).

Warren, E. (1977). *The memoirs of Chief Justice Earl Warren.* Garden City, NY: Doubleday.

Weiss, K. J. (2003). Confessions and expert testimony. *Journal of the American Academy of Psychiatry and the Law, 31,* 451–458.

Weisselberg, C. D. (1998). Saving *Miranda. Cornell Law Review, 84,* 109–189.

Weisselberg, C. D. (2008). Mourning *Miranda. California Law Review, 96,* 1520–1602.

Wermeil, S. (1995). William J. Brennan. In C. Cushman (Ed.), *The Supreme Court justices: Illustrated biographies 1789-1995* (2nd ed., pp. 446–450). Washington, DC: Congressional Quarterly.

Westover v. United States, petition for *certiorari,* No. 761 OT 1965, United States Supreme Court.

White, W. S. (1992). Regulating prison informers under the Due Process Clause. In D. J. Hutchinson, D. A. Strauss, & G. R. Stone (Eds.), *Supreme Court Review 1991* (pp. 103–142). Chicago: University of Chicago Press.

White, W. S. (2001a). *Miranda's* failure to restrain pernicious interrogation practices. *Michigan Law Review, 99,* 1211–1247.

White. W. S. (2001b). *Miranda's waning protections: Police interrogation practices after Dickerson.* Ann Arbor, MI: University of Michigan Press.

Wickersham Commission Report. (1931). *Report on lawlessness in law enforcement.* Washington, DC: Government Printing Office.

Wigmore, J. H. (1970). *Evidence in trials at common law* (Vol. 3) (Revised by J. H. Chadbourn.) Boston: Little, Brown.

Willemse, C. (1931). *Behind the green lights.* New York: Alfred A. Knopf.

Wrightsman, L. S. (2001). *Forensic psychology.* Belmont, CA: Wadsworth.

Wrightsman. L. S. (2006). *The psychology of the Supreme Court.* New York: Oxford University Press.

Wrightsman, L. S. (2008). *Oral arguments before the Supreme Court: An empirical approach.* New York: Oxford University Press.

Wrightsman, L. S. & Kassin, S. M. (1993). *Confessions in the courtroom.* Newbury Park, CA: Sage.

Yarborough v. Alvarado, 124 S.Ct. 2140 (2004).

Zalman, M., & Smith, B. W. (2007). The attitudes of police executives toward *Miranda* and interrogation policies. *Journal of Criminal Law and Criminology*, 97, 873–942.

Zelle, H., Romaine, C. L. R., Serico, J., Wolbransky, B., Osman, D., Wrazien, L., Taormina, S., & Goldstein, N. E. (2008, August). Adolescents' Miranda rights comprehension: The impact of verbal expressive abilities. Paper presented at the meetings of the American Psychological Association, Boston, MA.

Index